PLAYING
POKER
TO
WIN

howtobooks

3 Newtec Place, Magdalen Road, Oxford OX4 1RE, United Kingdom
Tel: (01865) 793806. Fax: (01865) 248780
info@howtobooks.co.uk www.howtobooks.co.uk

PLAYING
POKER
TO
WIN

A comprehensive guide to NO-LIMIT TEXAS HOLD'EM
for beginners and improvers

ANDREA SHAVICK & DAN SHAVICK

howtobooks

Published by How To Books Ltd
3 Newtec Place, Magdalen Road
Oxford OX4 1RE, United Kingdom
Tel: (01865) 793806. Fax: (01865) 248780
info@howtobooks.co.uk
www.howtobooks.co.uk

British Library Cataloguing in Publication Data
A catalogue record for this book is available from the British Library.

Cartoons by David Parkins
Cover design by Baseline Arts Ltd, Oxford
Produced for How To Books by Deer Park Productions, Tavistock, Devon
Typeset by Baseline Arts Ltd, Oxford
Printed and bound by Bell & Bain Ltd, Glasgow

NOTE: The material contained in this book is set out in good faith for general guidance and no liability can be accepted for loss or expense incurred as a result of relying in particular circumstances on statements made in the book. The laws and regulations are complex and liable to change, and readers should check the current position with the relevant authorities before making personal arrangements.

Contents

Acknowledgments

We would like to thank the following people for their invaluable assistance in the creation of this book: Rich Bradley, John Cooper, Dan Corder, Zoe Cunningham, Pete Kenny, Mark Greenberg, Chris Harris, Greg Hawkins, Richard Hill, Phil Marsden, David Moskovic, Stewart Reuben, Justine Shaw, Nick Tims, Sean Williams, and David Parkins for the cartoons.

Part I
Getting started

Chapter One:
Introduction

Poker is unlike other games

For a start, poker involves a degree of luck. In many games, such as chess or football, the better players or teams usually win. In poker, however, the better players don't win every hand or even every session. Anyone can play a hand perfectly and lose money, or play terribly and win.

But it's not all about luck. Good players will on average lose less with their bad cards and win more with their good cards. What's more, the best players will make the most money in the long run because *luck always evens out* if you play long enough. This isn't merely our opinion; it's a mathematical certainty.

Poker, as well as being a game involving luck, is also a game of incomplete information. In most games, again like chess or football, everybody has more or less the same information. In poker, however, some cards are hidden so that only the holder of those cards knows what they actually are. Because of this lack of information, poker isn't what's known as a solvable game. There is no definitive 'right move' in poker.

The aim of poker is to make educated guesses about what your opponents' cards might be – even though they will of course be trying to mislead you in this respect – and to play in the *same* way you would if you could actually see these cards. At the same time, you want to try to get your opponents to play in a *different* way than they would if they could see your cards. With all these hidden cards things can get pretty murky.

So poker is unusual because it involves (a) an element of luck and (b) incomplete information. These two qualities make it easy for many people to underestimate the game, believing it to be relatively simple, or even *mostly* governed by luck. It's not uncommon for players to have a few winning sessions, perhaps with the help of under-strength opposition or a healthy dose of good fortune, and to start believing they have the game cracked or are ready to enter the world championships.

A professional darts player who once appeared in a celebrity poker television programme made the rather arrogant claim that there isn't much difference in standard between many of the celebrity players and the poker professionals. To those who truly understand poker, his statement was preposterous, but he clearly had no inkling of how far off the mark he was.

It's true that the element of luck involved in poker sometimes obscures the skill factor over a few hands, or even over the course of a session or tournament. This is why very average players sometimes win tournaments. But such players won't make good money day in, day out.

In fact, poker is every bit as complex and subtle as games such as chess or bridge, and you could spend the rest of your life learning how to play it better and better. It's just that it sometimes takes a little longer for a winning edge to make itself apparent in poker.

Just as you shouldn't underestimate poker, you shouldn't be intimidated by the game either. When you first start playing, it can be difficult to make money at even the lowest stakes, and any player can have a couple of losing sessions and start doubting their own ability. But don't get disheartened. If you keep plugging away, and keep reading and learning, you can become a winning, money-making player.

Having said that, we wouldn't want you to think that poker is wholly about making money. As you read this book, it may seem at times like we're obsessed with profitability. We're not really, though – it's simply that making money is the part of the game it's easiest for us to dispense advice on.

People play poker for any number of reasons, most notably the game's inherent sociability and the mental challenges it provides. Whenever you play, you're sure to have fun too. It just so happens that we subscribe to the school of thought that says you have *more* fun if you play well and make money. And that's what this book is all about.

The poker phenomenon

Poker is the world's most popular card game but where it originates from no one really knows. Some say its earliest ancestor was the sixteenth century Persian game *As Nas*, others claim the honours for Europe, citing the French game of *Poque* or the German game of *Pochspiel* as likely contenders. Rather more well documented is the appearance of poker in the notorious gambling saloons on Mississippi steamers in the early nineteenth century.

Whatever its ancestry, the number of people playing poker has grown exponentially. Gone are the days of the shady underworld character losing his shirt in a smoke-filled backroom; poker is now entirely respectable and easily the most popular card game on the planet. At any one time, day or night, there are literally millions upon millions of people playing in homes, card rooms and of course, on the internet.

The emergence of the online card room is probably the most important reason for poker's recent stratospheric rise in popularity. Whereas previously you had to wait at least twenty-four hours to gain membership of a UK bricks and mortar casino, the internet is the epitome of convenience. You can play online whenever the mood takes you, anytime of the day or night, with instant access to thousands of games, competitions and tournaments at a click of the mouse.

Although the majority of players prefer playing for real money, you don't have to part with your cash if you don't want to. All the major online poker sites offer 'play money' games – which are great for when you're learning or when you just want to have fun. Countless online guides and tutorials are also available to give instruction, information, help and advice. And whether you're playing for free or big bucks, you always get to play real people, enjoy the camaraderie of the poker playing community and exercise your brain – all in one fell swoop.

Television has also done its bit to popularise the game. The broadcasting of poker tournaments and celebrity poker, and the launching of dedicated poker channels, has truly brought poker to the masses. You can't really improve your backhand watching Wimbledon, but you can certainly learn a thing or two from poker shows. Players' cards are revealed by cameras in or under the table, and commentators explain the thinking behind every move (even if their analysis is, at times, somewhat superficial).

It also used to be the case that poker was a heavily male-dominated pastime, but that has changed too. Although the number of women playing live games is still relatively low, a significant number of online players are female – and they're not all hiding in women-only poker sites either.

Incidentally, in this book we refer to individual players as 'he', but this is simply because it's too cumbersome to say 'he or she' every time. Be assured, women can be just as good players as men, if not better!

Finally, if you're looking for the big time then you won't want to miss the most important event in the poker playing calendar, namely the World Series of Poker (or *WSOP*). Launched in 1970 and played for the most part at Binion's Horseshoe in Las Vegas , the WSOP consists of a series of poker tournaments culminating in a week-long, no-limit Texas hold'em championship event. The winner of this event can expect to walk away with a minimum of several million dollars and the title 'World Champion of Poker'.

Games played at the WSOP are mostly variations of hold'em (limit, pot-limit and no-limit) with a smattering of omaha and seven card stud for good measure. There are ladies' events, gold bracelet events, celebrity and charity events, casino employee events and even a tournament for poker-playing computer robots. Buy-in prices vary, but entry for the championship event is, at time of writing, a cool $10,000.

Luckily it's quite possible to secure a cheap place by winning one of the smaller casino tournaments or online events, known as *satellites*. In recent years thousands of players have earned their seats online, including at least one world champion. Chris Moneymaker's win in 2003 is particularly memorable for the fact that he was a previously unknown player who managed to turn a $40 satellite stake into the $2.5million first prize.

The turnout for the WSOP has skyrocketed in recent years, with top prizes climbing ever higher and higher. But before you hop on a plane to Vegas in the hope of winning your share, we'd better teach you how to play.

How to use this book

This book is a comprehensive guide to the rules and strategy of no-limit hold'em, the fastest growing and most popular form of poker played today. It provides all the information you need to learn the game and make real money.

In **Part I** (which is where you are now) we explain the rules and aim of the game including the equipment you'll need, hand rankings and how the betting works. We also take you all the way through a hand (individual game), step by step.

If you're already familiar with the rules or have played before you might want to skip straight on to **Part II – No-limit hold'em strategy**. This is by far the largest section of the book and where we'll explore tactics and technique. It covers everything from pot odds to playing styles, starting hands to stack sizes, drawing hands to deception and much more besides.

Most sections have a simple summary at the end, so even if you don't follow everything the first time around you can still dip into the summaries and use the advice there to guide the way you play. Then you can revisit the material once you've had time to absorb it all.

Part II also includes plenty of quizzes to give you practice in each of the various ideas. We recommend that you do all the quizzes thoroughly (and without cheating) as they will help you develop a feel for the material much more quickly.

Part III is all about online poker. Here you'll find an insider's guide to playing poker on the internet, together with plenty of specific strategy hints and tips for online play.

In **Part IV – Poker Variants** we discuss some of the other popular games you might come across such as omaha, seven card stud, lowball and pineapple to name just a few. If you're wondering why you should learn any game other than hold'em, we have something to say on that subject too.

Part IV also includes a chapter on tournaments – how they work and how to adjust your strategy accordingly.

Strategy aside, when you play poker it's vital to have an understanding of how to manage your money. **Part V – The Money** is full of indispensable money management tips and includes advice on tracking results, selecting games (an essential skill for those of you who intend to win *big*), building a bankroll and increasing your earnings ... not to mention protecting those earnings from those who would get their hands on them dishonestly.

Our final section, **Part VI – Resources**, includes tables of odds and probabilities so you'll never have to get the calculator out. And although we've *tried* not to use too much jargon, Part VI also includes a comprehensive glossary, in case you find yourself wondering what a second-nut backdoor flush draw is.

There's even an online chat glossary for those of you who enjoy conversing with your opponents whilst taking their money.

For the latest information, lots of extra resources and links to recommended poker sites, please visit www.playingpokertowin.co.uk

Chapter Two:
Get started and learn the rules

In this chapter we will get you started playing no-limit hold'em and familiarise you with the basic rules and mechanics of the game. We'll explain what equipment you'll need, how each hand (individual game) is played, how and when you bet, and what cool phrases you should have prepared.

Note: If you're already familiar with the rules of hold'em then you might want to skip this chapter and move straight to **Part II** which covers strategy and technique.

Equipment

You don't need very much to play poker:

Table and chairs. 'Real' poker tables are rectangular with rounded corners but obviously any shape will do.

A new, or fairly new pack of cards (also called a *deck*). The reason your cards must be in good condition is because bent, dirty, torn or marked cards are easily identifiable. Even an inexperienced player will quickly cotton on if the card with the coffee stain on the back is an ace. Many web retailers, including eBay, sell good quality ex-casino cards at ridiculously cheap prices.

To speed up each hand you can use two packs; one to play with and one to shuffle. The packs should have different coloured backs to avoid mixing them up by mistake. Note: card rooms never use two packs because it's too prone to cheating, but it's fine for home games.

You may also decide to use a *postillion*, which is a playing-card sized piece of plastic that sits under the deck and ensures that the bottom card remains concealed.

Players. The minimum number is two, the maximum is around eleven, but the ideal poker game will have between five and ten players. If you have more than ten players then you can just split into two tables.

Playing with fewer players has its advantages:

- Each hand is faster, so there's less time sitting out if you're not involved.

- Each player will play a greater percentage of hands (we explain why later on) and so be more involved in the game.

- You don't need such a big table!

On the other hand, larger games tend to have bigger pots and may be considered more sociable. It comes down to personal preference but we favour around seven or eight players. There's a discussion on the relevance of the number of players to strategy in Chapter Thirteen.

Chips. Not the edible variety but small, round, coloured counters which represent money and with which you bet. Officially, the different colours denote different denominations as follows:

Colour	Denomination
White	1
Yellow	2
Red	5
Blue	10
Grey	20
Green	25
Orange	50
Black	100
Pink	250
Purple	500
Burgundy	1000
Light Blue	2000
Brown	5000

Genuine poker chips aren't expensive. For a small amount you can buy a really nice poker set which will include at least 200 chips (although probably only a handful of different colours) and a dealer button. Buy from online card rooms, poker equipment dealers or even your local department store.

If you haven't got any chips you can always improvise and play with real money or matches etc.

Dealer button. This a large round counter, usually white, which is placed on the table in front of the person who is currently the dealer, so everyone knows who they are. Players take turns to deal; for each hand the position of dealer moves around the table one person at a time in a clockwise direction.

If you decide to use a designated dealer (where the *same* person deals every hand) the button still moves around the table, in this case, symbolising the position of dealer. This ensures everyone takes it in turn to be the first player to bet and to experience the advantages and disadvantages of sitting in a different position relative to the dealer for each hand (more on this later).

Green baize or felt to cover the table. Often included in poker sets, this is an optional extra for those of you who want to pretend you're in a card room. It's a better surface to play on than a hard table top and makes the dealing easier.

The only other things you'll need are some atmospheric lighting, a bit of peace and quiet so you can all concentrate, black-out curtains and an inexhaustible supply of cigars and whisky. Ok, you can skip the curtains.

The aim of the game

Poker is organised into a series of individual contests, each lasting up to a few minutes or so. Each of these individual contests is called a *hand*. Unfortunately, the term *hand* also refers to the cards that a player has, in other words the cards with which he attempts to win the hand. It will be obvious from the context which one we mean at any point.

When we talk about a *game* of poker, we're not referring to an individual hand. A game is a series of hands played in succession, possibly a whole evening's worth. If you get confused by the terminology, there's a comprehensive glossary at the back of the book.

We will shortly talk you through an entire hand, step by step, but first here's a very brief run-down of what happens, condensed into three simple points:

■ Each player's hand consists of two *hole cards* which only they can see, and five *community cards*, which can be seen and used by everyone. The strength of each player's hand is judged on the best *five* cards out of these seven available.

- Players consider their hand and place bets accordingly or drop out if they don't want to bet. *The skill lies in knowing when, and how much to bet, taking into account the relative strength of the cards available to you and the cards you think other players have.* Strategy and playing skill is covered in detail in Part II.

- The winner is the player with the best hand at the end of the hand or, alternatively, the last player left in the hand at any point.

The best hand is determined by the following rules, which govern the ranking of hands.

Hand rankings

The best hand of five cards is determined by the following rules, known as hand rankings. Hands are shown ranked from highest (rarest) to lowest (most common) and include an example of each one, the odds against making that hand in hold'em, and some brief notes.

ROYAL FLUSH!

Hand Ranking Table

ROYAL FLUSH (30,940-to-1)

The top ranking hand and very, very rare. You need 10-J-Q-K-A of the same suit – plus the ability to stay calm.

STRAIGHT FLUSH (3,590-to-1)

Also incredibly rare. You need five cards of the same suit in numerical order. Aces can be high or low. In a tie between two straight flushes, the highest card wins.

FOUR OF A KIND (594-to-1)

Four cards of the same denomination, plus a kicker (a card that doesn't match the other four). In a tie, the highest denomination wins, followed by the highest kicker if these are the same.

FULL HOUSE (38-to-1)

Three of a kind plus a pair. In a tie, the higher three of a kind wins, followed by the higher pair if these are the same. So J-J-J-4-4 beats 8-8-8-A-A and 9-9-9-10-10 beats 9-9-9-7-7.

Hand Ranking Table

FLUSH (32-to-1)

Any five cards of the same suit not in numerical order. In a tie, the highest card wins, i.e. 2-5-7-J-K beats 4-6-8-10-J. If highest cards are the same, second highest wins and so on, i.e. 4-5-7-10-Q beats 3-5-7-10-Q.

STRAIGHT (21-to-1)

Five cards in sequential order, of mixed suits. Aces can be high or low, so both 10-J-Q-K-A and A-2-3-4-5 are valid straights. Middle value aces, e.g. Q-K-A-2-3, are not allowed. In a tie between two straights, the highest card wins.

THREE OF A KIND (20-to-1)

Three cards of the same denomination, plus two kickers. In a tie, the highest denomination wins, followed by the highest kicker if these are the same.

Hand Ranking Table

TWO PAIR (3.3-to-1)

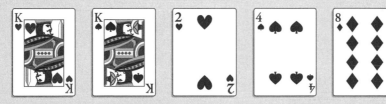

Two lots of two of a kind plus a kicker (odd card). In a tie, the highest pair wins, then the lower pair. If both pairs are similar, the highest kicker wins.

ONE PAIR (1.3-to-1)

Two of a kind plus three odd cards. In a tie, the highest denomination pair wins. If similar, highest kicker wins, i.e. 2-5-9-K-K beats 3-4-7-K-K. If the highest kickers match, the next highest kicker wins, and so on, i.e. 2-5-9-K-K beats 3-4-9-K-K.

HIGH CARD

The lowest ranked hand comprises five odd cards only. In a tie, highest card wins, i.e. 2-4-6-9-A beats 5-7-9-J-Q and 3-5-8-J-K beats 2-5-8-J-K.

All suits are equal in value and no one suit has precedence over another. If players have truly identical hands a tie is declared and the pot (the money) is divided between them.

Now we will take you through a hand of no-limit hold'em in a little more detail, but before we begin there are one or two things you need to know about the bets made at the start of each hand.

Understanding the initial bets

All hands have to start with some money in the pot – otherwise there'd be nothing to play for. This is achieved by a method of forced betting known as *posting blinds*. Before the cards are dealt at the beginning of each hand, the two players to the left of the dealer place forced bets.

The first forced bet is made by the player on the dealer's immediate left and is called the *small blind*. This can be any amount you all agree on, say £1. Then the player on his left places another forced bet, called the *big blind* which is usually double the small blind, in this case £2. These bets go into the *pot*, meaning they're placed in the middle of the table.

Note: We've used the example of a £1 / £2 game to keep the numbers simple while we explain the basic rules – but actually this is a *big* game for beginners as you'll see later.

This scheme may not sound particularly fair on those two players but, since the position of the dealer moves around the table after each hand, everyone gets to be small and big blind at some point. If you are the big blind in one hand, you will be the small blind in the next hand, and dealer in the hand after that.

Another way of getting money into the initial pot is by having an *ante*. Here everyone puts the same amount of money into the pot before the hand begins. If five players all put in £2, then the pot will be worth £10 before play begins. Antes have no effect on subsequent betting rules (although they will affect strategy). In hold'em, antes, when used, are used in addition to blinds rather than instead of them.

If you're playing casually with friends it's up to you to decide whether to use antes as well as blinds. We would recommend dispensing with antes altogether since they're rarely used outside of large live (as opposed to online) tournaments these days. For the purposes of describing the rudiments of the game we will assume you are playing with blinds and no antes.

We will now walk you through a basic hand of no-limit Texas hold'em – by far the most popular poker game in the world and the main subject of this book. (Although we do discuss other popular poker variants in **Part IV.**)

By the way, don't call the game *Texas hold'em* or you'll sound like a beginner (which you might be, but you don't want everyone to know that). Just call it *hold'em*.

Betting rounds

Each hand of hold'em consists of up to four betting rounds:

- Pre-flop
- The flop
- The turn
- The river.

In each round, cards are dealt and then the players bet. We'll discuss the rules of each round in turn.

Round one – pre-flop

Posting the blinds
The first round commences with the small blind and the big blind (see above) placing their bets.

Dealing the cards
The dealer first shuffles the cards thoroughly and cuts the deck (or, if the dealer is also playing, offers the deck to the player to his left to cut). He deals

a card face-down to each player in a clockwise direction, starting from his left and finishing with himself. He then repeats the deal (but not the shuffle or cut) so that players end up with two cards each. Players look at their cards, taking care not to let anyone else see them. These hidden cards are called *hole cards*, or *pocket cards*.

Once the blinds have been posted and the cards dealt, things should look something like this:

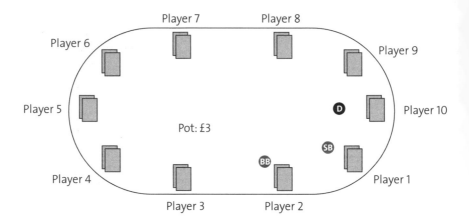

The betting
The player to the immediate left of the big blind (Player 3 in our example) now starts the ball rolling. He has three choices; he can *fold*, *call* or *raise*.

Folding (also known as *passing*) means withdrawing from the current hand completely. If you fold then you're no longer required to bet but you'll lose any money you've already put into the pot. You should normally fold if your cards are poor, although there is no necessity to do so – it's up to you. If you're folding, announce "fold" clearly so everyone hears, and push your cards face down into the muck in the centre of the table where all discarded cards are thrown. No matter how dire they may be, don't discuss your cards or tell anyone what you had until the end of the hand. Otherwise you may prejudice the continuing play.

Calling means *matching* the largest bet previously made in the round by adding this amount of money to the pot. Whenever you call, you will have contributed the same amount of money as the player who's contributed the most in total so far this hand. If you're first to act, the largest amount bet so far will be the bet placed by the big blind. So if the big blind put in £2, announce "call" and place chips to the value of £2 in the pot.

By calling you stay in the hand and add to the available pot. In general you should call when you think your cards are good enough to give you a chance of winning.

Raising means *exceeding* the largest bet previously made in the round so far. Using the example shown above, the biggest bet so far is £2 from the big blind (Player 2). So raising will mean matching his bet by putting in £2, and then adding more of your own, which is the raise. In general you should raise when your cards are good, or when you want your opponents to think your cards are good.

> *Note:* 'calling' used to be refered to as *seeing* the bet, as in "I'll see your £2". But this sounds hopelessly archaic these days and suggests you've been watching too many westerns.

In no-limit hold'em, you can raise as much as you like, up to the amount of money you have on the table. (It must actually be on the table from the start of the hand, not hidden in your pockets.) There are rules about what happens if a player doesn't have enough money to call the raise – see below for details. In other forms of poker, such as limit or pot-limit hold'em there are constraints on the amount you can bet – these are explained later.

Note the following points about raising:

- If somebody has already raised the original bet before you, then your raise is known as a *re-raise*.

- Before you raise (or re-raise) you *must* announce "raise" clearly so that everyone can hear you. Otherwise your bet is treated as a call even if you put enough chips in to raise. What you can't do is say something like "I'll call your £2 ... and I'll raise you £2", because other players might think you're finished in the pause in the middle. Once you've announced "raise" however, you can put in the chips required to call, and then subsequently and separately add your raise.

- On the first round of betting you can't *check* (unless you are the big blind) because the blinds force you to either fold, call or raise. But you can check on all subsequent rounds if no-one before you has bet. Similarly you can't bet on the first round (in the formal sense of the word), because only the first player to put money in is described as having *bet* – and in the first round, that's the blinds. Checking and betting are explained shortly.

Once the first player to the left of the big blind has made his move, the action continues around the table clockwise, with each player in turn choosing whether to fold, call or raise.

As the betting continues around the table, the players who are the small blind and big blind now get a chance to participate. Like everyone else they have the option of calling, raising or folding, although they are required to put less additional money in the pot than the others because they've already contributed their forced bets.

Completing the betting

The betting continues until it finally reaches the player sitting to the right of the last person to raise, at which point the end of the first round is reached. The last person to raise cannot do so again – you're not allowed to raise your own bet or raise, only somebody else's. If nobody raises, the betting ends after the big blind has acted.

By this point some players will have folded, and some will remain in the hand. If more than one player remains, they will all have contributed exactly the same amount of money to the pot during the round. If only one player remains, he wins the pot.

Round two – the flop

Dealing the cards

The second round begins with the dealer *burning* a card, meaning that he discards the top card of the deck. (This minimises the potential for cheating to occur.) He then places the next three cards *face up* in the middle of the table for everyone to see. These cards are known as the flop. They are community cards, also known as *board cards*, and any player can use them.

The betting

Another round of betting now follows, but this time starting with the player to the left of dealer (rather than the player to the left of the big blind); that's Player 1 in our example above. Every player who is still in the hand now has five cards – their two hole cards which nobody else can see plus the three community cards which are on the table.

The first player to act can either bet or check.

Betting means being the first player in a round to put money into the pot. Otherwise betting is exactly like raising as described above. If you don't want to bet, you can instead check.

Checking means doing nothing, i.e. not betting but not folding either. It's a sort of 'wait and see' move. If you check you'll get another chance to decide whether to bet or not a little later on in the hand (although you won't get another chance to bet in this round if everyone else checks too). You might check when your cards are not particularly good, or when you want your opponents to think they're not particularly good.

You can't check whenever you want however. A player has the option of checking only if he is the first player to act in a round, or if everybody acting before him in the round has also checked. As soon as somebody had made a bet, subsequent players in that round must either call, raise or fold – checking and betting no longer apply.

Completing the betting

As with pre-flop, the betting continues until it reaches the player to the right of the last person to bet or raise. If everybody checks, betting ends after the dealer has acted.

You have now reached the end of the second round. Again, some players will have folded, and some will remain in the hand, each of those having contributed the same amount of money to the pot. If only one player remains, he wins the pot.

Round three – the turn

A third round now commences with the dealer burning another card and placing a fourth community card face up on the table, next to the other ones. This is known as the turn (or sometimes *fourth street*).

Another round of betting takes place, starting as before with the player to the left of the dealer (Player 1), at the end of which some players will have folded and some will remain in the hand. If only one player remains, he wins the pot.

Round four – the river

You have now reached the final round. The dealer proceeds to burn another card and place a fifth community card known as the *river* (or sometimes *fifth street*) on the table. At this point all remaining players have seven cards – the five community cards and their two original hole cards. A final round of betting takes place as before.

The showdown

At the showdown, all players still in the hand show their hole cards if they wish to make a claim on the pot, starting with the last player to bet or raise. A player's hand is the best five cards out of the seven available to him, made up of any of the following combinations:

- Both hole cards plus any three community cards
- One hole card plus any four community cards
- All five community cards – known as playing the board.

Note: Players are not forced to reveal their cards at showdown unless either (a) they were the last to bet or raise or (b) they want to make a claim on the pot. We'll talk more about this shortly.

After examining the cards, the player with the best hand (according to the hand ranking table above) takes the pot. Everyone else gets nothing.

Once the hand is over, the dealer button moves one place to the left and the whole process starts again.

Other rules and FAQs

How much money do I need to play poker?

In casual home games, stakes and betting structures are by mutual agreement. When you're playing for tiny stakes or play money we recommend you stick to no-limit rules which permit you to bet or raise as much as you like (as long as you match or exceed the size of previous bets on that round). Playing this way is, for most people, more challenging and more enjoyable – especially when you have a great hand!

In general in no-limit hold'em, players should ideally sit down with at least fifty times the big blind in front of them. When you're just starting out, you will probably elect to play with blinds of a few pence or so, with each player having a few pounds on the table. Although blinds of a few pence might sound quite small, no-limit betting means that money can find its way into the middle very quickly, and pots can soon mount up.

Calculating how large a bankroll you need for serious games is covered in Part V, along with advice on how to best to manage your money.

How much am I allowed to bet?

In no-limit hold'em (which is the main subject of this book) you may bet or raise anything up to the amount of money or chips you have on the table in front of you, at any time. Generally, all raises must be *at least* the size of any previous bet or raise made in the same round.

So if the first player bets £10, for example, the second player can fold, call or raise. If they raise, the raise can be:

a) a minimum raise of £10, making £20 in total, or
b) a maximum raise of everything they have on the table (known as going ' all-in') or,
c) anything in between the two.

If the second player makes a minimum raise by putting in £20, the third player too can fold, call or raise. If they raise, the raise can be:

a) a minimum raise of £10, making £30 in total, or
b) a maximum raise of everything they have on the table (all-in), or
c) anything in between the two.

For a discussion of what happens when players start running out of money, see below.

The question of *when* to bet or raise is discussed in much greater detail in Part II which covers strategy.

What happens when players start running out of money?

A special rule comes into effect at this point, known as *table stakes*. It can get a little bit complicated...

Table stakes rules apply in all poker games and are particularly important when you're playing pot-limit and no-limit poker. As explained above, you can't bet any more than you have on the table in front of you. Although this idea in itself is straightforward enough, we need to explain what happens if you bet more than one of your *opponents* has on the table. What happens, you may ask, when one player is unable to match another player's bet? How can the hand continue?

This is what happens: let's suppose you want to bet £50 and you're up against two opponents, Pauline (think *Poor*-lean) with £30 and Richard (think *Rich*-ard) with £100.

- You announce "Bet, £50" and place your £50 in the middle of the table, although separate from the main pot for a reason that will become apparent shortly.
- Pauline announces "Call, £30 all-in" and places her chips in the middle, again separately.
- Richard announces "Call" and places £50 of his chips in the middle, separately of course.

Then the money needs to be sorted out. Firstly the amount that the poorest player (Pauline) was able to contribute is added to the main pot. In other words, all Pauline's chips, plus £30 of Richard's and £30 of yours are added to the main pot in the middle of the table.

However, Richard and you both contributed a further £20 each to the hand, and this is placed in a *side pot*. That side pot is played for between you and Richard only – Pauline can't win it because she didn't have enough money to match your bets.

There are now two pots in the middle of the table:

1) The main pot, being competed for by you, Richard and Pauline
2) The side pot, being competed for by you and Richard only.

Pauline has no money left and hence can't participate in any further betting that may take place in the hand. Any further bets made by you or Richard will be added to the side pot. What happens next will depend on whether either of you or Richard folds before the showdown or not.

- **If neither you nor Richard fold before the showdown** then all three of you show your cards (if you want to make a claim on the pot). The best hand of the three wins the main pot. The better of your hand and Richard's hand wins the side pot. Pauline can't win any money from the side pot, no matter how good her hand is.

- **If you or Richard fold before the showdown** then the one who remains (of you and Richard) wins the side pot automatically. Let's suppose for example that Richard folds to a bet from you. Then you take the side pot. There is still the main pot to consider, and it's between you and Pauline (who ran out of money but is still in the hand because she didn't fold). The remaining cards must still be dealt out even though Pauline has no money left. The main pot is then won by you or Pauline depending on whose hand is better.

There can be multiple side pots if more than one player runs out of money. If there are, say, five players in a pot then there can be up to four pots – the main pot and three side pots. Each player competes only for those pots to which they contributed money.

You can see from the above that there's never any point betting more money than any of your opponents have left on the table – if you're called, the extra chips are simply returned to you.

What is an *all-in*?

A player is said to be all-in when all his money is in the current pot. In the above example, Pauline goes all-in at the point where you bet £50 and she calls with the £30 in front of her. A player can go all-in not only when calling, but also when betting or raising. Once a player is all-in, he takes no further part in any betting. He is guaranteed to be able to show down his hand and claim his portion of the pot if he wins.

What's the maximum I could lose?

Forget what you've seen at the movies, you *cannot* be exposed for more money than you have on the table. In each hand, you can lose all the money in front of you, but no more. You cannot go and get a loan from your best mate when you're running out of money at some crucial point in the hand – it's against the rules.

What you can do, however, is go and get more money *in between* hands – this is known as *reloading*. You're just not allowed to reload in the middle of a hand.

How much you can lose in total, over the course of a session, is up to you. If you keep reloading and reloading, you can keep losing your money.

Is it possible to win with a weak hand?

Yes it's quite possible – if everybody else folds, or if everybody who doesn't fold has an even weaker hand. Strategy is discussed in detail in Part II.

What happens in the case of a tie?

In the case of a tie for the best hand, the pot is divided equally amongst the winners. Information on what constitutes a tie is provided with the hand ranking table above.

Do hands always reach showdown?

No. If everyone folds, the last player in the hand wins the pot. This can happen at any point, even in the first round.

Am I obliged to reveal my cards?

No. If you win before the showdown (because everyone else folds) you do not have to reveal your cards. Even if you do reach the showdown, the only people who are obliged to show their cards are the last person who bet or raised, and anybody who wants to make a claim on the pot. If they want to, other players can simply push their cards face down into the muck.

One reason players sometimes avoid showing their cards is because it reveals information about their playing style, for example how well or badly they played the hand or whether they've been bluffing. However, the advantage of showing your cards, especially when you're starting out, is that somebody might well notice that you won the hand even if you didn't realise you had. This usually applies only to beginners, but it can occasionally happen to experienced players too.

In a friendly home game it's quite common practice for everyone to scrutinise each other's cards in order to work out who's won the pot. You can certainly learn much more about the game that way, and you can also discuss the merits of each person's play – politely or otherwise!

When do players reveal their cards before the end of a hand?

When all, or all but one, of the players in a hand are all-in, there can be no more betting from anyone. Even if one player has money left to bet, nobody can match it. In many games, all the players involved turn their hole cards face up at this point, so everybody can see what everyone else has. Then the remaining community cards are dealt out as usual, but it's that much more exciting because it's obvious which cards will produce a win for each player.

This convention, revealing hole cards for all-ins, is commonplace in home games and tournaments. It's not usually the way things are done in British card rooms however, where you're obliged to show your hole cards only if you were the last bettor or want to claim the pot.

What's the difference between no-limit, limit and pot-limit?

No-limit, limit and pot-limit are not names of poker games – they just define the betting structure of the game, and whether or not the betting is capped. The maximum size of a bet or raise is determined by the type of game you're playing:

Limit and pot-limit betting structures are discussed later on in **Chapter Sixteen: Poker variants explained.**

What happens if cards are exposed or misdealt?

Honest mistakes are bound to occur from time to time. Dealers might flash a card now and then. Somebody might expose one of their cards by accident. The whole deck might get dropped or have coffee spilt on it.

The question is what to do about it? It depends on how high the stakes are. If you're playing a casual game with friends, you might decide not to do anything. If you're playing a big game, players may expect a tough line to be taken. Here are some suggestions as to what to do about the minor problems that frequently crop up in home games:

- **Exposed cards.** Cards which are exposed when they shouldn't be need to be taken out of the hand. A card accidentally revealed when the cards are cut, shuffled or dealt should be shown to all players and then placed in the muck. The same applies to any card found face up in the deck. However, this does *not* apply to hole cards inadvertently exposed by careless players. If you allow your opponents to see your cards, that's your look-out.

- **Wrong number of cards dealt.** Players who receive too many cards by accident can return the extra cards to the dealer, provided they haven't looked at them of course. Any extra cards that have been seen should be shown to all players and then mucked, as above.

- **Damaged cards.** Cards which are damaged in any way (torn, creased, stained etc) should never be used as even the most inexperienced player will be able to identify them pretty quickly. Use a new pack.

> Note: Player mistakes such as acting out of turn are covered below.

Is there any etiquette I should be aware of for casual play?

Even in a very casual home game there is some basic etiquette you should follow.

Don't act out of turn. Inexperienced players frequently act (e.g. fold, call or bet) before the person to their right has acted. Remember that the action goes round the table in a clockwise direction. However keen you are, *wait* until it's your turn before you place your bet or throw your cards in the muck. Acting out of turn annoys other players and can prejudice the hand.

In general, a player who acts out of turn should (a) wait until it is their turn, and (b) take the action they previously declared (assuming it's still possible). They shouldn't be allowed to change their minds. This is because in poker, *all verbal declarations are binding*, including those made out of turn.

Be decisive. Be aware of the consequences of changing your mind. If you say "fold" you will be expected to fold, if you announce "raise" you must raise. As mentioned above, *all verbal declarations are binding*.

Non-verbal declarations can also be binding. In fact, when it comes to folding, the rule that says your cards are dead once they hit the muck trumps the rule about binding verbal declarations. So if you say "raise" but inadvertently throw your cards in the muck by mistake, your hand is dead and you won't be allowed to continue.

Don't discuss your cards after folding until the hand is over. Discussing your cards *after* you've folded but *before* the hand has finished can severely prejudice the continuing game and is not allowed.

Of course you can always discuss your cards *after* the hand has finished.

As for discussing your cards while you are still in the hand – there's actually a rule about this called the *Moody rule* which forbids any discussion about cards between players. Having said that, the Moody rule is increasingly being dropped.

When the Moody rule isn't in force you can discuss your hand freely and even lie about it if you want – this is known as coffee-housing. It's now normally ok to say, for example, "I've got a pair of aces", whether that's true or not. So always treat with healthy scepticism any comments made by other players about their hands.

If the Moody rule isn't in force then the only real no-no is discussing your cards *after* you've folded but *before* the hand has finished.

Keep your chips on the table. Any chips off the table aren't in play so just keep yours in front of you on the table at all times. Never hide them in your pocket – that's against the rules. Sometimes people will expect you to keep your largest denomination chips at the front so they're visible, but actually there's no law against making it difficult for other players to see how many chips you have as long as they're actually on the table and therefore in play. However, you must always reveal the size of your stack, i.e. how much money you have on the table, when explicitly asked.

Keep your cards in view. The back of them, that is. For security reasons it's actually against the rules to completely hide your cards or keep them underneath the table. At least a corner of the back of each hole card must be visible to other players at all times, so no putting them between your knees or in your pocket.

When it comes to the way you hold your cards, we suggest you don't. (Don't hold them, that is.) Have a quick peek when you first receive them, ideally without lifting them off the table, and then keep them face down on the table in front of you. You can remember two cards, surely. Holding your cards up or worse, waving them around, is tantamount to inviting your opponents to take a good look.

Avoid slow play. Try to concentrate so that you know when it's your turn and other players don't have to wait too long for you to act. You should also avoid leaving the table during the middle of a hand because your cards are liable to be folded if you do so.

Be a good sport. Poker is a very sociable game; even players competing for millions of dollars in the World Series chat and joke with one another. So don't criticise your opponents' play, don't blame your bad luck on the dealer and don't get all grumpy if you hit a losing streak. Enjoy yourself.

Where can I find full rules?

Many poker sites (and poker books) use *Robert's Rules of Poker* authored by Bob Ciaffone, a leading authority on poker rules. See www.pokercoach.us.

Rules do vary, however, so check house rules wherever you play.

Where can I play for fun or for free while I'm learning?

We list a selection of good online poker sites which all have free or play money tables in **Appendix E: Online poker websites** towards the end of the book.

See also **Chapter Twenty: Increasing your earnings** for lots of ideas on how to get your game up to speed before you start spending too much money.

Strategy and technique is now coming up in **Part II**.

Part II
No-limit hold'em strategy

Chapter Three:
Strategy overview

In Part II we're going to take a long look at hold'em strategy and discuss the concepts and techniques you'll need to understand to become a winning player.

This part of the book assumes that you're already reasonably familiar with the rules and mechanics of the game, and it's likely you'll find it an easier read if you're well acquainted with the material in Part I or have played a few times before.

Before we delve too deeply into the detail, we'll start with a quick bit of poker philosophy and in the process debunk a very popular misconception – that poker is all about bluffing.

Value-based plays and deceptive plays

First let's try to piece together the main ideas behind playing a hand of poker. In the introduction to Part I we said that you have to try to work out what everyone might hold, and then act accordingly. But how would you act if you *did* know what everyone's cards were? That's the first question we need to address.

Suppose you knew that your hand were strong compared to other hands at the table. What then? Hopefully you can see that, in this situation, you should be more inclined to bet big and stay in the hand rather than to fold. On the other hand, if you knew that your hand were relatively weak you should be inclined to bet small or fold.

Extending this idea to real games, where the cards are hidden, we call this approach *playing for value*. You evaluate the relative strength of your hand compared with the likely hands of your opponents and play in a way consistent with that value. Strong hands merit strong betting, and weak hands merit weak betting.

But it can't be that simple – and of course it isn't. If you bet big only with your strong hands, then people will know when you have a strong hand, and they'll steer clear of you on those occasions (by folding) so you can't get their money. And if you never bet when you're weak, then they'll know when you're weak and they can run over you by betting you out of the pot (in other words, bet big to make you fold). In short, it's all too easy for your opponents to *read* you if you play too predictably.

To prevent this, you have to mix things up a little.

- Sometimes you check (bet nothing), or merely call (match) someone else's bet, with a strong hand so that your opponents don't know you have a strong hand. This is called *slowplaying* or *sandbagging*.

- Sometimes you bet, or raise someone else's bet, with a relatively weak hand to pretend you have a stronger hand than you really do – in the hope of muscling people out of the pot by making them fold. This is called *bluffing* or *stealing*.

When you play in a way that isn't consistent with the value of your hand, for example by slowplaying or bluffing, you are deliberately trying to mislead your opponents so they evaluate your hand wrongly and make a mistake as a result. Making such a deceptive play is frequently referred to as *making a move*.

But hold on a minute. If you play deceptively *too* often you'll have abandoned the principle of playing for value. You'd be spending all your time *not* putting money in the pot when your hand is strong or, conversely, betting *big* when you don't actually have a good hand to show down. That doesn't seem quite right either – and indeed it isn't.

The fact of the matter is that the majority of the time you should simply play for value – just bet your hands according to their strength. Against weak opponents, that's pretty much all you have to do and you'll make money. There's no point running big bluffs against them because they'll probably call your bets anyway even if logic dictates that they shouldn't. There's no point making fancy moves, because in all probability they won't notice what you're doing and it'll all just go straight over their heads. Against weak players, you can just play the percentages, by which we mean simply play for value, and you will profit from their mistakes.

This surprises many inexperienced players, who think that the whole point of poker is to pull outrageous moves on their opponents, time after time. Whilst you will occasionally make use of full-blown deception, your bread and butter will be solid, value-based plays (if you want to make money, that is).

Once you start facing stronger opposition however, an exclusively value-based approach will become less effective. You're going to have to make some deceptive plays against better players or they'll be able to read you too easily. Even so, deceptive plays should be used relatively sparingly because, unless you're fortunate enough to have an exceptionally good feel for the game, it's too expensive to depart regularly from good old straightforward value-based play.

As a result we'll worry about deception later in the book (in Chapter Ten). First you need to learn how to make solid, value-based plays. You need to know which hands to throw away, which hands to play, and how to bet on the hands you do play.

Summary: value-based plays and deceptive plays

Each time you act, you can either bet according to the strength of your hand, i.e. play for value, or you can try to play deceptively to mislead your opponents. Most of the time you should do the former and simply play for value.

Chapter Four:
The fundamentals of betting

Why the best hand bets

Poker is a game of both incomplete information (you don't know what your opponents hold) and future uncertainty (you don't know what cards are coming next). This can make it very difficult to work out what's going on for a beginner. We're going to simplify things for the time being by filling in the missing information and removing the uncertainty.

Things are actually more straightforward at the end of the hand than the beginning, so that's where we'll start.

On the river

Consider the following highly hypothetical example. There are ten players sitting at the table and £100 in the pot. The flop, turn and river have been dealt and the last round of betting is about to commence. Let's see how the players would act *if they could see each other's cards*.

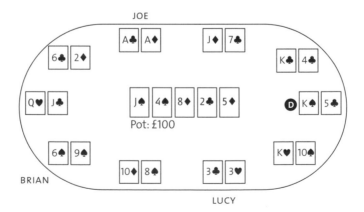

Everyone can see that Joe has the best hand. He holds a pair of aces, and none of the other players can beat that. How do you think the betting proceeds?

Well, we hope you worked that one out. Everybody checks round to Joe, who bets, and then everyone else folds. Do we need to explain why? Since it's the first hand, we will. Everybody checks because they know they're going to lose the pot to Joe, so if they put money in the pot it's just going straight into his pocket. They might briefly think that by putting in a big bet they could get Joe to fold. But then they would remember that, just as they can see Joe's cards, Joe can see their cards. Since Joe can see that he's winning, there's no way on earth he's going to fold. Therefore there's no point anyone other than Joe betting.

When it gets to Joe's turn, he bets – which is natural since he's winning. Admittedly there doesn't seem to be much point in Joe betting since everyone will fold anyway so he probably won't win any extra money by betting. But maybe, just maybe, somebody will misread their hand (or Joe's hand) and mistakenly think that they, rather than Joe, are winning. If that happens, Joe will get a call (or a raise) of his bet and win some extra money.

Ok, we've laboured the point enough. On the river, with all hole cards exposed, the best hand bets and everyone else folds. It's that simple.

On the turn

Now let's go back a round of betting, to the turn, and see how things are different earlier in the hand. Again, let's suppose that all the players can see each other's cards. Joe's still winning with two aces and nobody has a better hand at present. What happens?

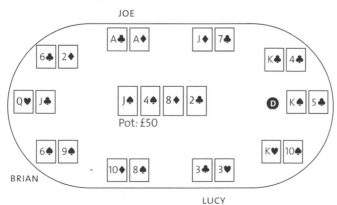

This one's a bit trickier because nobody knows as yet what the last card (the river card) will be. However, since Joe is in the lead at the moment – with two aces – it seems reasonable to think that he's favourite to win the pot. So is it the same as the previous example where all check to Joe, who bets, and then everyone else folds?

Not quite. It is reasonable for Joe to bet since, as before, he is in the lead. It is clearly in his interests to get his opponents to put money in the pot, because he's the player most likely to win it.

But this time it is not so obvious that all the other players should fold when Joe bets. Some of them might reasonably think there's a chance that the last card will improve their hand and that they will beat his pair of aces. Lucy, for example, has a pair of threes. If the river card is another three she'll be in the lead. Similarly, Brian needs only another spade to make a flush.

Here's the question then – under what circumstances is it correct to call a bet with cards to come when you aren't winning but have a chance of improving your hand?

The first thing you must consider in making such a decision is *how likely* you are to improve your hand with the remaining board cards that you haven't as yet seen. Is there a way of calculating how likely it is that the remaining card or cards will help you?

To answer that question, we first have to introduce a few new ideas.

Outs

We term any card that will improve your hand to a winning hand, an *out*. In practice, you don't always know which cards will give you a winning hand because you don't know exactly what your opponents hold. As we'll see, though, it's frequently possible to make some fairly safe guesses in this respect.

As an illustration, let's suppose you have been dealt:

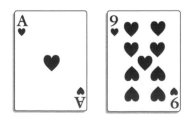

You're at the turn, with just the river card to come and the board is:

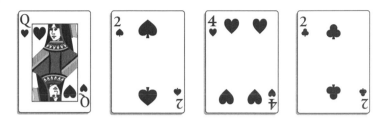

First question – what is your hand? Well at the moment, it's nothing much. You don't even have a pair, just an ace, you don't have a straight and you don't have a flush. But you do *nearly* have a flush – you have four hearts, so if the river is a heart, you will complete your flush. Therefore all the hearts are *outs* for you.

What's more, because you hold the ace of hearts, you will have the *best possible flush* if you make your hand. We need some terminology for all this:

- **Four flush** – four cards of the same suit
- **Flush draw**   a hand that can improve to a flush. If you have a four flush and there are more cards to come, you have a flush draw
- **Drawing hand** – a hand that isn't yet complete but has the potential to become a good hand if the subsequent board cards are favourable
- **Nut flush** – the best possible flush given the cards on the table. You have the nut flush if you hold the highest card of that suit that's not already on the board – usually the ace.

Now you need to work out your chances of making a heart flush on the river. This bit gets a little mathematical, but it's really not too difficult so please bear with us.

First you count your outs – in this case, any of the remaining hearts in the deck. Two of the hearts are in your hand and two of them are on the board. Since the deck started with thirteen hearts, there are now nine hearts still out there. You have nine outs in this case. (Of course, some of the hearts might be in your opponents' hands – but you don't have any information on that one way or the other here so it doesn't affect the probabilities.)

Next you need to count the number of unseen cards. You have seen two cards in your hand and four on the board for a total of six seen cards. Since the deck started with 52 cards that means that there are still 46 cards unseen. Nine of those 46 unseen cards are hearts, which will make your flush, and the remaining 37 of them are not hearts and won't help you at all. Therefore your chances of making your flush on the river are 37-to-9 against, or a little over 4-to-1. This can also be expressed as about 19.6%. (By the way, 4-to-1 isn't the same as 1-in-4, which would be 25%. See Appendix A: Odds and probabilities for an explanation of this if you need it.)

So you will make your flush on the river 19.6% of the time. Remember, it is *always* a 19.6% chance. It doesn't matter whether you feel lucky or unlucky or hot or cold or whatever. Nineteen point six percent of the time that last card will be a heart and make you your flush – and there is nothing that anyone can do to change that (except by cheating).

Extra outs

So those are the chances of making a flush. But are there any other hands that you think might win for you?

Recall that the board is Q♥ 2♠ 4♥ 7♦ and you hold A♥ 9♥. Suppose you're up against a single opponent. Perhaps you suspect him of having a hand like queen-x (in other words a queen plus another card) which would give him just a pair of queens overall, or something similar in strength to this. Do you have any extra outs? Yes, you do. If an ace comes on the river then you will improve to a pair of aces but leave your opponent on a pair of queens. How many extra outs is that? The answer is three – the remaining three aces in the deck.

Now your total number of outs has risen to nine hearts plus three aces for a total of twelve. Since there are still 46 unseen cards, there are now only 34 cards that don't help your hand. Your chances of making the winning hand on the river are now 34-to-12 against, or just less than 3-to-1, or around 26%. Look how much those three extra outs have helped you.

To reiterate our earlier point: in practice you don't know exactly what your opponent has, so you don't know exactly what your outs are. Instead of a pair of queens he might have, say, two pair in which case an ace is no good to you and you'll need to make the heart flush to win. On the other hand he might not even be able to beat your ace-high and you might already be winning. You have to make an educated guess, and in this case you might reasonably guess that you're not winning at present but that you have twelve outs.

Technical note

If you assume in the above example that your opponent actually has a queen (rather than merely a hand 'like' queen-x), then there aren't 46 unseen cards, there are 45. Therefore you calculate your chances of making the winning hand to be 33-to-12 against (instead of 34-to-12), or 26.7% (instead of 26%). In practice, however, you can almost always ignore this sort of adjustment in hold'em because its effect is minimal.

Non-nut draws

Now let's suppose instead that you hold:

(with a board of Q♥ 2♠ 4♥ 7♦ as before). How many outs do you have? Again you might decide you have twelve outs, for the same reasons as above: nine hearts and three kings. But is your hand as good?

If you are up against a single opponent with queen–x then yes – because all twelve outs will win you the hand. But in general K♥ 9♥ isn't anywhere near as good as A♥ 9♥ because, even if you hit your flush, there's a chance that your king high flush might lose to another player's ace-high flush if they happen to be holding two hearts including the ace. In this case you're not drawing to the nut flush, and we say that your outs are not *nut outs*.

In general, you should downgrade your assessment of non-nut drawing hands for precisely this reason. Many poor players will play any two suited cards in the hope of making a flush – and then lose all their money to a better flush when they hit it. Don't make this mistake.

A handy rule – 2x / 4x

Finally, we'd like to draw to your attention a useful rule of thumb for calculating how likely you are to make your hand given how many outs you have.

- With one more card to come, the probability of making your draw expressed as a percentage is roughly two times your number of outs.
- With two more cards to come, the probability of making your draw expressed as a percentage is roughly four times your number of outs.

For example, if you have eight outs after the flop then you are roughly 16% to make your draw on the turn, and 32% to make it by the river. Bear in mind however that this rule yields approximate numbers. (The actual numbers in this case are 17.0% and 31.9%.)

Quiz: outs

In each of the questions below, you are facing one opponent. You are told what your hole cards and the four board cards are, plus how good a hand you will need in order to win. Your job is to count how many outs you have on the river, i.e. when the last board card is dealt.

Question 1. You hold 6♠ 7♥ and the board is 5♣ 8♦ 2♥ K♠. You will win the hand if you make a straight – how many outs do you have?

Question 2. You hold 9♣ 10♣ and the board is 2♦ J♠ 3♣ 5♣. You will win the hand if you make a flush – how many outs do you have?

Question 3. You hold 6♦ 6♥ and the board is 7♠ 4♦ Q♥ 10♣. You will win the hand if you make three of a kind – how many outs do you have?

Question 4. You hold 9♠ 9♥ and the board is 10♣ K♦ 8♦ 9♦, giving you three of a kind, nines. But there is a real likelihood of an opponent holding a straight or flush. You will win if you can beat any straight or flush – how many outs do you have?

Question 5. You hold A♦ 8♦ and the board is 8♣ 7♦ 2♦ 3♥, giving you a pair of eights. You will win if you can beat a player holding a pair of kings in their hand – how many outs do you have?

Question 6. You hold J♣ 10♣ and the board is 8♦ 4♠ 10♥ 9♥. You will win if you can beat a player holding a pair of aces – how many outs do you have?

Question 7. You hold 8♠ 9♠ and the board is A♣ 6♠ K♥ 7♠. You will win if you can beat three of a kind – how many outs do you have?

Question 8 (difficult). You hold Q♥ K♥ and the board is 8♥ 10♠ 10♣ J♥. Your opponent has a pair of sixes in their hand – how many outs do you have?

Now we're going to ask you to calculate the rough odds against hitting one of your outs. You need to count your outs and then divide the number of non-outs remaining in the deck by the number of outs to get the answer. You should try to do this in your head.

Question 9. On the turn, you have the following four cards to a straight: 7-8-10-J. What *approximately* are the odds against you making your straight on the river?

(a) 5-to-1 (b) 7.5-to-1 (c) 10-to-1 (d) 20-to-1.

Question 10. On the turn, you have the following four cards to a straight, 5-6-7-8. What *approximately* are the odds against you making your straight on the river?

(a) 5-to-1 (b) 7.5-to-1 (c) 10-to-1 (d) 20-to-1.

Question 11. You hold K♦ 2♦ and the board is K♣ 7♣ K♥ 8♣. If you make a full house or better, you will win. What *approximately* are the odds against this happening?

(a) 2.5-to-1 (b) 3.5-to-1 (c) 4.5-to-1 (d) 5.5-to-1.

The last few questions in this quiz ask you to calculate the approximate probability of hitting one of your outs, expressed as a percentage.

Question 12. On the turn you hold a flush draw, with nine outs. What approximately are the chances of making your flush on the river?

Question 13. On the flop you hold an inside straight draw, giving you four outs. What approximately are the chances of making your straight on either the turn or the river?

Question 14 (very difficult). You are dealt 7♥ 7♠ and the flop comes 6♦ 7♦ J♦. What approximately are the chances of making a full house or better on either the turn or the river?

Answers to quiz

Answer 1. You have 5-6-7-8, and hence eight outs to make a straight – any four or any nine.

Answer 2. This is a standard flush draw. There are thirteen clubs in all, and four are in your hand or on the board. Therefore there are nine clubs remaining in the deck, and you have nine outs.

Answer 3. The only way you can make three of a kind is if another six comes. There are four sixes in all, two of which are in your hand. You therefore have a paltry two outs.

Answer 4. To beat a straight or flush, you've going to have to make a full house or four of a kind, which sounds like a tall order at first. But this will happen whenever the board pairs on the river, i.e. if any ten, king, eight or nine comes. There are sixteen of these cards in all (tens, kings, eights or nines), six of which are in your hand or on the board. There are therefore ten of them remaining in the deck. You have ten outs.

Answer 5. Your outs are:
- any eight, for three of a kind – there are two of these remaining
- any ace, for two pair (aces and eights) – there are three remaining
- any diamond, for a flush – there are nine remaining (it's a standard flush draw).

You have two plus three plus nine outs, a total of fourteen.

Answer 6. Your outs are:
- any seven or queen for a straight – eight of these
- any ten for three of a kind (tens) – two of these
- any jack for two pair (tens and jacks) – three of these.

You have a total of thirteen outs.

Answer 7. Your outs are:

■ any five or ten for a straight – eight of these
■ any spade for a flush – nine of these.

But – we mustn't double-count. Two of the spades are the five and ten of spades, and they have already been counted as cards that will make your straight. You therefore have a total of fifteen outs, not seventeen.

Answer 8. Your outs are as follows:

■ Any heart will make you a flush, except for the six or ten which make your opponent a full house – seven of these
■ Any nine or ace will make you a straight – there are eight of these although two of them are hearts and have already been counted, so call it six
■ Any queen or king will give you a higher two pair than your opponent – there are six of these
■ Any eight or jack will leave two pair on the board and you'll have a higher kicker than your opponent – there are six of these.

Your number of outs is a whopping 7 + 6 + 6 + 6 = 25. You are actually a 58% favourite to win the hand.

Answer 9. This straight draw needs a nine to complete, and there are only four of those. Of the forty-six cards remaining in the deck, you therefore have four outs and 42 non-outs. The odds against making your straight are therefore 42 divided by 4, or 10.5-to-1. The answer is (c).

Answer 10. This time your straight draw has eight outs, needing a four or a nine to complete. You therefore have 38 non-outs. The odds against making your straight are therefore 38 divided by 8, or 4.75-to-1. The answer is (a).

Answer 11. Your outs are any seven, eight or two for a full house (there are nine of these remaining), or the last king in the deck for four of a kind. You therefore have ten outs, and 36 non-outs. The odds against hitting one of these are therefore 36 divided by 10, or 3.6-to-1. The answer is (b).

Answer 12. You have nine outs and there's one card to come. Your chances are approximately nine (the number of outs) times two (multiply by two with one card to come), or 18%.

Answer 13. You have four outs and there are two cards to come. Your chances are approximately four (the number of outs) times four (multiply by four with two cards to come), or 16%.

Answer 14. You will make a full house if the board pairs. You therefore have seven outs on the turn: one seven, three sixes and three jacks. But if you miss on the flop you will have ten outs on the river: the seven you had on the turn plus the three cards in the deck matching the turn card. So you have seven outs for one card, then ten outs for one card. Your chances are approximately seven (the number of outs on the turn) times two plus ten (the number of outs on the river) times two, or 34%.

The actual figure in this case is just under 33% (remember that the 2x / 4x rule yields approximate numbers). You can remember than whenever you have three of a kind on the flop, you are 33%, or about 2-to-1 against, to make a full house by the river.

Pot odds

Now we'll return to the hand we were looking at earlier. You hold:

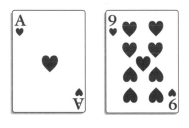

and the board is:

Suppose you've concluded on this particular occasion that you need to make a flush on the river to win, and your nine outs make you around 20% to do so. Your opponent bets. Do you call?

You'll need a little more information to make your decision because it's not only the number of outs that determines whether or not you should call a bet. You must also consider the size of the bet, and how it relates to the *size* of the pot.

Whenever you call a bet, you should think of it as making a wager. If you win the hand, you will win the money in the pot. If you lose the hand, you will forfeit the money that it cost you to call.

All wagers (in poker or otherwise) involve *odds*, which are calculated as the size of your potential winnings divided by the size of your stake. When you are contemplating making a call in poker, the *pot odds* are defined as the total size of the pot divided by the amount you have to call.

If an opponent has made a bet that is small in relation to the size of the pot then the odds are good because, by calling, you are risking a small amount of money for the chance to win a relatively large amount. If on the other hand the bet is large in relation to the size of the pot then the odds are poor, because you will be risking a large amount of money for the chance to win a relatively small amount.

It follows naturally that, all other things being equal, you should be more inclined to call bets if the pot odds are good, that is, if the bet size is relatively small in comparison with the total size of the pot. Or, to put it another way, if the total pot size is relatively large in comparison with the bet size.

Calculating pot odds

To be a half decent poker player you have to be comfortable with calculations involving pot odds. They involve a slight grasp of maths and probability, but nothing too demanding. This next section is arguably the hardest in the whole book, but it's so fundamental that it's well worth making the effort to understand it.

Even if you don't like manipulating the figures in detail you should at least have some idea of when the odds are favourable and when they're unfavourable. If you can do that, you'll be well ahead of most casual players.

If you're not familiar with the ideas and terminology behind odds in gambling then we suggest you read over Appendix A: Odds and probabilities at this point. If on the other hand you can work out in your sleep that 3 to 1 against is the same as 1-in-4 which is the same as 25%, then you'll be just fine.

Anyway, back to the hand. Let's suppose there's £100 in the pot and your opponent bets £20, so it will cost you £20 to see if you can make your flush.

First let's consider what happens if you fold. If you fold, you neither win nor lose money – your balance stays the same. Does that seem like the wrong way of looking at it to you? Does it seem like the money in the pot is in some sense partly yours, because you've already invested in it?

That's a beguiling notion, but it's wrong. The money in the pot isn't yours, it's the pot's. It doesn't matter that you may have put money in the pot earlier on in the hand – that's history now. Therefore folding is *always* a break-even move regardless of the decisions you may have made previously. To put it another way, *do not* throw good money after bad because of a feeling that you've already invested in the hand. Make each decision on its own merits.

Now what instead happens if you call? There's £120 in the pot (the £100 that was there at the start of the betting round, plus £20 from your opponent) and it costs you £20 to have a shot at winning it – that's pot odds of 120-to-20, or 6-to-1. These are the odds that that the pot is laying you if you call the bet.

As we saw earlier, your chances of hitting the flush are just over 4-to-1 against, which is somewhat unlikely. But the pot odds, which are 6-to-1, are greater than your actual chance of winning the hand. This is exactly what all gamblers are looking for – a winning edge. You should call.

Do you find this counter-intuitive? Even though you're going to make your flush less than one time in five, it still makes sense to match your opponent's bet. The reason for this is that the one time you do make the flush, you also win the money that was already in the pot. This sum is large enough to justify the risk of losing an extra £20.

We can actually work out how profitable this move is if we wish, and the technique for doing so is described in Appendix B: Expectation (and it uses this example as an illustration). It turns out that your expected profit, often just called expectation, is in this case around £7.40. So every time you make this call, you expect to win £7.40 on average. It may not *seem* like that since you either win £120 or lose £20, with nothing in between. But if you made this exact same call a thousand times, you are likely to win something reasonably close to 1,000 x £7.40 = £7,400 in total. This is because, as we mentioned earlier, luck *always* evens out in the long run.

You don't need to be able to calculate your expected profits during a hand. In general, you just need to remember that a call is profitable if the pot odds are greater than the odds against making a winning hand.

- Pot odds equals total pot size (including all bets already in) divided by bet size (how much you have to call).
- Odds against making a winning hand equals number of non-outs (cards that don't help you) divided by number of outs (cards that do).

The larger the pot odds, the better for you, and the more you should tend to call. The smaller the odds *against* making your hand, the better for you, and the more you should tend to call. When the pot odds are bigger than the odds against making a winning hand, a call is profitable. The greater the difference, the more profitable is the call.

When we talk about a profitable call, we mean a call which has positive expectation and hence will make you money in the long run if you make many such calls. You will often hear a profitable call referred to as *good call* or a *correct call*.

Working out whether a call is profitable or not sounds complicated but it becomes easier with practice. Fortunately there's some practice for you coming up right now.

Quiz: pot odds

Question 1. The pot contains £100 and your opponent bets £50. What odds is the pot offering you if you call?

Question 2. The pot contains £78 and your opponent bets £78. What odds is the pot offering you if you call?

Question 3. The pot contains £60 and an opponent bets £60. Another opponent calls. What odds is the pot offering you if you call?

Question 4. The pot contains £50 and an opponent bets £25. There are four callers. What odds is the pot offering you if you call?

Question 5. The pot contains £125 and an opponent bets £75. Another opponent raises a further £125, betting £200 in all. What odds is the pot offering you if you call?

In each of the following questions, you are at the turn with just the river card left to be dealt. You are told what your hole cards and the four board cards are, plus how good a hand you will need in order to win. Your job is to (a) count how many outs you have and hence work out the odds of making a winning hand, (b) work out the pot odds on offer based on the betting and (c) determine whether or not a call is profitable (based solely on a comparison of these figures).

Question 6. You hold K♠ J♠ and the board is A♠ 7♦ 2♠ 6♣. The pot contains £50 and your single opponent bets £25. You will win if you make a flush – do you call?

Question 7. You hold J♥ J♣ and the board is J♦ 6♦ 10♦ 5♦. The pot contains £60 and there is a pot-sized bet (£60) and two callers. Since one of your opponents must have a diamond flush, you will need to make a full house or better to win. Do you call?

Question 8. You hold 6♥ 7♥ and the board is 4♣ Q♠ 8♦ K♥. The pot contains £100 and your opponent bets £25. You will need a straight to win. Do you call?

Answers to quiz

Answer 1. You are calling £50 into a pot that contains £150 (the £100 that it started with plus your opponent's bet). Your odds are 150-to-50, or 3-to-1.

Answer 2. You are calling £78 into a pot that contains £156. Your odds are 156-to-78, or 2-to-1. Note that all pot-sized bets offer you 2-to-1 If you're the first caller.

Answer 3. You are calling £60 into a pot that contains £180 (the £60 it started with, plus a bet and a call of £60). Your odds are 180-to-60, or 3-to-1. All pot sized bets offer you 3-to-1 if you're the second caller.

Answer 4. You are calling £25 into a pot that contains £175 (the £50 it started with, plus a bet and four calls of £25 each). Your odds are 175-to-25 or 7-to-1. The more callers there are, and the smaller the initial bet, the more favourable are the pot odds. These are very good odds indeed.

Answer 5. You are calling £200 into a pot that contains £400 (the £125 it started with, plus the bet of £75 and raise of £200). Your odds are 400-to-200, or 2-to-1.

Answer 6. You have nine outs to make the flush, the nine remaining spades in the deck. The odds against hitting it are 37-to-9, or just over 4-to-1. The pot contains £75 and it will cost you £25 to call, so the pot is offering you 3-to-1. Since the pot odds (3-to-1) are worse than the odds of making your hand (just over 4-to-1), you should fold.

Answer 7. You have ten outs to make the full house or four of a kind (three fives, three sixes, three tens and one jack). The odds against this happening are 36-to-10, or 3.6-to-1. The pot contains £240 and it will cost you £60 to call, so the pot is offering you 4-to-1. Since the pot odds (4-to-1) are better than the odds of making your hand (3.6-to-1), you should call.

Answer 8. You have four outs for the straight (the four fives). The odds against hitting one are 42-to-4, or just over 10-to-1. The pot contains £125 and it will cost you £25 to call, so the pot is offering you 5-to-1. Since the pot odds (5-to-1) are far worse than the odds of making your hand (over 10-to-1), you have a clear fold. Note that even though your opponent's bet was relatively small (compared with the pot size), you can't call with a draw this weak. You have too few outs.

Implied odds and uncertainty

In our discussion of pot odds thus far, we've made an assumption that all you will win if you hit your draw (i.e. improve your hand) is the pot *as it currently stands*. In practice however, you may win extra money from your opponent(s) and this extra money needs to be factored into the equation. In other words:

■ Total winnings equals pot size now plus opponents' future contributions

Suppose once again that you are drawing to a flush and contemplating calling a bet from an opponent on the turn. If you make your flush, you believe you will surely have the best hand. Where might any extra money come from if you decide to call? There are two possible sources:

1. Any players still to act after you in the current round may call the bet too, making the pot bigger than it is at present before the next card is dealt.

2. You may win extra money from your opponents on the river if they call a bet from you then, or make a bet of their own.

At the point you have to make your decision, however, you don't know exactly what your opponents' future contributions will be. They might not put any more money into the pot at all, or they might be kind enough to go all-in when you have the nuts. All you can do is work on the basis of a reasonable guess of what they might do, your *estimated* total winnings if you make your hand.

Your *implied odds* are then defined as follows.

■ Implied odds equals estimated total winnings divided by bet size (how much you have to call)

Implied odds are just like pot odds, except you add your expected future winnings to the pot size. Your implied odds are therefore usually better than your pot odds, because you reckon to make *some* further money if you improve your hand.

In the previous section we said that a call is profitable if the pot odds are greater than the odds against making a winning hand. We're now going to refine that slightly, and say that a call is profitable if the *implied odds* are greater than the odds against making a winning hand. Since implied odds are usually somewhat better than pot odds, it is often the case that implied odds indicate that a call is justified even when the pot odds don't.

Estimating implied odds

Implied odds can come into play on earlier betting rounds too, not just the turn. You might have a drawing hand on the flop and be considering calling a bet. In this case you have to worry about:

- What happens if you make your hand on the turn? Will your opponent make contributions to the pot on both the turn and the river?
- What happens if you miss your hand on the turn? Will your opponent bet again, forcing you to pay even more to try to beat him?

All in all, implied odds are a very tricky thing to evaluate precisely – a rough estimate is usually the best you can hope for. In general, however, your implied odds are better if:

- Your opponents are loose or aggressive, meaning that they bet or call more readily than others. Loose and aggressive opponents are more likely to pay off your hand if you hit it.
- Your hand would be *well disguised* if you made it, so that your opponents are unlikely to suspect you of having such a hand. Flushes are poorly disguised because when three suited cards appear on the board, most half-decent players start worrying about a flush being a possibility.
- You are up against many opponents rather than one. This way, if you do hit your hand, the chances are better that some of your opponents will call your bet.

And, although strictly speaking it doesn't affect the implied odds, we'll reiterate the important point that you should be very wary of drawing to non-nut hands. You want your hand to be virtually unbeatable if you make it, rather than a possible second best.

So, in practice, deciding whether you have the correct odds to call a bet may involve much more uncertainty than the rather clear-cut examples we've covered so far.

Dealing with uncertainty

Have you noticed that we have now seen several different types of uncertainty:

- You don't know what cards are coming next. However, you can calculate the *chances* of any particular combination arising very precisely.
- If you successfully draw a winning hand, you don't know how well your opponents will pay off your hand, if at all. Evaluating the implied odds is always going to involve some estimation and approximation.
- You don't know exactly what your opponents hold. You may make the hand you were drawing to and still lose to an even better hand (that is, if you weren't drawing to the nuts). Alternatively, you may miss your draw completely but still have the best hand and win the pot.

How are you supposed to make a decision with all this uncertainty floating around? You can't know exactly what the right move is of course, but you should try to pick the option that on *average* will produce the best return. To put it another way, you should seek the course of action that fares best according to a balanced assessment of all the possibilities.

Some people have a very good intuition for this kind of decision making – they are the naturally gifted poker players. But such decisions can also be reasoned out mathematically. We've provided some specific guidance on how to do this in the section on evaluation of multiple possibilities in Chapter Thirteen.

Quiz: Implied odds and uncertainty

Question 1. You are dealt 5♣ 6♣ in the big blind and three players call. The small blind folds and you check, making the pot £9. The flop comes 3♦ 4♥ J♠. You check and the player to your left bets £10. The other two players in the pot both call, making the pot £39, and it's now your turn. You believe you will win if a two or a seven comes, making you a straight. Do you call?

Question 2. You are dealt A♦ K♣ on the button and raise. One player calls you and the pot is now £15. The flop comes 7♦ 8♠ 9♦ and both you and your opponent check. The turn is 10♦ and your opponent bets £15. It looks like he has a straight (although a flush is a possibility too), so you're going to need to make your ace-high flush to win. Should you call?

Question 3. You are dealt A♠ 9♠ in the big blind. Four players call, including the small blind, and you decide to check. The pot is now £25. The flop comes J♠ 2♠ 7♥ and the small blind leads out with a bet of £20. It seems likely that he has at least a pair of jacks. Do you call?

Question 4. You are dealt K♥ 5♥ in the small blind. Three players call the big blind, as do you. The big blind checks and the pot is now £10. The flop comes A♥ 10♥ 3♣. You check, as does the big blind. The next player bets £10 and one player calls. It's now your turn and there is £30 in the pot and one player (the big blind) to act after you. Do you call in the hope of making your flush?

Answers to quiz

Answer 1. You have eight outs to make your straight and there are 47 unknown cards out there. The odds against hitting are therefore 39-to-8 or just under 5-to-1. You have to call £10 into a pot which is now £39, making the pot odds just under 4-to-1. These pot odds, 4-to-1, are therefore just less than the odds against making your hand, 5-to-1. On the basis of the pot odds alone, a call isn't justified.

But surely if a two or seven does come you'll be able to make some extra money on the turn or river, either by one of your opponents betting or them calling your bet. You decide it's reasonable to assume you'll win at least an extra £20 if this happens. So you can imagine the pot to have £59 in it rather than £39, and your implied odds (for a call of £10) are just under 6-to-1. This figure is clearly bigger than the odds of making your hand, so you call.

Answer 2. You have nine outs to make a flush and there are 47 unknown cards out there. The odds against hitting are therefore 38-to-9 or just over 4-to-1. You have to call £15 into a pot which is now £30, making the pot odds 2-to-1. These pot odds, 2-to-1, are much less than the odds against making your hand, 4.2-to-1. On the basis of the pot odds alone, a call isn't justified.

Do you have much greater implied odds? Probably not. If another diamond comes, your opponent is likely to be worried about you having a flush and not likely to bet or to call a big bet from you. Even if you think you can extract a further £30 from him if you hit – which seems unlikely – your implied odds are only (30 + 30) divided by 15, or 4-to-1. This is still a little less than the odds of making your hand so you fold.

Don't call pot sized bets with straight or flush draws against one opponent. If you had two opponents rather than one in this situation then you would instead be calling £15 into a pot of £45, giving you pot odds of 3-to-1 and implied odds that should make it over 4-to-1. Against two opponents rather than one, a call is more easily justified.

Answer 3. You have nine outs to make a flush which will almost certainly win for you. You may not have any extra outs although it's possible that an ace will put you in the lead. You thus have somewhere between nine and twelve outs – we'll call it ten. The odds against hitting are therefore 37-to-10 or 3.7-to-1. You have to call £20 into a pot of £45, making the pot odds just over 2-to-1. On the basis of the pot odds alone, a call isn't justified.

What about implied odds? Unfortunately these aren't much help here. It's possible that the other two players involved in the pot might call after you, and then you could work on the basis that the pot was £85, giving you the odds you need. But it's probably more likely that they'll fold, leaving you heads up (playing one other person). Worse still, one of the other players might raise rather than call or fold, and that will surely make you have to fold your hand. There are just too many ways of this one going wrong so you fold.

Answer 4. Although you don't have an ace, you still have the nut flush draw since the ace of hearts is on the board. You therefore have nine good outs and the odds against hitting one are 38-to-9 or just over 4-to-1. You have to call £10 into a pot of £30, making the pot odds 3-to-1. On the basis of the pot odds alone, a call isn't justified.

However, the implied odds are some help here. Firstly the big blind might call the bet in this round if you do since he's the last to act (so doesn't need to fear a raise from a player acting after him) and has good pot odds (4-to-1). If he calls then there'll be an extra £10 in the pot and your call will be a more or less break-even move.

Moreover, if you do make a flush you'll almost certainly be able to extract a little extra money from your opponents anyway – perhaps £25 you might guess. All in all it might be reasonable to assume you can make an extra £20 – £30 this hand if you make your flush, making the implied odds somewhere between 5-to-1 and 6-to-1. The only potential problem to worry about is the big blind raising immediately after your call, but that seems unlikely since he checked this round already. You decide to call.

Note the difference between this and the previous question. Although the situations seem superficially rather similar, the indications are much more favourable this time. In particular, the pot and implied odds are a little greater, and there's less chance of a raise behind you because (a) there's only one player to act rather than two, and (b) he's already checked in this round. These factors are more than sufficient to make the difference between a fold and a call.

How much to bet

We've discussed calling in some detail, and talked about what makes a profitable call. Now we're going to consider betting, and what constitutes a good bet. First however we need to examine the relationship between betting and calling a little more closely.

The effect on the bettor of a profitable call

We've seen that calling a bet with what you believe currently to be the worst hand can be a winning move – as long as your chances of improving are good enough and the pot odds justify it. When you call in such a situation, you gain. But what effect does it have on your opponent when you make a profitable call?

Let's return to our earlier example. You hold:

and the board is:

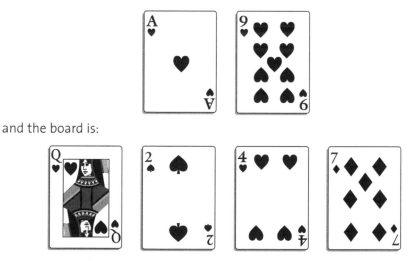

so you have a four-flush. There's £100 in the pot and your opponent bets £20. If you fold, your opponent wins the £120 now in the pot. If on the other hand you call then:

- around 80% of the time you fail to make your flush, and your opponent wins an extra £20, for a total of £140
- around 20% of the time you do make your flush and your opponent gets nothing.

It turns out that your opponent's expectation (expected winnings), averaged out over these two cases, is approximately £112.60.

Since this figure is less than the £120 your opponent would get if you folded, he has suffered by your calling him, and he expects to make a loss as a result. You may have noticed that his expected loss is £120 minus £112.60, or £7.40, which precisely equals your expected gain which we calculated earlier. Hopefully you can see why this would be, since you and your opponent are both competing for exactly the same prize.

Let's just take stock of this important point. If you make a move which is profitable for you, it costs your opponents money. The more profitable that move is for you, the more it harms them.

But conversely this must mean that whenever your opponents make profitable moves, it must cost you money! In order to stop this happening, you have to try to deny your opponents opportunities to make profitable moves. But how?

Preventing a profitable call

Let's swap the hands over and suppose that you hold the stronger hand and your opponent has the flush draw. How can you protect yourself against the loss you would effectively incur if you bet £20 and your opponent called? The answer is simple – bet more money. By doing so, you can make it too expensive for your opponent to call.

This table shows how the size of your bet (measured in comparison with the pot size) affects the pot odds that you offer your opponent, an includes an example based on a pot of £100.

You bet	Example based on £100 pot	You offer pot odds of:
A fifth of the pot	£20	6-to-1
A quarter of the pot	£25	5-to-1
A third of the pot	£33	4-to-1
Half the pot	£50	3-to-1
Two-thirds of the pot	£66	2.5-to-1
Three-quarters of the pot	£75	2.33-to-1
The pot	£100	2-to-1
Twice the pot	£200	1.5-to-1
Ten times the pot	£1,000	1.1-to-1

You don't need to memorise these figures. You can just reason them out when needed, for example: "There's £100 in the pot now. If I bet £50 (half the pot) then my opponent will have to call £50 into a pot of £150. That's odds of 150-to-50, or 3-to-1."

You can clearly see that, the more you bet, the worse the odds you are offering your opponent. In our example above, you need to bet enough so that the pot odds your opponent is getting are *worse* than the odds against making his flush. Since it's about 4-to-1 against him making his flush, you need to bet at least a third of the pot for this to be true.

But don't forget about your opponent's *implied* odds too. He might reason that you will call a bet on the river if he makes his flush. If he's right about this, his implied odds are better than the 4-to-1 you're offering him. You would therefore need to bet more than, perhaps, half the pot (giving him only 3-to-1) to make his call incorrect, and hence unprofitable for him.

However much you bet, make sure that your opponent doesn't have the implied odds to justify a call. Then, if he does call, it will cost him money. (By which we don't mean that he'll lose money *every* time of course, just that making that sort of call will cost him money in the long run.) And if it costs him money, it makes money for you. The correct thing for your opponent to do in this case is to fold, leaving you to win the pot. This is a good result for you.

As before, we need to emphasise that, in practice, you don't know what cards your opponents actually hold and so don't know how many outs they have. Unless you've got the nuts, they might even be beating you of course.

But if you are in fact winning, it's not that common for an opponent to have more than around ten outs to beat you. Ten outs would make an opponent around 3.5-to-1 against improving. You won't go too far wrong if, whenever you have an opponent whom you suspect is drawing, you never give him (implied) pot odds that are better than this.

Betting the right amount

Let's sum up what we've learnt about betting so far:

■ You should generally bet when you believe you're in the lead.

■ You should bet a sufficient amount that no other player has the odds to call correctly (because a correct call is profitable for your opponent and hence costs you money).

Because you always need to consider the odds that you will be offering your opponents to call, your bets should *always* be considered in relation to the pot size. If you ignored this fact and, for example, made a £10 bet every round, the odds you would be offering your opponents would be getting more and more attractive as the pot grew. There aren't many scenarios where it would be in your interests to do this.

Instead you should first work out what odds you want to offer your opponents, and then size your bet accordingly. It turns out that – as a very general rule – you will usually want to make a bet of somewhere between 50% and 100% of the pot size, thereby offering pot odds of somewhere between 3-to-1 and 2-to-1 to the first person to call you.

Subsequent callers will receive better odds, because they are calling the same amount but into a larger pot. As a result you need to bet a little bit more against many opponents, to stop later callers from getting odds that make a call correct for them. Conversely, you can bet a little bit less than you otherwise would when you're up against just one or two opponents.

Once again, pause to contemplate the fact that you don't know exactly what your opponents hold or how many outs they may have. If you believe your hand is winning then a bigger bet may earn you more money. But if it turns out you are losing, it will cost you more. Playing good poker is all about treading this very fine line.

Small bets

The problem with bets much smaller than 50% of the pot is that they offer very attractive odds for almost anybody with half a decent hand. If you honestly believe that you're in the lead, then you will usually want to bet at least this much to stop weaker hands from outdrawing you too cheaply, in other words not allow them the odds to make a correct call. (And don't forget about their implied odds.)

Moreover, betting usually reveals information about your hand, namely that you believe it to be strong. If you're going to give this information away to your opponents, you should at least make sure you get a reasonable amount of money out of them in return.

As a result, with more cards still to be dealt, bets of less than half the pot are not usually made by players who believe they are winning. They more normally occur:

- When a player is trying to discover where he stands, and how strong his opponents are – these are often called *probe bets*.
- On the river, after all the cards have been dealt, when a player is trying to extract a little extra money from an opponent with a weaker hand.

Big bets

Bets that are bigger than the pot size are called *oversize* bets, and making an oversize bet is known as *overbetting the pot*. One problem with overbetting the pot is that you stand to risk a lot (your bet) for a smaller reward (the pot). Generally speaking, risking a large amount to win a smaller amount isn't a good idea. In practice, oversize bets are liable to be called only by the very strongest hands, so you shouldn't make them unless you have a very strong hand yourself.

Players tend to overbet the pot when:

- They have a hand that they are sure is winning, but which is vulnerable to being outdrawn – for example when they hold a straight but there is a flush draw, or some other obvious danger, on the table.
- They believe that, despite the size of bet, they will be called by a relatively weak hand for some reason.
- They are bluffing, and want to maximise their chances of making everyone fold.
- They are nearly all-in and decide that there's no point holding back their little remaining funds for later rounds.

Raising

If you're raising somebody else's bet, rather than opening the betting yourself, don't forget to factor in the amount you're about to call when working out how much to raise.

Suppose that the pot is £100 and an opponent bets £50. You decide to make a raise which offers your opponent pot odds of 2-to-1. Recall from the table above that you need to make a pot-sized raise in order to achieve this.

How much is a pot-sized raise in this case? First you have to call the £50, making the pot £200 (the £100 it started with, plus £50 from each of you and your opponent), then you raise a further £200. In other words you have to put in £250 overall. Any less than this, and you will be offering the original bettor pot odds of more than 2-to-1.

Summary: the fundamentals of betting

If you think you're in the lead, you should bet (or raise if somebody else bet), and you should bet enough so that your opponents don't have the odds to call you. Usually you should make bets that are between 50% and 100% of the pot size.

If you think you're behind, don't bet if you don't have to – you don't usually want to get money into a pot in which you're not favourite. If there has been a bet in front of you then you should weigh up the possibilities, count your outs and call if you think you have the implied pot odds for the call to be profitable.

There will be many, many exceptions to these guidelines, but they are nonetheless the general principles that will underpin almost every aspect of your poker strategy.

How did you get on with this chapter? There was a lot to absorb so we hope you followed it all. If not, make sure you revisit it at some point soon – we promise it will make more sense the second time around. And once you've grasped these fundamentals, you will have a better understanding of poker than, maybe, three-quarters of all players. That's encouragement for you!

Chapter Five:
General playing considerations

In the previous chapter we learnt about the general principles of betting, and what you should do given a reasonable assessment of the relative strength of your hand, in other words how strong it is compared with your opponents' hands. The next step is to examine the ways in which you go about making such an assessment.

In this chapter we'll look at the various factors that will influence your decisions during the course of a poker hand. These are:

- Hand strength
- Number of players
- Other players' actions
- Position
- Playing styles
- Blind and stack sizes.

Some of these considerations involve very big and obvious ideas, but some are rather more subtle. The challenge you face is to:

- remember all the things you need to take account of – and there are a lot
- correctly evaluate the importance of each consideration – which isn't at all straightforward but becomes easier with practice
- weigh up the situation and select the very best course of action – a knack for which is what separates the pros from the amateurs.

We'll start with hand strength.

Hand strength

Your cards are the main thing that distinguishes you from your opponents during a hand of hold'em. You might be tempted to think that they are the *only* thing that distinguishes you – but as we'll see shortly there are other considerations, such as position and stack size (funds), which will also influence the way you play.

Your hand is made of up your hole cards, which are specific to you, and the community cards. Taking the hole cards first, let's observe the rather obvious fact that some hands are better than others. Pre-flop, a pair of aces is unquestionably the best hand, whereas a hand like 2-7 unsuited is just about as bad as it gets (2-7 is the lowest hand that is neither paired nor able to make a straight with three other cards). Other hands fit somewhere in the middle.

Although it's not a precise science, we can rank all the starting hands according to their playing strength. Here are the top ten, for example. (The full list is at the start of the next chapter.)

Rank	Hand	Rank	Hand
1	A-A	6	A-K
2	K-K	7	A-Q suited
3	Q-Q	8	A-J suited
4	A-K suited	9	K-Q suited
5	J-J	10	A-Q

When you're sitting there having just been dealt a pair of aces, you are in the enviable position of knowing you have the best hand at the table. Nobody else can be beating you (although it's possible, if extremely unlikely, that another player has aces too). Similarly when you've got 2-7, you're in little doubt as to your strength (and it's not good). But with the intermediate hands it's trickier to know where you stand.

Matters are further complicated by the arrival of the community cards. We hope it doesn't sound too obvious to remind you that you that community cards are *shared*. One of the most common mistakes made by inexperienced players is to place too great an emphasis on the absolute strength of their hand, i.e. how it scores in the hand rankings, without thinking sufficiently about what their opponents are likely to hold given what's on the board.

For example, you may see that you have made a flush and think – *a flush, that's good, isn't it!* – and start throwing all your money at the pot. But if the board is:

and your hand is:

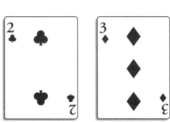

then you're not in very good shape. Anybody with a higher club in their hand will be winning, and that will usually be a reasonably likely outcome. So it's vital to pay sufficient attention to the shared nature of the community cards and always try to identify your relative strength so that you don't overplay or underplay your hand.

THE IMPORTANCE OF RELATIVE STRENGTH !

- To *overplay* your hand – to bet it more strongly than its strength justifies.
- To *underplay* your hand – to bet it less strongly than its strength justifies.

There are two key ways in which you try to determine the relative strength of your hand:

- A simple assessment of probabilities – what are the chances of somebody having a better holding (i.e. hand) than yours
- Reading the betting patterns (and the demeanour or body language) of the other players to further refine your picture of what hands those players are likely to hold.

Both of these tasks are explored later on in the book; but they're both made much easier if you are good at *reading the board*. This means having an awareness of what hands are possible given the community cards that have been dealt so far in the hand. Since this isn't always as easy as it sounds, we'll have a quick quiz to get you up to speed.

Quiz: reading the board

Each question below consists of a sample board in which the cards have been dealt, from left to right as usual. For each board:

(a) Say what is the nuts, i.e. the best possible hand an opponent could hold, at each stage of the hand:

- *on the flop, using the three leftmost board cards*
- *on the turn, using the four leftmost board cards*
- *on the river, using all five board cards*

(b) Repeat the exercise, but assume that your opponent doesn't hold paired cards in his hand.

Question 1. The board is:

Question 2. The board is:

Question 3. The board is:

Question 4. The board is:

Question 5. The board is:

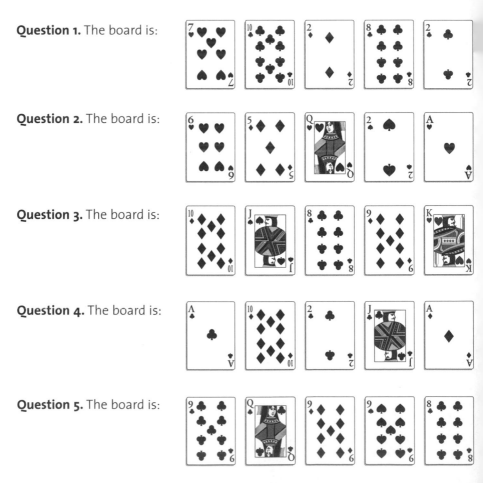

Answers to quiz

Answer 1.
(a) **Flop** three tens; **Turn** straight, jack high; **River** four twos
(b) **Flop** two pair, tens and sevens; **Turn** straight, jack high; **River** full house, twos over tens

Answer 2.
(a) **Flop** three queens; **Turn** straight, six high; **River** flush, ace-high
(b) **Flop** two pair, queens and sixes; **Turn** straight, six high; **River** flush, ace-high

Answer 3.
(a) **Flop** straight, queen high; **Turn** straight, king high; **River** straight, ace high
(b) **Flop** straight, queen high; **Turn** straight, king high; **River** straight, ace high

Answer 4.
(a) **Flop** three aces; **Turn** flush, ace high; **River** four aces
(b) **Flop** two pair, aces and tens; **Turn** flush, ace high; **River** full house, aces over jacks

Answer 5.
(a) **Flop** four nines; **Turn** four nines; **River** straight flush, queen high
(b) **Flop** full house nines over queens; **Turn** four nines; **River** straight flush, queen high

Number of players

Next we'll consider how the number of players at the table, or in a hand, should influence the way you play.

Many poker books assume for the bulk of their discussion that play is progressing at a full table, with somewhere from perhaps nine to eleven players in action, and make relatively little reference to how the game changes when you have fewer opponents than this. Presumably this is because their authors spend much of their time playing in live games in card rooms, where this is usually the case.

Although working with the assumption of a full table simplifies matters somewhat, we don't believe that it's necessarily the best approach. If you're relatively new to poker, you're likely to spend a good amount of time playing either with friends or online, and you may well find yourself having to play (or choosing to play) at shorter-handed tables. If that's the case, advice tailored for full tables is likely to be misleading. At the very least it may obscure the more important underlying principles, namely how to evaluate your hand given the specifics of each situation.

So why does the number of players matter? Very simply, the fewer opponents you face, the less the chance of one of them having a good hand, and the greater the chance that you will win. Since only one player can win each pot then:

- At a ten-seater table, you will on average win one in every ten pots.
- At a two-seater table, you will on average win one in every two pots.

Your cards aren't any better at a two-seater table than a ten-seater table – the reason you win more pots is simply because your opponents' cards, viewed collectively, are weaker. It's much easier for one of nine opponents to pick up a better hand than yours than for a single opponent to do so. We'll try to quantify this a little.

Let's suppose you're playing *heads-up* (one on one) and you're the first to act after the cards have been dealt, so you have no information about your opponent's hand. Which sort of hands should you be raising with? Well, we discovered earlier that you should generally bet or raise if you believe you have the best hand – no rocket science there. And we also established that all starting hands can be ranked from best to worst. But when there are only two of you playing, it's more likely than not that your hand is the best hand *whenever it's in the top 50% of all hands*. You can see why this is: because half the time your opponent will have a hand that's in the bottom 50% of all hands.

So, half the time that you pick your cards up in a heads-up game you can expect to have the best hand, even though you'll often have what would be considered a fairly ropey holding in a fuller game. Under these circumstances and with no information about your opponent's hand, it's quite reasonable to go ahead and raise. (Don't get hung on the numbers here, by the way. We're not saying that you should raise *exactly* 50% of the time, or *only* with hands in the top 50%. We're just giving you a *rough* idea of what constitutes a reasonable criterion for raising in this scenario.)

What happens in a three-player game? Under what circumstances should you, as the first player to act, make a raise? This time, for your hand to be best, it has to be better than both the hands held by the other two players at the table. It turns out that your hand is more likely than not to be the best at the table when it's in the top 30% of hands, i.e. better than 70% of all hands. So, roughly speaking, it's reasonable to raise with hands in the top 30% in a three-player game.

Now let's consider a ten-player game. This time, for your hand to be best, it must be better than *all* nine hands held by the other players at the table. Now it turns out that it's more likely than not that your hand is the best at the table only when it's in the top 7.5% of hands, i.e. when it's better than 92.5% of all hands. So in a ten-player game, the first player to act must really have quite a strong hand in order to raise – the top 7.5% includes only hands like ace-jack, nine-nine, or better.

In practice, there are reasons why you must be *even stronger* than this to raise from first position – as you'll find out in the discussion of position that follows shortly.

Technical note

For those that are interested, we'll briefly explain how the figures of 30% and 7.5% we quoted above were derived.

To have the best hand in a three-handed game, you must beat both other hands. If your hand is in the top 30% of hands then you are 70% likely to beat one hand, and 70% likely to beat the other one too. So your chances of beating both are 70% of 70%, which is about 50%. And if you're 50-50 or better to beat both hands, that makes you the favourite.

To have the best hand in a ten-handed game, you must beat all the other hands at the table, but this time there are nine of them rather than two. If your hand is in the top 7.5% of hands then you are 92.5% likely to beat each individual hand. So the chances of it beating all nine others are 92.5% to the power of nine, which is roughly 50%. And being 50-50 or better to beat all the other hands at the table makes you the favourite.

The following table (which you don't need to commit to memory) will help you work out how to adjust your game when playing against different numbers of opponents.

No. of players (including you)	Percentile to be favourite
2	50%
3	29.3%
4	20.6%
5	15.9%
6	12.9%
7	10.9%
8	9.4%
9	8.3%
10	7.4%
11	6.7%

Once again, you shouldn't take the numbers too literally but you can in principle compare the percentiles here with the ones in the starting hand chart in the next chapter to get an idea of whether you're likely to be favourite given any particular holding and number of opponents.

In other words, in a very short-handed game, you can raise with any two half-decent cards, but in a ten-player game, you need a pretty good hand to do so. Here's a table showing examples of some of the weakest starting hands that rate to be winning, varying with the number of players at the table (and in the absence of any other information).

No. of players (including you)	Minimal hands that rate to be winning
2	Any queen or king
3	Any ace
4	J- 10; low pair
5	A- 10; Q-J
6	K- J; suited ace
7	8- 8
8	K- Q
9	A- J
10	9- 9
11	10- 10; two suited picture cards

A similar rule applies to calling (as opposed to betting / raising). To call, you have to believe that you have a chance of improving to the best hand. With ten players at the table, you're going to need to make a much better hand to win than if you face only a few.

Now, here's a very important point. One thing that many players overlook is that you have to make an adjustment for the number of players in the hand *all the time*. If you're on the button in a ten-handed game and everyone folds to you, it's really little different from being in a three-handed game – because there are only two other people left in the hand (the small blind and big blind) and they haven't yet acted so they could have anything.

It's true that if the first seven people to act all fold then it's slightly more likely that the remaining players have something playable. But this effect is fairly insignificant, mostly because having a playable hand is less about whether your two hole cards are *individually* good, and more about how they relate to each other and whether they work well in combination.

Whenever you're on the button and everyone folds to you, you should play the hand much as you'd play a three-handed game, and your starting requirements are therefore drastically reduced. And of course, this principle can be extended. If you're one place to the right of the button and everyone folds to you, you can play more or less as if you were first to act in a four-handed game, and so on.

To sum up, when there are fewer players in a game or in a hand, your hand is more likely to be winning. This is an illustration of the importance of *relative strength*. Poker isn't about absolute strength, i.e. what you actually hold – it's about relative strength, i.e. what you hold in relation to what your opponents hold.

Many inexperienced players don't understand the effect that the number of players has on their relative strength. As a result they don't play tight enough in full games, and don't loosen up enough in short-handed games, or short-handed pots.

Other players' actions

We've just seen that in a ten-player game, your relative strength is greatly increased if all or many of the players ahead of you decide to fold; all of a sudden, mediocre hands can rate to be the best at the table against the few remaining hands. This suggests that your assessment of the relative strength of your hand is strongly influenced by the actions of other players at the table – and indeed this is the case.

Let's contrast the previous example – where everyone ahead of you folds – with the situation where you're on the button and *everyone* ahead of you calls the big blind. There are now two very good reasons why you can't value your hand anything like as highly in this case:

- Rather than being up against only a few players, all nine other players are still in the hand this time. Even if you like your hole cards, you're going to need to get quite lucky with the community cards to beat that number of other hands, whatever they are.

- In fact, the other players are likely to be holding some quite reasonable cards between them – they presumably wouldn't all have called with trash. Moreover, as you'll see shortly, players who act early in the round actually require a better than normal hand to call. All in all, it looks like you'll be up against some pretty good hands.

So in this case you have to tread very carefully. You're going to need a premium hand to get heavily involved with this pot. On the other hand, however, you're getting very good odds for your money if you decide to call – so it's ok to get *lightly* involved. If the blinds are £1 / £2 then there will be £17 in the pot when it's your turn to act, and it will only cost you £2 to call. Those are mouth-watering pot odds of 17-to-2, or 8.5-to-1, which to a certain extent offset the otherwise unfavourable circumstances (lots of other players competing for the pot). You're justified in making a call with any two half-decent cards in this case, provided that:

- You believe that the two players left to act – the blinds – are unlikely to raise, which would force you to throw away a non-premium hand.
- You're prepared to fold on the next round of betting unless you catch a good flop.

To sum up: if there are many callers ahead of you, you should downgrade the relative strength of your hand accordingly, but the favourable pot odds might indicate that a call is in order. Remember too that the players to your right will also have (or should have) reasoned the same way, and that some of their calls might owe more to the odds being offered than the strength of their hands.

So that covers the case with callers ahead of you. What about raisers? We saw earlier that a raise by the first player to act in a ten-player game should normally suggest a hand in the top few percent of all hands. What does it mean if somebody else then re-raises? Well, it suggests that the re-raiser can beat most hands in the top few percent.

In practice, one would probably need a hand like ace-king or better to re-raise in this situation (unless there were other factors in play at the time). And what if there were another re-raise following that one? Well, that player would have to be holding a huge hand like ace-ace or possibly king-king to justify such a move. If they were holding a hand like queen-queen or worse, there's too much chance that one of the other players would be holding a better hand.

You see then that one or two raises or re-raises from early players in a full game means that all of a sudden you need an *extremely* strong hand to play. But before you get too carried away and start thinking "right, two raises means I need a pair of aces or kings to be ahead", let's just look at a superficially similar example with a very different analysis.

Suppose you're in the big blind. All players fold to the player on the button who raises, and then is re-raised by the small blind. What now? In this case, remember that the player on the button doesn't need a powerhouse to have raised – they can do so with any reasonable hand (in the top 30% or so). The raise from the small blind therefore says that they can beat most hands in the top 30%. Maybe they'd raise then with a hand like, say, king-queen or better. In this case, sitting in the big blind, you would be justified in re-raising with a hand like queen-queen which could very easily be the best of the three remaining.

The above illustrates one of the key differences between strong players and weaker players. Weaker players won't notice the difference between the two situations. If there are raises and re-raises from the first three players to act, all are likely to hold good hands and the third raiser will normally be very strong indeed. If all players fold to the button however, and there are then raises from the button, small blind and big blind, you wouldn't expect to see those players show down such strong hands because they're effectively playing a three-handed game rather than a ten-handed one.

In summary then, what's gone on ahead of you in the betting makes a huge difference to how you evaluate the relative strength of your hand. But don't be too simplistic about this evaluation. It's not just about whether players fold, call or raise. It also depends on other playing considerations such as the pot odds they were being offered at the time of their bet, and the number of players left in the hand.

Position

In a hand of poker, your *position* is your place in the order of play on betting rounds. If you are one of the first to act, you are said to be in *early position* and if you are one of the last to act, you are said to be in *late position*. If you're about halfway down the order, you're in *mid-position*.

In hold'em this means that players on the button and just to the right of it are always in late position, and those in the blinds and just to their left are always in early position. Note that the first round of betting is a special case for the blinds since they act *last* on this round, but *first* on every other round.

So how does position affect your play and why does it matter? The answer is that being in later position than your opponents is a huge advantage because each betting round you get to see what they do first, before you act, whereas they are betting in the dark without any information whatsoever.

We hope that by now you can start to see why position might be important. In the previous section we considered how the player on the button might evaluate his hand differently depending on whether the players in front of him have folded, called or raised. In some circumstances, he might consider any two reasonable cards a playable hand and even worth a raise. In other circumstances, he might throw away a hand like queen-queen without a second thought. But in all cases the player on the button, because he has good position, can make his decision once he's seen the other players act.

What's more, there doesn't need to be a whole bunch of players in the hand for position to be crucial. Let's suppose that after the pre-flop round of betting there are just two players left in the hand and you're the second to act, or as we say *in position*. If your opponent checks to you, there's a good chance that he's weak (although it's admittedly by no means certain). Knowing that, you can check as well if you'd like to see the next card for free.

Alternatively you can bet, either for value (if you have a good hand) or as a bluff if you're very weak. Because your opponent is quite likely to be weak too, there's a reasonable chance the bluff will work in this case. Yes, your opponent might have been slowplaying a good hand and raise you if you decide to bet – but that sort of play is generally quite risky and shouldn't be overused as we'll see later.

If on the other hand your opponent bets rather than checks, you can be reasonably sure they've got some kind of hand. Knowing that, you can throw your hand away if it's no good or call if you think you're behind but have the pot odds to make the call profitable. If you think you're ahead, well then you can raise your opponent and make him put even more money in the pot.

In all these cases you can react to what your opponent has done and tailor your move accordingly. If you're first to act however, then all these advantages lie instead with your opponent.

When you are in position, you will lose less money on the hands you lose, and win more money on the hands you win. You may even win some hands you would otherwise have lost. Inexperienced players will often underestimate the importance of position, or pay no attention to it whatsoever. But remember this: if you put a good player on the button and leave them there all night – without rotating the deal – they would probably make money without ever looking at their cards (providing that nobody knew that's what they were doing!). As the poker saying goes, *position is king*.

In poker, *every* holding becomes more valuable when you have favourable position and is less valuable when you have unfavourable position. Hands that are unplayable in early position may become easy raises in late position, especially when none of the other players has shown much strength. Other hands that look quite promising must often be thrown away if you find yourself first to act.

If you're new to poker it will probably take you quite a while to develop an intuitive feeling for the importance of position and how to balance your strategy accordingly. At the very least, make sure it's one of the things you consider in every hand you play. The more you're aware of it, the quicker you'll develop a feel for its significance.

Note: the one time you can discount position is when you (or your opponents) are all-in. With no more betting to be done, position is worthless – it certainly doesn't make your cards any better. Therefore if you have the opportunity to go all-in, you should be more inclined to do so if you're out of position, to reduce your opponents' positional advantage. If you're in position, you can be more restrained with your money, because you'll have the opportunity to outplay your opponents later in the hand.

Playing styles

In any game of poker, a lot depends on the playing style adopted by you and your opponents. You need to have an understanding of your opponents' playing styles so that:

- You can better decipher what their bets mean.
- You can better predict what course of action they might take during a hand.

Of course, whenever you yourself are involved in a hand, your opponents will be reacting to you too. Your analysis of their behaviour must to a certain extent factor in how *they* perceive *you*. No-limit hold'em is a game in which the cards that are dealt often matter less than the personalities and styles involved. Hence the old expression – *play the man, not the cards* – which, if not sound advice on all occasions, is at least a useful reminder of this fact.

Knowing and understanding your opponents' playing styles is so important that we've dedicated a whole chapter to it later on. For now we'll just introduce a couple of terms to which we make occasional reference in the meantime. A player's style is described as:

- loose if they play a lot of hands, or play under-strength hands
- tight if they play relatively few hands, or only strong hands
- passive if they check or call much more than they bet or raise, or make small bets
- aggressive is they bet or raise frequently, or make large bets.

We'll define and examine these traits more thoroughly in Chapter Eleven.

Blind and stack sizes

Another factor that should influence the way you play your hands is how big the stacks are – in other words how much money you and your opponents all have in front of you on the table, in comparison with the size of the blinds and the size of the pot.

If you find yourself nearly all-in during a hand, i.e. you have little money left, then it often makes your decisions easier. You don't have to worry so much about the playability of your hand, your position and so on – you can just shove your remaining chips in the middle if the odds are in your favour, and deal the cards out.

If on the other hand you have a large stack and are contemplating taking on an opponent who is similarly well endowed, you have to worry about much more than just the current bet – you must consider much more carefully whether the whole ensuing battle would be likely to work in your favour or not.

As with playing styles, there's too much to say on this topic to squeeze it all into this brief introduction, so we'll revisit it in more detail later on. You should note however that in all the discussions that follow, unless otherwise stated, we will be assuming that available funds (stack sizes) are many times bigger than the blind and / or pot size.

Chapter Six:
Pre-flop play

Thus far we've looked at some of the general principles that influence your decisions during the course of a hand of hold'em. Over the next few chapters we're going to look in more depth at the specific features of each stage of the hand, and how those general principles should be applied. We'll start, of course, at the beginning with pre-flop play – when all you have is the two hole cards which make up your starting hand.

As a general rule, pre-flop play is about working out whether your starting hand is strong compared with your opponents' hands, that is, determining your relative strength. If your hand is strong you want to get money into the pot so that you can:

■ win more money
■ eliminate players with weak cards who might otherwise outdraw you.

If you're not so strong then you may want to see a cheap flop, especially with good drawing hands like small pairs, suited cards (which can make flushes) or *connectors* (which are good at making straights). Otherwise you'll want to fold.

Bear in mind that it doesn't really help you very much to count your outs pre-flop because, with just your two hole cards, there are still too many different things your hand could become. Even when you are hoping for a specific outcome on the flop, it's difficult to calculate the chances of it happening when *three* cards are about to be dealt simultaneously. Therefore, pre-flop, it's best to learn the odds of improving (provided shortly) rather than work them out on the fly.

Many players see too many expensive flops. They play hands that don't justify being played because they think "what if the flop came XXX". The problem is that, whatever your hand, the flop is relatively unlikely to help you very much. If you hold suited cards, you're quite unlikely to flop a flush draw, let alone a flush. Similarly, if you have a pair, you're unlikely to make three of a kind on the flop.

Therefore if you're thinking about calling a pre-flop raise, make sure that you legitimately have the pot odds to do so. Alternatively, when debating a call, you should often ask yourself what you will do if (a) you miss the flop completely and then (b) the pre-flop raiser puts in a bet on the flop.

If the answer is 'fold', then you may be better off folding sooner rather than later – because very frequently, as we'll find out later, this is exactly what happens.

One final word of caution. On television you'll often see professionals making big raises or going all-in with hands that we're about to tell you aren't very strong and don't justify this kind of treatment. Most of the time this will be because those professionals are involved in *tournament* play, with large blinds and (perhaps) few opponents. Such situations demand a very different strategy, as we explain later on.

> Note: It is conventional to describe pre-flop raises as a multiple of the big blind rather than a multiple of the pot size. After the flop, bets and raises will generally be described as a multiple of the pot size.

Starting hands overview

We'll begin with a quick introduction to the starting hands you can be dealt. The following table lists the top third of starting hands in rough order of their playability, from best to worst.

Hands with an '**s**' after them (e.g. A-Ks) are suited hands, i.e. contain two cards of the same suit. *Probability* refers to the probability of being dealt a hand this good or better. *Odds* expresses the same information but, unsurprisingly, as odds. So the odds of being dealt, for example, Q-Q or better are about 73-to-1.

Rank	Hand	Probability	Odds
1	A-A	0.45%	220.0
2	K-K	0.90%	109.5
3	Q-Q	1.36%	72.7
4	A-Ks	1.66%	59.3
5	J-J	2.11%	46.4
6	A-K	3.02%	32.2
7	A-Qs	3.32%	29.1
8	A-Js	3.62%	26.6

Rank	Hand	Probability	Odds
9	K-Qs	3.92%	24.5
10	A-Q	4.83%	19.7
11	10-10	5.28%	17.9
12	A-10s	5.58%	16.9
13	K-Js	5.88%	16.0
14	Q-Js	6.18%	15.2
15	9-9	6.64%	14.1
16	A-J	7.54%	12.3
17	K-Q	8.45%	10.8
18	J-Ts	8.75%	10.4
19	A-9s	9.05%	10.1
20	8-8	9.50%	9.5
21	A-8s	9.80%	9.2
22	K-Ts	10.11%	8.9
23	A-7s to A-2s	11.92%	7.4
24	K-J	12.82%	6.8
25	Q-J	13.73%	6.3
26	10-9s	14.03%	6.1
27	A-10	14.93%	5.7
28	Q-10s	15.23%	5.6
29	7-7 to 2-2	17.95%	4.6
30	9-8s	18.25%	4.5
31	8-7s	18.55%	4.4
32	7-6s	18.85%	4.3
33	6-5s	19.16%	4.2
34	5-4s	19.46%	4.1
35	K-9s	19.76%	4.1
36	J-9s	20.06%	4.0
37	J-10	20.97%	3.8
38	Q-9s	21.27%	3.7
39	Q-10	22.17%	3.5
40	A-9	23.08%	3.3
41	K-10	23.98%	3.2
42	10-9	24.89%	3.0
43	A-8	25.79%	2.9
44	9-8	26.70%	2.7
45	8-7	27.60%	2.6
46	7-6	28.51%	2.5
47	6-5	29.41%	2.4
48	5-4	30.32%	2.3
49	A-7 to A-2	35.75%	1.8

This list refers to the general playability of hands and is fairly *subjective*. Whilst (for example) A-A is definitely better than 5-4 in anyone's book, it's debatable whether, say, J-J is better than A-K. You might come across this kind of table in various places in the poker literature or on the internet, but it's unlikely that any two will rank all the hands – or even the top five or ten – in exactly the same order. This list merely represents our opinion on the topic.

In the end, how you decide to play each hand will depend on the character of the hand itself and the situation you're in. It doesn't particularly matter whether two closely ranked hands are in exactly the right order or not. What this list should give you is a *general* overview of how valuable each hand is, which is useful when you're starting out.

Let's quickly note a few points which we'll explore in more detail later on.

Pairs perform quite well in this list. This is because they start with an advantage over any unpaired hands. The non-paired cards will have to match some of the board cards to improve. Pairs can also match a board card to make a *set* (three of a kind), with two of those three in your hand. Although this happens relatively rarely, it's a very powerful hand and you can often win a big pot when you make a set.

Suited holdings (two cards of the same suit) perform better than their *off-suit* (unsuited) counterparts. The sole reason for this is that suited cards are much more likely to make a flush. As with sets, your odds of making a flush by the river are pretty small (around 6%), but when you do make a flush you will often win a nice pot with it.

With suited holdings you ideally want at least one high-value card so that if you make your flush it's less likely that somebody else will have made a better one. In practice, suited holdings really need to have an ace in them to have any special value, unless they obtain their value in other ways (either by being connected or containing two high cards, or both – see below).

Connected holdings (two cards with consecutive values, also known as *connectors*) are more valuable than other unpaired holdings solely because they are more likely to make a straight.

Less well connected cards, such as one-gaps (e.g. 9-7), two-gaps (e.g. 9-6) and three-gaps (e.g. 9-5) can also make straights but are less likely to do so. To see this, just consider that there are four ways that 9-8 can make a straight (5 to 9, 6 to 10, 7 to J and 8 to Q), three ways that 9-7 can do so (5 to 9, 6 to 10, 7 to J), two ways that 9-6 can do so (5 to 9 and 6 to 10) and only one way that 9-5 can do so.

Since the odds of making a straight are pretty slim anyway, these poorly connected holdings are only marginally more playable than completely unconnected ones. Note also that connectors are less likely to make straights if they are very high or very low. For example, 9-8 can make four different straights (see above), but 2-3 can make only two straights: ace to 5 and 2 to 6.

Two high cards. Other than pairs, suited cards and connected cards, the only hands of any value are those with two *high cards* in them (a high card is any card ten or better). Even so, these are nowhere near as valuable as most beginners imagine. Look for example at K-J in 24th place and K-10 in 41st place. In this category, two high cards, only those hands with an ace in fare particularly well.

If your hand isn't in any of the above categories then it is, as they say, *trash*. You should usually throw it away at the earliest opportunity since it won't stand up to much pressure from other players.

Many inexperienced players insist on playing ace-x (or even king-x) unsuited because they think that any hand with an ace in it can't be that bad. But at a table of ten players, there are eighteen cards in your opponents' hands in total so it's overwhelmingly likely that one or more other players have an ace too. If that is the case then it also very likely that their kicker (second card) is going to be bigger than yours – and you're going to be a big underdog against them. Weaker hands such as these are occasionally playable, but usually only against a very small number of opponents – and with extreme care.

Starting hands guide

Now we'll look at each of the starting hands more closely and discuss how they should be handled. There's a lot of information here and you don't need to learn all of this in detail, at least not initially. It's sufficient to get the gist and perhaps absorb the contents of the summaries at the end of each section.

Then you can revisit the material as you become more experienced, treating it as a reference guide to be consulted whenever you need a refresher.

You should also bear in mind that the guidelines that follow are necessarily simplistic, because they reduce the myriad possibilities into a few simplified categories. They describe the generally correct play at a *typical* table.

Sometimes you will need to depart from these guidelines in marginal situations if the circumstances merit it, but as long as you do so with good reason that's fine. Remember though that there is such a thing as a downright bad play. We've tried to make our feelings loud and clear about these.

We'll start right at the top, with a pair of aces.

Pair of aces

Pocket aces, often referred to as *aces, pocket rockets* or *bullets* – call this hand what you will – it's as good as it gets in hold'em. You are dealt aces on average only once every 221 hands, but surely there are few sweeter sights in this world! Ok, we shouldn't get carried away – and in fact you shouldn't either. Without wanting to spoil the party, here is the most important thing that you need to know when you hold a pair of aces:

■ *Pocket aces are not strong enough to slowplay pre-flop.*

By which we mean the following: an inexperienced player sees a pair of aces in his hand and gets very excited – well, who wouldn't? He thinks that his hand is so strong he must win a huge pot with it. He gets scared to bet too much in case everybody folds, so instead he sneaks in with a call or small raise in the hope of getting his unsuspecting opponents to stay with him.

Having lured a few in, he throws increasing amounts of money at the pot on the flop, the turn and the river, without giving sufficient thought to why his opponents might still be in the hand. Come the showdown, he probably hasn't improved and still holds just a pair of aces. His opponents, on the other hand, show down two pair or three of a kind or a straight made early on in the hand when it was nice and cheap to stay in. Result – he loses his entire stack because he played too weakly early on and too strongly at the end.

Now, maybe you don't quite believe this cautionary tale and think we're exaggerating the risks. But take a look at the following table which shows the chances of ace-ace winning against various numbers of opponents holding any two *random* cards.

No. of opponents	Odds of ace-ace winning
1	85%
2	73%
3	64%
4	56%
5	49%
6	44%
7	39%
8	35%
9	31%

As you can see, by the time you get to five opponents, the aces aren't even favourite to win. And at a full table they're a worse than 2-to-1 underdog. Now further bear in mind that your opponents in the hand won't have two *random* cards – they will have better than average cards otherwise they wouldn't still be there. You can see that even with a hand as strong as aces, you don't want to be up against too many opponents. One or two opponents is fine – after that you're losing your edge.

What's more, the truth of the matter is that most players won't put a large amount of money in the pot on later rounds with a hand that can't beat a pair of aces. For your opponents to call big bets after the flop, they're usually going to need to hold something like two pair or better. Hopefully you can see why this would be – they're making value-based plays too, after all – but can you see the implications?

What this means is that you will usually win a big pot with aces only when one of the following happens:

■ Most of the money goes in the pot early on in the hand, usually pre-flop, or

■ Your pair of aces improves to a better hand somehow, for example if an ace appears on the board too. But you can't count on this happening too often.

So, all of the above is pointing towards the following two principles when playing aces:

- You don't want to play against too many opponents – ideally one or two.
- You want to get as much of your opponents' money in the pot pre-flop as you can. If the money goes in too late, you may already be beaten if you are called.

By a happy coincidence these two ideas are highly compatible – because if you stick in a big raise, most players will usually fold (but hopefully not all of them).

Raising with aces

The next question of course is how much to raise. Let's look at the options.

You could go *all-in*, by pushing your entire stack into the middle, daring other players to call you. This will definitely reduce the field, but it's doubtful it will get much money in the pot (other than yours). Who would call such a big bet? This move seems to shout from the rooftops, "I've got aces" so in all likelihood everyone will fold.

The only way you're likely to get callers when you go all-in with aces is if other players know you might make the same move with other hands too. But all-in moves don't work well with other hands because you'll only be called by players with pocket aces or perhaps other very strong hands like pocket kings. That's the general drawback with over-size raises; you either win a small amount or lose a lot.

You could instead make a *minimum raise* by putting in a bet of double the big-blind. Let's suppose that you're in a game with £1 / £2 blinds, and that one player has called the big blind ahead of you. After you've put in your £4 there will be £9 in the pot and it's £4 to call. That means that the players following you are getting pot odds of over 2-1, which is reasonably attractive for them. Worse still, the small blind has to call only £3 rather than £4 (because he has already put in his £1 blind) and is therefore getting odds of at least 3-1, more than this if anybody has called behind you. And the big blind and caller ahead of you have to put in only £2 to call, meaning that they're getting odds of at least 4.5-1.

In practice, with a raise this small, you're quite likely to get a caller behind you, and that will encourage further callers who see the pot odds growing with each additional call. You may thin the field a little, but you won't usually narrow it down to the one or two opponents you desire.

It seems then that if you bet too much, you'll scare everyone off and win only the small amount of money already in the pot. If you bet too little, you won't discourage callers sufficiently and you'll be playing against too many opponents on the flop. So you should find a balance between the two. The right amount to bet depends very heavily on the circumstances of the game and who your opponents are, but on average a bet of maybe four times the big blind should do the trick. Bear in mind however:

- If the game is very *loose* in that many players are calling bets then you may need to bet more than this, for example five times the big blind, to shake enough opponents off.
- If the game is tight or short-handed you may want to bet slightly less than this, maybe three times the big blind, to entice one or two callers in.
- If you are in late position with several callers ahead of you, you will need to bet more. This is because (a) players who have already called the blinds are likely to have reasonable cards and therefore will be more inclined to call a raise, and (b) with quite a bit of money already in the pot, you need a bigger raise to avoid giving your opponents favourable pot odds.
- If you are in early position, you can afford to bet less since other players will have more respect for raises from early position (or should do) and will have relatively poor pot odds.

Even if you decide that, say, four times the big blind is the right amount for the situation, you should of course mix your play up a little and raise by different amounts at different times to throw your opponents off the scent; sometimes you might raise three times the blind and sometimes perhaps five times or more. (Mixing up your play in this way isn't really a significant departure from value-based play because you're choosing from a short-list of sensible plays all of which have a good chance of achieving your aims. This idea is discussed in more detail in Chapter Ten.)

By the way, if you do bet a reasonable amount and everyone folds, don't be too disappointed. Anybody who'd had a good hand would have called, so you can assume that nobody had much of a hand. Without good cards, they wouldn't have paid you off unless the board cards matched their hand very well. And if that had happened, well you wouldn't have been such a strong favourite anyway. Just be happy that you picked up a small pot with your aces rather than losing a big one.

So let's just pause and sum up what we've learnt so far: pocket aces shouldn't be slowplayed pre-flop. You should aim to raise an amount that is likely to encourage no more than one or two callers. In a typical situation, this amount might be around four times the size of the big blind.

Slowplaying aces

We should briefly discuss a fairly common tactic for playing aces which departs from this guideline. Many players will simply call the big blind from early position, hoping that another player will raise behind them and they can then either call the raise or re-raise. You'll hear this tactic referred to as *slowplaying aces from early position*.

The first potential problem with this approach is that it's of course possible that nobody else will oblige you by raising. In this case you're going to find yourself in an unraised pot with maybe five or six other players, some of whom could hold frankly anything. Once the flop has been dealt, it's highly possible that your pair of aces won't be winning any more and you'll have to tread with extreme caution. Even if you go on to win the hand, it's far too risky to bet big if others are showing interest.

In this situation you should usually make a bet on the flop betting round and be prepared to check or fold subsequently if you get any action. It's best to avoid getting into this situation in the first place however, so make sure you *flat-call* with aces (i.e. call rather than raise) only on aggressive tables where most pots are raised pre-flop, and only from very early position where there are plenty of people behind you who have the opportunity to raise.

The second potential problem with slowplaying aces is that it can reveal too much about your hand. Suppose you call when first to act and then re-raise when a player raises behind you? What sort of hand do you think he's going to put you on?

The fact of the matter is that this sort of move is too risky with all but the strongest holdings. Your opponent will know you have a monster (a *monster* is a great hand). This isn't so bad in itself but if you instead raise rather than flat-call, and then your opponent re-raises, there will be a lot more money in the pot by the time he finds out quite how strong you are. Moreover, let's suppose you *always* slowplay aces in early position. What does that tell your opponent when you raise, rather than call, as you often will? It tells them that you don't have aces. Some players always slowplay the top hands like aces and kings from early position, which means that when they raise their opponents can know they're winning with hands like Q-Q.

In short then, if you are going to slowplay your aces, only do it from early position at aggressive tables, and don't do it all the time – make sure you mix it up with raises. You should bear in mind too that you probably wouldn't harm your game very much if you made it a rule *never* to flat-call the blinds with aces – and you'd stay out of a lot of trouble as a result. This is especially true against inexperienced players.

Playing aces against a raise

Next we need to consider how to handle aces in the case where somebody has raised the blinds before the action gets to you or, if you're really lucky, where somebody has re-raised your raise. As before, your first thought should be for the number of opponents you are likely to face. By the time the flop is dealt, you ideally want to be against one or two other players at most. Therefore, if there are currently more than this number of players active in the pot, you *must re-raise* if you think that's what's needed to thin the field. If you do raise, make sure that you raise enough to give your opponents unattractive pot odds. You may need to make a pot-sized raise for this to happen, given that some players have already called a raise.

If, on the other hand, it's already obvious that the number of opponents is small enough for you to be comfortable, then you can choose between calling and raising. Once again, we would urge you to curb any natural predilection merely to call in order to disguise the strength of your hand. True, calling will sometimes be right, but on the other hand:

- You might still be winning after the flop, but you are *definitely* winning (or at least tying) right now. The playing-for-value rule of betting when you're in the lead says you should raise.

- If you re-raise and take down the pot, i.e. your opponent(s) fold, you've won a decent sized pot (it was already raised) for no risk, which is not a bad outcome.
- If you re-raise and get callers, then they're putting even more money into a pot in which you're the favourite. That's profit for you (well, expected profit anyway).

In fact, the only justification for calling rather than raising is if you think you can get your opponents to put more money in the pot later on by doing so even *if they don't make their hand*. Suppose your opponent has A-K for example. They might call a re-raise pre-flop without too much thought. But if the flop comes and misses them (has no ace or king in it) then they probably won't call another bet. In this case you'll cost yourself money by waiting till the flop to bet.

The one downside of re-raising – especially if you're putting in the third raise – is that it does reveal quite how strong your hand is. Your opponent will (or certainly should) start to suspect that you might have a hand like aces or kings. This however is usually a small price to pay for getting more money in the middle and cutting down the number of players.

To call or to re-raise then? There is no right answer. The best thing to do will depend on the situation and your opponent(s). What do you think they hold, and what do you think they think you hold?

Another important factor is position – which one of you will act first after the flop? If you're in position (i.e. last to act) then you can be more inclined to call rather than raise because it will be easier for you to extract money later on. If your opponent checks, then you can bet and it might look to them like you're stealing (i.e. bluffing) rather than strong, making them more inclined to call. If they bet then you can raise if you're confident you're still in the lead, or you can perhaps call or fold if you suspect they might have overtaken you on the flop.

Playing aces post-flop

One final note on playing aces. It's fine to fall in love with them pre-flop because there's no better hand at that stage. But sometimes you need to be prepared to fall out of love with your aces after the flop if you have reason to believe you're beaten. Even if you've narrowed the field to one or two opponents, they can still flop two pair or a set and clean you out.

One trait that all successful players have is being able to let go of a good hand if it looks like they're up against a great hand. If you've been betting and raising your aces and your opponent has taken everything you've thrown at him and even raised you back, you'd better start wondering whether you might be beaten. Your opponent is even more likely than normal to have the goods in this situation because, given that you've been doing quite a bit of betting and raising yourself, they must have an extra strong hand to think they're winning. A bluff would be too risky for them since the evident strength of your hand makes you likely to call.

Summary: pair of aces

- Don't slowplay aces pre-flop.
- Raise an amount that is likely to be sufficient to produce no more than one or two callers. In a typical game, this amount might be around four times the size of the big blind.
- If you are going to flat-call the blinds, only do it from very early position in aggressive games, and even then don't do it all the time.
- Re-raise as necessary to get as much money in the pot pre-flop as possible and thin the field. Remember that as the pot grows, so must the size of your raise.
- Sometimes you can call a raise rather than re-raising, to mix your game up and to try to get more money later on in the hand.
- On occasions, be prepared to throw your aces away after the flop if you don't improve – especially if there were a lot of callers or one of your opponents is showing a lot of strength.

Pair of kings

Well, that was a lot of information to absorb about just one hand. Fortunately it gets easier from here on because there are many similarities in the ways different hands are played. In particular, you can play pocket kings pre-flop in largely the same way you play aces, but with just a couple of caveats.

The first difference you should be aware of is that kings aren't always as easy as aces to play *after* the flop – because an ace can appear on the board, and will do so 23% of the time. That's nearly one time in four (or just over one time in five if you prefer to be optimistic). If the flop brings an ace then your lovely kings are all of a sudden losing even to trash hands like ace-x which have now paired up, and the kings will be a big underdog in this situation.

This means that the thing you most fear with kings is an ace arriving on the flop – even if none of your opponents actually holds an ace, they're almost certainly going to fold if you bet, since they will fear that *you* have an ace based on your pre-flop betting. In short, you're either going to win a small amount or lose a large amount if an ace arrives. Aces on the flop are the Achilles heel of pocket kings.

So how can you protect yourself against the possibility of an ace coming? You should be able to work out the answer to this of course – bet even more pre-flop. By betting a little bit more strongly pre-flop, you are more likely to win the pot there and then, and never even make it that far. Even if you do get to the flop, by betting more you are likely to have further reduced the number of opponents and are therefore less likely to be up against somebody playing an ace.

To be clear, we're not saying that you should actually *aim* to win the pot pre-flop with kings – with a hand this strong you'd like at least one caller. It's just that kings like multiple callers a bit less than aces do.

So this argument suggests that pocket kings should be bet a little more strongly than aces pre-flop. Whilst you're aiming for no more than one or two opponents with aces, you should probably aim for one opponent with kings. In a typical game, a raise of maybe five times the big blind might achieve this, but once again the correct amount to raise depends so much on your position, opposition, and so on.

The other consideration with kings is that – unlike aces – *it is possible you are already losing*. It's tempting to think that the chances of somebody else having aces when you've got kings is so remote that it's not worth contemplating, but that's not quite true. Firstly let us remark that the chances of somebody having aces are independent of whether you've got kings or any other hand (without an ace in it), so that's irrelevant. In fact, at a table of ten players, one in every 27 times you hold kings somebody will hold aces. It will happen to you sooner or later and then you'll believe it.

The good news is that you'll very rarely have to modify your play because of this risk. Even very good and experienced players won't throw away pocket kings pre-flop very often – maybe a handful of times during their careers. But let's suppose you're on the button in a ten-player cash game and there's a raise from early position. You re-raise with your kings and the big blind re-raises all-in, and it's a big raise. Then the early position raiser goes all-in too. In most games of a reasonable standard, the likelihood of one of the other two players having aces with this betting pattern is high. It's certainly safe to say that their play (in either case) would be questionable even with a holding like pocket queens.

(Note that the same analysis wouldn't apply during e.g. the latter stages of a tournament or other situation when the blinds are big compared with stack sizes – because players will have loosened up as a result. In this case, your kings are more likely to be winning.)

So we're afraid that we can't tell you whether your kings are beaten pre-flop or not, but you shouldn't spend much time worrying about it.

Very rarely you'll come across a situation where your opponent's play is screaming aces. Give yourself a chance of getting away cheaply in that situation, but make sure you don't form a habit of folding kings against weaker hands. If in doubt, and if your bankroll can stand the potential loss, it's usually going to be best to hang in there rather than talk yourself out of it. If you're not all-in pre-flop then you can take a view on how to proceed when the flop is dealt.

Summary: pair of kings

- Kings should be played in a roughly similar way to aces pre-flop.
- You're scared of an ace coming on the flop however, so bet slightly more than you would with aces to further discourage callers.
- Very occasionally, if the signs are compelling that an opponent has aces, you may choose to fold kings pre-flop.

Pair of queens

If you've absorbed the ideas laid out above on playing kings and aces then you should have no trouble working out what to do with queens. Like these other two big hands, pocket queens rates to be the best hand at the table in the absence of any other information, i.e. before the betting starts. You will almost always raise with queens to thin the field before the flop comes. Are there any times when you should flat-call with queens?

You might decide to call the big blind, hoping for a raise behind you so you can then re-raise or perhaps call. This isn't a very good play with queens, though, since, as strong as they are, they're not really strong enough to justify a re-raise in this situation. Having said that, you may occasionally choose to flat-call the big blind in the name of mixing up your game. You should do this only if you're the first one into the pot and only from very early position.

If there is a raise ahead of you then you might decide to call rather than re-raise, to disguise your hand and in the hope of winning more money later on. In general however, this isn't a very good play to make with queens either. The chance of an overcard (ace or king) falling on the flop is quite high – around 41%. When that happens it's going to be quite tricky to play the rest of the hand since anyone holding a king or ace will be in the lead. You're quite happy to pick up the pot pre-flop and, even if you get to the flop, you don't want many callers. This suggests that a raise is usually preferable.

There's one further advantage to raising rather than calling – it helps define the relative strength of your hand more effectively. Your opponent may fold, which is fine because you win the pot without further risk. They may call, which means that they must surely have a very good hand and you will need to tread carefully. However you have succeeded in getting more money into a pot which you are *probably* winning. Or your opponent may re-raise, which – if they are a half decent player – strongly suggests that you're beaten.

Most opponents would not raise and then re-raise in this situation without kings or aces because it's too likely that *your* re-raise indicates an extremely strong hand. It's up to you whether you call this re-raise or not – it depends on how you read your opponent. (You may be tempted to think they're bluffing but bear in mind that, at a ten-player table, an opponent will have aces or kings roughly once every 13 times that you hold queens – it's not that uncommon.)

Note: you might argue that the fact you encountered a re-raise in this situation implies that raising was the wrong move in the first place. However, by raising you were able to determine that your opponent probably had a better hand than you because he re-raised. Had you just called, you'd have seen the flop, but then where would you be? With aces or kings your opponent is probably going to bet into you whatever the flop brings and you're no closer to knowing what he holds. Sometimes raising early in the hand can provide you with information that helps you get away more cheaply later on.

Summary: pair of queens

- Queens should be played in a roughly similar way to kings and aces pre-flop.
- You're scared of overcards (aces and kings) appearing on the flop, so bet and raise strongly to discourage more than one caller.
- You should normally re-raise any raises, unless your opponents' betting patterns suggest that you might be losing, or if you want to mix up your game a little and the indications are that calling won't let too many players in too cheaply.
- If you suspect you might be losing – up against aces or kings – then it's down to your judgment whether you call and see what happens on the flop, or simply fold and cut your losses.

Other pairs: jacks down to twos

For the purposes of this discussion, we've grouped together all the paired hands from jacks downwards. Although these hands vary in strength, with the higher pairs being much more valuable than the lower ones, the considerations when playing these hands have much in common.

If you can win the pot pre-flop by putting in the first raise with these hands, that is usually a good result. Once you get to the flop then the chances are that there will be overcards on the board (cards of a higher value than your pair) and you won't be sure where you stand. Here are rough guidelines for a game of around ten players when the pot is as yet unraised:

- With tens and jacks, from any position, you should usually raise but occasionally just call.

- With mid-pairs – sevens, eights and nines – you should occasionally raise from early position, but usually call. From later position you should be inclined to raise if you're one of the first into the pot (i.e. one of the first players not to fold), but otherwise just call.
- With small pairs – two, threes, fours, fives and sixes – you should usually call, but make the occasional raise when you're in late position and one of the first into the pot.

As with all the advice in this book, always remember that these guidelines may need to be tailored to the particular circumstances of the game you're in – particularly the number of players and their playing styles. (In shorter-handed games, for example, your pair is more valuable, so you can be more inclined to raise with it rather than merely call.) The important thing is that you understand *why* these plays are recommended, which you should do if you understand the general concepts we've introduced thus far.

Now let's consider what you should do in pots where there has been a raise (but no re-raise) ahead of you. The first thing to point out is that the majority of these paired hands aren't good enough to justify a re-raise because you're not necessarily likely to be winning. However, with the bigger pairs such as tens and jacks you can usually venture a re-raise if you're in late position, or if you suspect the raiser isn't in fact that strong for some reason.

However, when faced with a raise you're usually left with a choice between calling and folding. With the higher pairs you will usually call since there's a fair chance you'll be winning when the flop comes, assuming it helps neither you nor your opponent(s). For the smaller pairs however, it becomes less and less likely you'll be ahead – both because of the possibility of overcards on the board hitting your opponents' hands, and the chance that one of your opponents holds a higher pair than yours as their hole cards.

This means that if you call pre-flop with small and mid-pairs, you're really treating them as *drawing hands*. You're hoping that the flop will improve your hand and you'll make a *set* – three of a kind, with one of the community cards matching the pair in your hand. Sets are very powerful hands in hold'em because:

- If you flop a set, you will very frequently end up with the best hand and win the pot.

■ Your hand is very well disguised because two of the three cards in the set are hidden – it's difficult for opponents to realise quite how strong you are so they're more likely to call bets, or bet into you themselves.

In short, when you flop a set you can usually expect to win a very handsome pot. Now here's the bad news – this won't happen very often. If your hole cards are a pair, the odds against flopping a set or better are just over 11%, or around 8-to-1. Given that the odds of starting with a pair are 16-to-1, you'd make a set only one in every 150 hands, even if you played all pocket pairs as far as the flop (which of course you shouldn't).

Anyway, with odds of 8-to-1 against making a set, you need very attractive pot odds to make a call profitable. As a general rule, calling with small pairs in the hope of making a set is a good idea only when:

■ there are likely to be several callers of the flop – ideally four or more, although three might be sufficient depending on the game, or:
■ the actual pot odds (not implied odds) are long enough, perhaps 5-to-1 or more.

If either of these conditions is true, you should have the implied odds to make the call. Can you see why your odds are better with several callers? Each of the other players is matching your bet pre-flop, which improves your pot odds. But moreover, with more opponents there's a greater chance that one of them will hit a reasonable hand on the flop (e.g. one or two pairs) and hence invest further money later on in a hand you hope to win if you hit your set.

What you especially should avoid is calling big raises with small pairs in a heads-up situation – the implied odds don't justify it and it's not a profitable move.

Some other points to bear in mind when deciding whether to call:

■ With smaller pairs you can afford to call a little more readily if you are in late position. If the flop misses everyone, all may check round to you. Then you can bet and hopefully win the pot. If instead there is a bet on the flop, you may sometimes decide to raise anyway if you suspect the bettor isn't particularly strong. Your favourable position should normally prevent you getting into too much trouble even if that move fails to win the pot right there.

- Be more reluctant to call if there are other players still to act behind you. One of these may re-raise and force you to fold when it comes back round. If this looks likely, you'd rather save your money and not call in the first place.
- If your opponents are loose and / or aggressive then your implied odds are better and a call is more favourable. The reverse is of course true if your opponents are tight.
- If you call, there is a very slim chance that you might flop a set while one of your opponents flops a better set. When that happens, you're probably going to lose a big chunk of money. Fortunately this happens very rarely, but the risk of it means that you should be slightly more reluctant to call with the smaller pairs, and more careful subsequently if a large number of players see the flop. Don't get too paranoid though – it would almost always be wrong to fold a set post-flop because you suspected somebody of having made a better set.

As a final note on pocket pairs from jacks downwards, you should be well prepared to throw them away if there has been a raise and then a re-raise ahead of you. In this sort of situation, you want to be playing only with premium hands – and even pocket tens and jacks don't really cut it. If you're in late position and know your opponents well then you may decide to venture a call, but you'd normally be asking for trouble.

Summary: pairs, jacks and lower

In unraised pots, either call or raise depending on the value of the pair and your position, but be less inclined to raise if there are a number of callers ahead of you. If you raise, you should raise an amount that gives you a chance of winning the pot there and then.

With a single raise ahead of you then:

- Re-raise if you hold one of the larger pairs and have good position.
- If you're not strong enough to raise then call if the implied odds are favourable, which is usually true if several players are going to see the flop.
- Fold otherwise.

With a raise and re-raise ahead of you then even with the higher pairs you should normally fold, unless you've a good reason to think that you may be winning.

Ace-King

Ace-king, often called *big slick*, is the best non-paired hand in hold'em. In fact, in terms of its playability, it's stronger than all but the highest paired hands. As with the big pairs though, ace-king isn't a good enough hand to slowplay pre-flop. If you don't hit the flop, i.e. if no ace or king comes, then your hand isn't very much – just ace high. In fact, you'll pair an ace or king on the flop only 32% of the time, so you're quite happy to win the pot pre-flop with this hand.

All this suggests that you should put in a decent sized raise with ace-king, and indeed that's generally what you should do in unraised pots, from any position. In a typical game, 3-4 times the big blind should normally do the trick.

Just a quick note here. When holding ace-king some players might be tempted to think along the following lines: "I have a good hand, but it isn't that great. I'll simply flat-call the blind pre-flop and then play strongly if I pair up on the flop." Beware though – this is seriously flawed thinking. Firstly it violates the principle that you should bet when you're ahead. Ace-king will typically be the best hand at the table, and you can't give weaker opponents a cheap chance to outdraw you. If you merely call the blind what will usually happen is one of the following:

- you'll miss the flop and give up the pot without a fight
- you'll hit the flop and win a small pot immediately when you bet
- you'll hit the flop but lose a big pot to somebody who hit the flop better than you did, e.g. made two pair or a set.

In short, if you win then you'll win small, and you risk losing big. Playing ace-king this way certainly isn't optimal, and it may even be very costly. Don't do it.

So you should almost always raise any unraised pots. What about raised pots? In most games, with just one raise ahead of you, ace-king will usually still reckon to be the best hand. (An exception might be if a good, tight player has made a raise from very early position in a full game – you might then surmise there's a good chance they hold a very big pair.) And you know by now what to do if you think you have the best hand – re-raise of course.

A re-raise in this situation puts big pressure on players who have raised with hands like medium pairs or ace-queen or ace-jack. They may fold right there, giving you a risk-free win, or they may call and see a flop where you will hold the initiative – because you showed the most strength pre-flop.

Occasionally however you may decide simply to call a pre-flop raise with ace-king, and then slow down if you miss the flop altogether. This is a slightly passive play, but not an unreasonable one. You don't want to let too many players see the flop however, because of the chance one of them will hit something like two pair and turn a mediocre hand into a winning one.

If there are two or more raises in front of you, or if your raise is re-raised, then you need to start worrying about somebody having one of the two hands you fear most: pocket aces or pocket kings. You're a big underdog to these hands, especially to aces, so you may want to fold if you think that's what you're up against. You should note however that your opponents are less likely to hold aces or kings when you hold ace-king, because you've got some of the cards that make up these hands. (To be precise, they're half as likely to hold one of these hands as they would be if you held no king or ace.)

If you don't have reason to believe your any of your opponents hold aces or kings then you're actually in pretty good shape with ace-king. If you can play all the way to the showdown then you're only slightly worse than 50:50 against any pair, and a solid favourite against any other unpaired hands. (And you're actually a strong favourite against unpaired hands with an ace or king in them.)

What this means is that you might sometimes decide to take a deep breath, close your eyes – not literally of course – and either shove in a big re-raise or go all-in with this hand. (Recall that all-in is a more favourable option if you're out of position, although bear in mind our earlier comments about the inadvisability of huge, oversize raises.) If you're not up against kings or aces then worst case it's a coin flip if you're called. And a bet like this can put enormous pressure on your opponents, possibly even making them lay down very big hands because they fear that *you* hold pocket kings or aces.

Having said that, raising a re-raise is a risky move and you probably shouldn't do so unless you think there's a reasonable chance your opponents will fold.

One final note on ace-king suited versus unsuited. Naturally the suited hand is stronger than the unsuited one because it's more likely to make a flush. This gives you roughly an extra 3% chance of winning if you get to the showdown, and your hand is very much more playable if you flop a four flush. Of course, if you go on to make a flush, or hit it on the flop, then you might win a big pot if somebody else has a good but slightly worse hand. So although that 3% extra edge isn't very big, it can sometimes make you a lot of money when it comes into play.

In fact, ace-king is strong enough a hand that you can play the suited and unsuited variants in more or less the same way. As we'll see shortly however, this isn't true of some weaker hands, where the unsuited combinations need to be played more cautiously.

Summary: ace-king

- From any position, you should usually raise any unraised pots by an amount that gives you a chance of winning the pot pre-flop – perhaps 3-4 times the big blind (although you may occasionally mix it up by flat-calling).
- You should usually re-raise an opponent's raise, although occasionally you may decide to call and see what the flop brings.
- With two or more raises ahead of you, or a re-raise of your raise, you will normally call. If you're worried about kings or aces however, you may fold. If you're not unduly worried about that prospect you might even re-raise or go all-in.

Ace-Queen

Ace-queen is a similar hand to ace-king and will often be played in a similar way. Whilst ace-king is in trouble pre-flop only against pocket aces or kings however, ace-queen is in addition a big underdog to two more hands, namely pocket queens and ace-king. Moreover, ace-queen always feels quite uncomfortable whenever a king falls on the flop.

We say that ace-queen is *dominated* by hands such as A-A, A-K and Q-Q because it is weaker than they are yet has cards in common with them. This gives it very few ways to win against them.

In practice, these factors make ace-queen significantly weaker and less playable than ace-king. Whilst it is a good enough hand to justify a pre-flop raise in many *unraised* pots, you should almost never re-raise with ace-queen at a full table. You may decide to do so in short handed games however, or their equivalent. If you're in the big blind and all have folded to the button for example, who then raises, you might choose to *re*-raise since you wouldn't necessarily expect to be up against a very strong hand – it's reasonable for the button to raise with some quite weak holdings in this situation.

Ace-queen is also not usually strong enough for a call if there are two raises ahead of you, or if your initial raise incurs a big re-raise. Of course there will be exceptions to this, for example if you have specific reason for believing your opponents would re-raise with hands weaker than yours, or the pot odds are very good indeed, but in general ace-queen should be folded in the face of this sort of betting strength.

Ace-queen's vulnerability is to a certain extent mitigated by being suited, because of the possibility of making a (nut) flush and winning a big pot. As a result, ace-queen can be played a little more strongly in the suited variety.

Summary: ace-queen *suited*

- From any position, you should usually raise any unraised pots.
- A single raise of a reasonable size can usually be called, but don't re-raise unless you have good reason to think you could be winning.
- You should normally fold to re-raises.

Summary: ace-queen *unsuited*

- You can often raise any unraised pots, although be more inclined merely to call if the indications are unfavourable, e.g. if you are in early position or if there are a lot of callers ahead of you.
- You may want to fold to a raise, unless the indications are favourable, e.g. you have good position or reason to believe you might be winning.
- Fold to any re-raises.

Ace-Jack and Ace-Ten

The problems that ace-queen faces are magnified dramatically as the value of the second card diminishes to a jack or a ten. At a full table, it becomes increasingly likely that someone else will hold a *better ace* (an ace with a bigger kicker) and you'll be in real trouble as a result. Here's a table showing the chance of being dominated in this way at a ten-seater table:

Your hand	Probability 1+ opponents has a better ace (ten-seater table)
A-Q	8%
A-J	15%
A-10	22%
A-9	28%
A-8	34%
A-7	39%
A-6	44%
A-5	49%
A-4	53%
A-3	57%
A-2	61%

(And don't forget that there are many hands you can be losing to that *don't* have in ace in.)

So ace-jack and ace-ten should be played carefully. Even if nobody actually holds a better ace than you, the *risk* of this happening means that you won't be able to play your hand very strongly, and you'll have to bet more cautiously or fold in the face of strength from your opponents. This simple and obvious analysis seems to elude many inexperienced players, who as a result are frequently guilty of overplaying these hands.

Note: the suited variety of these hands retain their strength quite well – because it doesn't matter what your kicker is if you make the nut flush.

Summary: ace-jack and ace-ten *suited*

- In unraised pots, your decision is between calling and raising. You should be more inclined merely to call if you're in early position or hold the ten. From later position you should usually raise, although a call may be in order if there are callers ahead of you that you respect.
- You should often fold to a raise unless the indications are favourable, e.g. you have good position or reason to believe the raiser isn't that strong, in which case you should call (although you may occasionally re-raise if you're heads-up against an opponent who's probably under-strength).
- Don't even think about calling any re-raises.

Summary: ace-jack and ace-ten *unsuited*

- In unraised pots, your decision will depend upon your position. In early position, you should be inclined to fold these hands, more so if you have the ten. However, in mid or late position these hands become increasingly worth a call, and should usually be raised if there aren't many (or any) callers ahead of you likely to have a better hand.
- Be very wary of calling any raises, and don't call any re-raises.

Ace-x

By ace-x, we mean an ace paired with any card nine or lower. The value of the kicker (second card) is important, since ace-nine is better than ace-eight which is better than ace-seven and so on. But we're grouping all these hands together because they play similarly.

Hopefully by now you're aware of our feelings about Ace-x *unsuited* – it's trash. You can play ace-x if you're the first one into a pot and you're in late position, and you should usually raise with it because you'd like to win the pot right there. You can also play ace-x in very short handed games when 'any ace' becomes a reasonable hand. But in a full game with other players having called or still to act, you should normally just throw it away. Go on, throw that ace away, it's worthless. Really, we mean it!

Ace-x *suited* however is much more playable. You might hit a nut flush with it, and you might win even when you don't, perhaps because of that ace. These two factors in combination make it much more robust. Ace-x suited plays best against a large number of opponents because its flush potential makes it a good drawing hand. If you strike gold and end up making your flush, you should get paid off nicely.

Summary: ace-x *suited*

- In late position, with several callers ahead of you, you will have good odds to call and see the flop. Hopefully, cards of your suit will appear.
- You can call a raise too sometimes if the situation is favourable. It's a similar decision to calling a raise with a small pair in the hope of making a set. You need good odds (i.e. lots of other callers), good position and little expectation of a re-raise behind you for it to be a profitable move.
- In late position, with no callers ahead of you, you can play as if your ace were unsuited and raise in the hope of taking the pot down there and then.
- If none of the above applies then you're probably better off folding.

If you do make it as far as the flop, be very careful if you pair up your ace but your flush draw isn't in play. Your kicker is weak and you need to consider the likelihood of somebody else having an ace with a better kicker.

Summary: ace-x *unsuited*

Unless you're playing short-handed, throw it away.

King-queen

King-queen is by no means a bad hand and even the unsuited variety is nearly favourite in a ten-player game. As you'll see from the table of starting hands however, it isn't an absolutely premium hand, and it is vulnerable in the sense that whenever you make a pair on the flop with it, there's always a chance that you'll be out-kicked (by ace-king or ace-queen). You will often fold this hand pre-flop if you have unfavourable position or meet much resistance.

Summary: king-queen *suited*

- As first into the pot, you should usually raise. However, be more inclined merely to call if you're in early position, especially if there are aggressive players behind you who might re-raise.
- With other callers ahead of you, a call is more favourable. Despite its high card value, your hand is also a suited connector – you might make a straight or a flush with it – and it therefore plays quite well against multiple opponents. Remember though that if you make a flush, it won't be the nut flush unless the ace of your suit appears on the board.
- You should usually fold to a raise unless you suspect the raiser to be weak. However, you may occasionally venture a call if you have good odds and position, and a re-raise behind you seems unlikely.
- Fold to any re-raises – your hand isn't strong enough.

Summary: king-queen *unsuited*

- As first into the pot, you may fold, call or raise depending on your position. Be more inclined to fold in early position (yes, fold – really!) and raise in late position of course.
- With other callers ahead of you, you should usually call. However, you may want to fold if you're in early or mid-position and many pots are being raised pre-flop.
- You should normally fold to any raise or re-raise.

King-jack and queen-Jack

Don't get too excited just because you have two picture cards. These hands really aren't that strong and are nowhere near as valuable as most beginners might expect. As with king-queen, they risk being out-kicked even when they hit the flop but their slightly lower card value means that risk is even greater.

The suited holdings are a little stronger than the unsuited holdings and should be played as such, by which we mean you should be a little more inclined to call rather than fold, or raise rather than merely call. However, we can group both flavours together for the purpose of discussing strategy.

Summary: king-jack and queen-jack

- As first into the pot, you may fold, call or raise depending on your position. Be more inclined to fold in early position and raise in late position.
- With other callers ahead of you, you should usually call. However, you may want to fold if you're in early or mid-position and many pots are being raised pre-flop.
- Fold to a raise unless you have good odds and position, and a re-raise behind you seems unlikely.

Suited connectors

A suited connector is any two cards of the same suit with consecutive values. Suited connectors therefore range from ace-king suited down to three-two suited. We've covered ace-king, king-queen and queen-jack above, and those hands are really special cases because they have high card value too.

At the other end of the spectrum, the very small suited connectors aren't really playable because of their low card value and the fact that they don't make enough straights – so they're much less likely to make the winning hand. Here, then, we're just considering jack-ten suited down to six-five suited, or maybe five-four suited at a stretch.

Whenever you play a suited connector, you're really hoping to flop a straight draw or flush draw, or maybe even a straight or flush if you're very lucky. Of course there are other hands you can hit such as two pair or trips (a pair on the table with a third in your hand) but this will be pretty rare.

Suited connectors have much in common with small pairs because:

- they are drawing hands – they really need to hit the board well to improve.
- when they do improve, they often improve to very good hands that are likely to win the pot.
- they often make for well disguised hands that your opponents won't suspect you of having – because you're less likely to be playing two low cards – and hopefully therefore win you a big pot.

(If you've forgotten how to play small pairs pre-flop, you may want to revisit our discussion on them above.)

But on the other hand, suited connectors require considerably more care than small pairs because (a) small pairs are easy to throw away when they miss the flop and (b) when small pairs improve on the flop, they improve to a made hand that's extremely likely to be winning at that point, i.e. a set.

Suited connectors in contrast:

- often improve to flush draws and straight draws that may not complete until the turn or river and present you with difficult decisions in the interim
- often make hands which aren't the nuts even when they do improve or complete, e.g. low flushes, bottom two pair, or trips with a low kicker.

As a result of all this, suited connectors are not hands that beginners should play as readily as small pairs – they require a lot more skill and judgment to make profitable. The adjustments you should make are as follows.

- Be even less inclined to play them out of position. Suited connectors are drawing hands and are much more effective from late position. (Drawing hands are discussed further at the end of Chapter Seven: Playing the flop.)
- Avoid getting involved with them unless the odds (effective and implied) are clearly very favourable. Typically this means having three or more opponents in the pot with you.

Summary: suited connectors

- The bigger suited connectors are slightly more playable than the smaller ones because of their high card value.
- As first into the pot, you may fold, call or raise depending on your position – be more inclined to fold in early position and raise in late position. Also bear in mind the value of your cards – you can hang around more readily with jack-ten or ten-nine.
- With other callers ahead of you, you should usually call. However, you may want to fold if you're in early or mid-position and many pots are being raised pre-flop.
  ... continued on next page

- With a single raise ahead of you and favourable position, call if the implied odds are favourable, which is usually true if several players are going to see the flop, and fold otherwise.
- Fold to any re-raises.

Other miscellaneous hands

There are other hands near the top of the starting hand list not really covered in the above discussion, although they are all at best marginal (barely playable) hands at a full table. Examples include: king-ten and queen-ten.

By now you should have got enough of an idea to work out what to do with each of them. Think about:

- Which other hands are similar to yours and how those hands would be played.
- How strong your hand is, i.e. how far it is down the list and which other hands dominate it.
- Whether it's a drawing hand that plays better multi-way (i.e. against several opponents) and therefore favours calling, or a hand that fares better against few opponents, and is therefore better played with a raise.
- What your position is. Late position is always good, but it's especially important when playing marginal hands or drawing hands.

All this sounds like a lot to bear in mind while you're in the middle of a hand. Don't worry though, once you've got some playing time under your belt it will all become much easier. If in doubt with a marginal starting hand, just fold. Folding a marginal holding at the first opportunity is never a particularly bad option.

Trash

Once you get a certain way down the list, everything else is trash. Don't play those hands, just throw them away. Don't decide that they're your favourite hand and that you must play them to the river, because if you do it will cost you money. You may get away with it once or twice but with an inevitable certainty it will hurt you in the long run.

You might decide to bluff with one of the weaker hands. But why bother? There are plenty of half-decent hands, so if you do decide to bluff then at least do so with a small pair or suited connector – at least you'll have a chance of turning them into something good if your bluff is called.

The only time trash hands become playable is when the game (or hand) becomes very short-handed. Only then should you consider betting and raising with, say, any ace or hands like king-nine unsuited.

Quiz: Pre-flop play

In all the following questions the blinds are £1 / £2 and there are ten players seated at the table. Unless otherwise stated, all players involved have plenty of money left in front of them. Your job is to say how you'd play each of the hands you are dealt.

Question 1. You're in mid-position and are dealt a pair of aces. There's one caller ahead of you. Do you (a) fold (b) call £2 (c) call £2 with the intention of re-raising if somebody else raises (d) make a minimum raise to £4 (e) raise to £8?

Question 2. You're in the big blind with a pair of aces. A tight player *under the gun* (first to act) raises to £8. All fold to you. Do you (a) fold (b) call (c) make a minimum raise to £14 (d) raise to £25?

Question 3. You're on the button with a pair of kings. There is a call from early position and then a raise to £6. Do you (a) fold (b) call (c) make a minimum raise to £10 (d) raise to £20?

Question 4. Following on from the previous question, you raise to £15 with your pair of kings on the button and have £90 left. The player in early position raises to £50 and has another £75 left. The first raiser goes all-in for £80. Do you (a) fold (b) call (c) go all-in for £90?

Question 5. You're in the small blind with a pair of queens. There is a caller in mid-position and a raise to £8 from late position. Do you (a) fold (b) call (c) make a minimum raise to £14 (d) raise to £25?

Question 6. You call from early position with a pair of sixes. The player immediately after you raises to £10 and there are three callers from mid or late position. Do you (a) fold (b) call (c) make a minimum raise to £18 (d) raise to £40?

Question 7. You are in mid position with a pair of twos. There's a call from the player under the gun, and then a raise to £8. Do you (a) fold (b) call (c) make a minimum raise to £14 (d) raise to £25?

Question 8. You are in late position with ace-king (unsuited). There are two calls ahead of you, one from early position and one from mid position. Do you (a) fold (b) call (c) make a minimum raise to £4 (d) raise to £8?

Question 9. You are on the button with ace-queen (unsuited) in a tight and cagey game. The first two players to act call and then a player in mid position raises to £10. Do you (a) fold (b) call (c) make a minimum raise to £18 or (d) raise to £35?

Question 10. You are on the button with ace-seven spades and there are three callers from mid and late positions. Do you (a) fold (b) call (c) make a minimum raise to £4 (d) raise to £8?

Question 11. You are on the button with ace-six hearts and all fold to you. Do you (a) fold (b) call (c) make a minimum raise to £4 (d) raise to £8?

Question 12. You are in the big blind with king-four off-suit. There's a call from mid position and a raise to £8 from late position. The small blind calls. Do you (a) fold (b) call (c) make a minimum raise to £14 (d) raise to £25?

Answers to quiz

Answer 1. With aces you ideally want to reduce the field to one or two players (plus you). In this situation you're going to have to raise to do this. A raise to £4 isn't enough since callers will be getting reasonable pot odds. The correct answer is (e). Slowplaying the aces, answer (c), is no good in this instance – you should only attempt this from early position, and as the first person into the pot in aggressive games.

Answer 2. If a tight player raises from under the gun at a ten-seater table then they've got a great hand, either a big pair or perhaps ace-king or ace-queen suited. But you've got a better hand. Making a minimum raise is a silly thing to do because you're giving away the strength of your hand and not really getting much extra money in the pot even if you're called. So if you're going to raise then you should make a decent sized raise to £25. But what about calling? Since everybody else has already folded, the field has already been reduced to two. And since your opponent has a strong hand, he's very likely to bet on the flop anyway even if he doesn't hit it. The best option in this instance is probably (b), to call, although a case could be made for (d) too.

Answer 3. You ideally want to reduce the field to one opponent with kings. Calling almost certainly won't achieve that since one of the blinds or the early caller will probably call too. So you have to raise. A minimum raise is a bad idea because it gives away the strength of your hand without getting much extra money in the pot, and risks not driving out enough players. The correct answer is (d), raise to £20, which is just short of a pot-sized raise.

Answer 4. We said you should hardly ever fold kings pre-flop. But in this case, unless you know your opponents to be poor or loose players, you're almost certainly beaten. The player in early position flat-called and then raised your re-raise; that should set alarm bells ringing. It seems very likely that at least one of your opponents holds aces, making you a big underdog. You could hope that, for example, one has ace-king and the other a pair of queens – but they would both have played badly if that were the case. You've committed a relatively small amount of your stack to the pot so far, so you should go for option (a) and fold. If you'd had less money remaining, the longer pot odds might have made a call more compelling.

Answer 5. There's no particular reason to think your queens aren't winning, – the raise from late position could have been made with plenty of hands you can beat. So folding isn't the right option. The problem with calling is that you risk drawing in other callers by giving them favourable pot odds, plus it doesn't allow you to find out where you stand with the raiser in late position. Since you're playing against him out of position, you'd be quite happy to win the pot right now. Raising is the correct option here, and it needs to be more than a minimum raise to give him a tough decision. The correct answer is (d), raise to £25.

Answer 6. There's £43 in the pot and it costs you £8 to call. That's pot odds of nearly 5.5-to-1. Your pair of sixes is almost certainly not winning at this point, so you won't raise. You might however flop a set which would be very likely to win. The odds of this happening are 8-to-1, so on the pot odds alone a call isn't justified. But with four opponents the implied odds are good – clearly in excess of 8-to-1 (unless, for example, your opponents are very tight). You go for option (b) and call.

Answer 7. Your pair of twos isn't very likely to be winning at the moment, although it's just possible that the two players into the pot ahead of you both have unpaired high cards. But even if this were the case, the flop will bring overcards and your hand won't be playable.

What about calling in the hope of hitting a two on the flop? There's £13 in the pot and it costs you £8 to call. That's pot odds of less than 2-to-1, which are feeble for your 8-to-1 shot of making a set of twos. Calling is made less attractive still by the risk that nearly everyone behind you will fold, or that somebody behind you will raise, thereby forcing you to put more money in the pot or fold. In either case, your implied odds are shot to pieces. The answer is (a) – this is about as clear as folds get.

Answer 8. The good thing about ace-king is that, although you're rarely a big favourite over other players, you're rarely a big underdog either. This allows you to put other players under pressure without too much risk to yourself, even if they turn out have a better hand. You need to find out what the two callers are up to, and raising is the way to do this. By raising you'll also drive out players thinking about playing 'any two cards' because of the attractive pot odds, and hence obtain a better idea of where you stand post-flop. A minimum raise is too small to achieve this, so you go for option (d) and raise to £8.

Answer 9. Careful here – there's some real strength being shown from your opponents. Two calls in the first two positions represent reasonable hands in a tight game, and the raise on top seems to represent a hand like ace-king or a big pair. Your ace-queen is in danger of being dominated, and might not be good enough even if you hit the flop. If an ace comes, you could be losing to ace-king or a pair of kings, and if a queen comes you could be losing to a pair of kings or a pair of aces. You must also bear in mind that there are still four players to act behind you even if you call (the two blinds and the two early callers) and one of them could raise. You haven't committed any money to this pot as yet and it seems prudent to keep it that way. You go for option (a) and fold.

Answer 10. You're definitely not strong enough to raise in this position since there's a good chance that one of the callers has an ace with a higher kicker. But you're getting great pot odds (nearly 5-to-1) and you might catch a nice flop such as two pair or a couple of spades, giving you a nut flush draw. You're in good position to take advantage if that happens, or to steal if nobody else shows much interest in the pot. You go for option (b) and call.

Ace-x suited is best played as a drawing hand.

Answer 11. This question is superficially similar to the previous one, but there's a key difference. This time all the players ahead of you have folded so you're now playing a three handed game. Your ace-x suited is of little value played as a drawing hand against just the two blinds because the odds aren't very good. But with just two other players remaining, it does rate to be the best hand at the table. You should raise. The ideal amount seems to be about £6 since £8 is a little strong with so little money in the pot and so few players to act after you. But £4 definitely isn't enough. Given the choices available, you go for option (d) and raise to £8.

Answer 12. Your hand is trash so to even consider playing it you'd need exceptionally good odds, hoping to flop, say, two pair or trips. (If you call and flop a pair, you're likely to be out-kicked or up against a higher pair and get yourself in trouble.) Alternatively you might play king-four if you reckoned you could win the pot there and then with a bluff. But the odds are poor and a bluff doesn't look likely to work since a few players have already shown interest in the pot. We've spent longer on this hand than it deserves just by explaining our reasoning. You go for option (a) and fold as quick as you can.

Chapter Seven:
Playing the flop

In hold'em, the flop is a very significant moment. In one fell swoop, three of the seven cards that make up your hand are revealed. You'll refine your strategy for the hand on the turn and the river if you make it that far, but the flop is where you'll make your big decisions.

When we discussed pre-flop play, we were able to provide a methodical breakdown of the different situations that can arise, because the number of distinct possibilities pre-flop is relatively small. Although we weren't able to provide completely prescriptive advice in every case, a beginner could become a reasonably competent pre-flop player quite rapidly by learning and following our guidelines.

Once we get to the flop however, this is no longer so easy. Many more factors come into play and it's not really possible to provide specific advice for each circumstance. Ultimately, learning how to play post-flop is going to require a lot of playing experience, so you can develop a feel for each situation and how best to handle it.

Of necessity then, our advice now becomes more general – unfortunately we're getting past the point where poker can in any sense be played by rote. We can't tell you exactly what to do, but we can tell you what factors to consider. How good a player you become will be determined by how well you analyse each situation, act on the factors in play, and – most importantly of all – refine your strategy and understanding by learning from each of your own successes and failures.

In Chapter Five (which covers general playing considerations) we discussed the various factors that influence your play during a hand of hold'em – such as your cards, your position, etc. On the flop you must continue to bear all these in mind, but pay particular attention to the key considerations for this stage of the hand, namely:

- whether the flop helped you, and how much
- whether the flop is likely to have helped your opponents
- **t**he outcome of the pre-flop betting round.

Let's look at each of these in turn.

Did the flop help you?

This is the easiest part of the flop to assess. If the flop helped you, or *hit you* as people often say, then it made your hand better. This can happen in a number of ways.

You flop a pair. This happens when your hand is unpaired, and one of your cards matches one of the cards on the flop. If you match the highest value board card, we say you have *flopped top pair*. You can also flop *middle pair* and *bottom pair* too. Flopping top pair is quite a good result in general – you are sure to be beating anyone who's flopped a different pair to yours. Flopping middle pair is better than bottom pair or no pair, but obviously not as good as top pair.

If your hole cards are paired, then you are guaranteed to have a pair after the flop even if the board cards all miss you. We say that you hold an *overpair* if your pair is of a higher value than all three flop cards, or an *underpair* if one or more of the cards on the flop is higher than yours. Note that an overpair is better than any flopped pair, which is why pocket aces is such a great hand.

Whenever you flop a pair, you should always consider your kicker too. There's always a chance that somebody flopped the same pair as you (especially if you paired a high card – players are more likely to see the flop with high cards) and if that's the case, your kicker will make or break the hand for you.

You flop two pair. This happens when your hand is unpaired, and both of your cards match cards on the flop. Once again, it's significant which two of the three board cards you match. If you match the two highest value board cards then you have *flopped top two pair*. You can also flop top and bottom pair, and bottom two pair. Whenever you flop two pair, you have a great hand that stands a good chance of winning the pot (though you should watch out for straights and flushes – more on that later).

If your hole cards are paired then you can also have two pair after the flop – but only if two of the flop cards are paired. When people talk about flopping two pair, they don't usually mean this scenario.

You flop three of a kind. This is a lovely thing to happen. However, there are two different ways of flopping three of a kind, one much better than the other:

■ You have two unpaired cards, and one of your cards matches two of the board cards (i.e. the board pairs). This is called *flopping trips*. Although it's a great result, there are two potential problems. Firstly notice that there's one remaining card out there somewhere that matches the pair on the board. If that card is held by one of your opponents then they too have trips. In this case, your kicker (second hole card) may come into play. The other problem is that your hand is poorly concealed. As soon as you start betting too strongly, people may start to suspect what you hold.
■ You have a pair in your hand, and one of the board cards matches your pair. As we saw earlier, this is called *flopping a set*, and it's an extremely powerful hand. Neither of the potential problems described above can apply here. It's unlikely that anybody else has a set, and your hand is very well concealed. Lovely.

Note that people often use the term *trips* to mean any three of a kind, including sets. However, in this book we'll restrict our usage of the term trips to the definition above, that is, a pair on the board with a matching hole card.

You flop a full house or four of a kind. Urrrrrgh ... now, stay calm, breathe nice and slow, and try not to break into song. Actually, great as they may look, flopped full houses and quads (four of a kind) come along extremely rarely and aren't usually that profitable. The problem is that the board will be paired (because if the board is unpaired then a flush is the best possible hand) and hence quite scary looking. Furthermore your opponents will rarely have anything worth playing since you've got a high percentage of the cards that match the board. If you show too much strength in your betting, you're unlikely to get any callers.

In an ideal world, you'd win at poker by waiting for the nuts and then getting all your money – and all your opponents' money – in the middle. But in real life it hardly ever works like that. You make your money by hard graft and showing good judgment on the marginal hands. Be thankful for that though – if poker were that simple, you wouldn't be able to get ahead of the pack and make a profit.

You flop a straight draw. You flop a straight draw when there are four cards to a straight out of the five visible to you (your two cards plus the three flop cards). Straight draws come in two varieties:

- You have an *inside straight draw* if the four cards have a gap in the run somewhere that needs to be filled in order to make the straight; for example if you hold 5-6-8-9 and are looking for a 7. Inside straight draws are also variously known as *gutshot, belly-buster* or *middle pin* straight draws. All inside straight draws are characterised by having exactly four outs (the four sevens in the example above). For this reason, A-2-3-4 and J-Q-K-A are also considered inside straight draws despite not having any gap. They each have exactly four outs: A-2-3-4 needs a five and J-Q-K-A needs a ten.
- You have an *outside straight draw* (also known as an *open-ended straight draw* or *up-and-down straight draw*) if the four cards to the straight are consecutive and don't include an ace. An example is: 4-5-6-7. All outside straight draws are characterised by having exactly eight outs (four threes and four eights in the example above). With twice the number of outs of an inside straight draw, outside draws are obviously far more playable in practice.

Interestingly, there are also some eight-out straight draws that don't contain four consecutive cards, e.g. 2-4-5-6-8 or 7-9-10-J-K, and in fact they all have the pattern X_XXX_X. These are known as *double gutshot* or *double belly-buster* straight draws. They can be considered outside straight draws for our purposes; the number of outs is the key differentiating feature.

You flop a straight. You flop a straight when the five cards visible to you are consecutive. This is a very nice thing to happen, but you should check whether you can be beaten or if you have the nuts. For example, if the board is:

then:

- 8-9 is the nut straight
- 4-8 is the second nut straight
- 3-4 is the worst straight.

You flop a flush draw. You flop a flush draw when there are four cards of the same suit out of the five visible to you. You have the nut flush draw if you hold the highest card of that suit that's not already on the board.

You flop a flush. You flop a flush when the five cards visible to you are of the same suit. Nut or near-nut flushes are much better hands than smaller flushes.

You flop a straight flush. Unless you play a lot of poker, this may not ever happen to you. When it does, you'll be praying that somebody has the nut flush or nut flush draw and pays you off.

So, those are the various ways that the flop can help your hand. Let's just look at the chances of each of these happening to put them in perspective:

You hold	You flop	Probability
Any two unpaired cards	No pair	67.6%
Any two unpaired cards	One pair	29.0%
Any two unpaired cards	Two pair	2.0%
Any two unpaired cards	Trips	1.3%
Any two unpaired cards	Full house or quads	0.1%
A pair	No set	88.2%
A pair	A set	10.8%
A pair	Full house or quads	0.1%
Connectors (4-5 to 10-J)	Outside straight draw	9.8%
Connectors (as above)	Inside straight draw	18.9%
Connectors (as above)	Straight	1.3%
Suited cards	Flush draw	10.9%
Suited cards	Flush	0.8%
Suited connectors (4-5 to 10-J)	Straight flush	0.02%

As you can see, by far and away the most likely thing to happen on the flop for you is ... nothing whatsoever. Most flops will miss your hand completely, regardless of what you've got.

You should also notice that flopped flushes and straights happen pretty rarely, and even flush and straight draws aren't that common. Plus, when you hit a draw, more often than not you won't complete your hand even if you play to the river. This is precisely why suited cards and connectors really need to have something else going for them to be playable. They need either some high card value, or to be *both* suited and connected rather than merely one or the other.

We'll just wrap up this section by observing that it's perfectly possible for the flop to hit your hand in more than one way. For example, you might make top pair *and* a flush draw, or middle pair *and* a straight draw. These hands are particularly playable because they are made hands that also have good opportunities to improve.

Did the flop help your opponents?

Once you've seen the flop and worked out what it's done for you, the next thing to consider is what it might have done for your opponents. One very simple point that often eludes beginners is that some flops are more likely than others to hit people – we say that every flop has a different texture. Some textures are fairly safe, and some are dangerous.

Let's look at the possibilities that the flop may bring.

High cards. Flops with high cards are more dangerous than those with low cards – because players who hold high cards are more likely to stay and see the flop than those who don't. If the flop comes, for example:

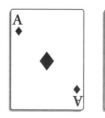  

or

then you should be very careful, especially if there are several players still in. It's almost certain that somebody will have one or even two pairs, and quite likely that somebody will hold a straight or straight draw.

Flops with two high cards, e.g. A-Q-2, or one high card, e.g. K-8-3, are not usually as dangerous as those with three, but still demand caution. The basic rule is simple: the more high cards on the flop, the more dangerous it is.

Pairs. When the flop has a pair in it, the most dangerous outcome is that somebody has made trips – three of a kind. There are two cards out there that make trips, and the more players there are, the more likely it is that someone has one of them.

Number of players (other than you) seeing the flop	Probability someone has trips when flop is paired
1	8.4%
2	16.5%
3	24.1%
4	31.5%
5	38.4%
6	45.0%
7	51.2%
8	57.0%
9	62.4%
10	67.5%

So you need to be careful when the board pairs if you don't have a piece of it. Note however that if there are just one or two other players seeing the flop then paired boards are in some ways safer than unpaired boards. Since there are only two different card values on the flop (rather than the three there would be if the board were unpaired) then:

- there is less chance that one of your opponents has paired the board, because there are only two card values that will pair rather than three
- a flopped straight is impossible
- a straight draw is less likely.

So if you raised pre-flop with a pair of tens for example, and got one or two callers, you'd much rather see a flop of:

than one of:

With the paired flop, it's much less likely that one of your opponents has improved sufficiently to beat you. Don't go too far with this line of reasoning though – paired boards are always tricky, and if you're losing to trips you're usually going to be a big underdog.

Also remember that, whenever the board is paired, someone can in theory have made a full house or quads (unlikely as it may be). Whenever you're drawing to straight or flush and the board has paired, spare a moment to contemplate whether you might be *drawing dead*, in other words playing a hand which can't possibly win however it improves.

Finally, note that paired boards offer good bluffing opportunities because you can *represent* having made trips even if you haven't. Unfortunately, so can your opponents.

Three of a kind. Once in every 425 hands, you'll see a flop that comes three of a kind. If you've got a pocket pair, try not to get too excited about the fact you've flopped a full house – it's the worst kind of full house there is. You're still losing to anyone:

- with a higher pair than you – they have a better full house
- who holds the other card in the deck matching the board – they have quads.

If you don't have a pocket pair or quads, you're probably done with the hand unless you decide to bluff at it.

Connecting cards. The danger of flops with connecting cards, or nearly connecting cards, is that somebody will have made a straight, or a good straight draw. If somebody starts betting heavily into a flop of e.g. 5-6-7 or 8-9-J, then you have to start worrying about a possible straight. The higher the connecting cards, the more likely the possibility is, since people are more likely to play high connectors than low connectors.

If only two of the cards connect, then a flopped straight isn't possible, but a straight draw is. This likelihood is greater if the cards are closely connected rather than loosely. For example, K-6-5 makes three outside straight draws (with 3-4, 4-7 or 7-8) whereas K-8-5 makes only one (with 6-7).

Suited cards. The possibility here – obviously – is that one of your opponents will have made a flush or flush draw. The most scary flop in this category is one with three cards all of the same suit, sometimes called a *monochrome* flop. Anybody with two cards in that suit has a flush, and anyone with one card in that suit is drawing to a flush.

Even if there are only two cards of a suit on the flop, that's still something that should register with you. Anybody holding two cards of that suit has a flush draw, and they will improve to a flush by the end of the hand more than one time in three.

When the flop comes with three different suits, that's called a *rainbow flop*. You don't really have to worry too much about flushes in this case since even if an opponent has three cards to the flush, they're going to need to get two more cards of that suit on the turn and the river to complete the flush. That's called making a *backdoor* flush, and it's not very likely to happen.

So, in summary, rainbow flops are safer than non-rainbow flops, with monochrome flops being the most dangerous of all.

Carefully consider the texture

As in the previous section, you should note that the flop will frequently bring more than one of the above possibilities. For example, if the flop comes:

then you might easily be up against:

- one pair
- two pair
- a set
- a straight or straight draw
- a flush or flush draw
- a straight flush.

Or several of the above. If on the other hand the flop is:

then:

- there are no possible straights or straight draws at this point
- there are no possible flush or flush draws
- pairs are less likely because there are fewer high cards on the board, and people don't play hands with sevens and twos in them as often as hands containing high cards (or, at least, good players don't)
- you're less likely to be up against two pairs, because K-7, K-2 and 7-2 are all poor holdings that usually don't make it as far as the flop (again, depending on the skill level of your opponents)
- even a set is less probable, because opponents holding 2-2 or 7-7 are more likely to fold pre-flop than those holding J-J or Q-Q.

So K-7-2 rainbow is a much *safer* flop than K-Q-J suited.

All in all, the texture of the flop is crucial in your assessment of the relative strength of your hand, and hence in how you decide to play the remainder of the hand. For each flop you should consider:

- How likely is the flop to have helped your opponents?
- How *many* of your opponents may have been helped by the flop?
- What *kind* of hands will the flop have helped? Are they hands that your opponents are likely to be playing, given due consideration to the pre-flop betting?
- Are most of the hands that the flop helped likely to be *made hands* – i.e. hands that are already complete, such as pairs or sets – or *drawing hands*, such as straight and flush draws?

The outcome of pre-flop betting

When you're considering what course of action to take on the flop (and indeed the turn and the river too) it's important to remember how the betting proceeded during previous rounds, because this provides information about what cards your opponents might be playing. The pre-flop betting *sets the tone* for the flop round, and all your betting decisions on the flop will be made with reference to what you perceive to be the relative strength and weakness – and likely holdings – of your opponents.

For each of the players remaining in the hand, you should think about:

- What actions they took pre-flop: call, raise or re-raise
- What were the circumstances under which they acted, e.g. were there a lot of callers ahead of them or were they the first into the pot
- How their play compared to what you know of their usual pre-flop play
- Whether you are able to put them on a range of possible hands, or at least make a rough assessment of their likely hand strength.

In general you won't be able to form that much of a picture of what's going on based solely on the pre-flop betting, but you may be able to rule out a few possibilities. If you hold all the information in your head and gradually add to it as the remainder of the hand unfolds, you can often draw some reasonable conclusions in the later rounds.

Bearing all this in mind, we're first going to make some observations about pots where there was no raise pre-flop, and so none of the players contributed more to the pot than the amount of the big blind.

When there was no raise pre-flop

Here are some fairly obvious statements about pots that were unraised pre-flop:

- They are cheaper to participate in.
- Because they're cheaper, players can call with weaker starting hands.
- Because players can call with weaker starting hands, more players will call.
- Some players, especially those in late position, may be playing almost any two cards if there were callers ahead of them, because the pot odds can get so tempting under those circumstances.
- The small and big blind have contributed even less money than the other players and are effectively playing random cards.

This combination of more players and weaker holdings makes unraised pots very unpredictable. If there had been a sizeable raise pre-flop then you could perhaps count on the raiser and callers to have *some* kind of hand at least. But in unraised pots, you can't really draw any conclusions – and this means you have to tread more carefully.

It means, for example, that some flops that might normally be considered safe are potentially dangerous. On a flop such as:

it's usually unlikely for somebody to have hit two pair if there has been any pre-flop action – because people don't often play hands like Q-6, Q-2 or 6-2. But if everyone has any old cards, this is a more realistic possibility. Or if the flop comes:

it's usually unlikely for someone to have made a straight, because 2-5 and 5-7 really shouldn't withstand a pre-flop raise. But if there was no pre-flop raise then these become possible holdings. Just remember that unraised pots are inherently unpredictable.

Here's another statement about pots that were unraised pre-flop – they tend to have less money in them than raised flops. This rather obvious point means that you're not as incentivised to try to win such pots. The combination of unpredictability plus lack of size makes unraised pots rather unappetising. If you get a piece of the flop then by all means try to pick up such pots with a bet – but there's no sense in losing your stack over them.

Suppose for example that, pre-flop, you called in early position with pocket aces hoping for a raise behind you – but sadly no raise came. Six players see the flop which comes:

Now, you might reason that your pair of aces is good enough to be winning, because you're beating anyone with a pair of any kind, and in fact you might well be right. It's fine for you to go ahead and make a bet on the flop, and in this case we'd recommend making it of a reasonable size – maybe near to pot-sized – so that players with straight draws (2-3, 3-6, 6-7) don't have the odds to call.

But suppose you get callers or raisers – then what are you going to do? Do you still think you're in the lead? You might decide you are, and carry on betting on the turn and river, only for your opponent to turn over a hand like:

In this situation, you can't really argue with your opponent's play. He saw a cheap flop and hit a nice hand. Look how easily he overtook your lovely pair of aces. But if there had been a raise pre-flop, he almost certainly would have folded. And if he hadn't, well good luck to him – he'll need it if he's going to call raises with those sort of cards.

To sum up, hands that are unraised pre-flop are:
- small
- unpredictable.

So don't pursue them in the face of too much resistance from your opponents unless you have a very strong hand.

When the pot was raised pre-flop

Several features distinguish raised pots from unraised ones. They are obviously bigger and somewhat more predictable, as should be clear from the previous section. This makes them both worth fighting for and easier to read. In fact, the more betting and raising there was pre-flop, the more you should be able mentally to restrict your opponents to a range of possible hands.

But there is another aspect of such pots that is particularly significant to flop play – the *identity* of the pre-flop raiser. Or, if there was a re-raise, the identity of the *last* pre-flop raiser. Recall from the previous section that most flops fail to improve most hands. This means that much of the time, the player who has the best hand pre-flop still has the best hand *after* the flop.

This in turn means that the player who showed the most strength pre-flop – the last raiser – is the player who is favourite to win the hand. Or at least, they are usually *considered* to be favourite by the other players; certainly the initiative lies with them unless wrested away by an opponent.

Hopefully you know by now what the player who reckons they're in the lead is supposed to do – they bet of course. Therefore it is very common to see the pre-flop raiser make the first bet on the flop, regardless of whether the flop improved their hand or not – we call such a bet a *continuation bet*.

All good players make continuation bets when the time is right, and you should too. Let's take a closer look.

The continuation bet

We've established that the pre-flop raiser will often lead out with a bet (a continuation bet) once the flop is dealt. Just to be clear, to qualify as a continuation bet, a bet must be:

- the first bet made on the flop, *and*
- made by the last player, or only player, to raise pre-flop.

Some players, particularly looser, more aggressive players, seem *always* to make continuation bets after raising pre-flop. This is very rarely the correct strategy as we'll see. On the other hand, some players, usually tighter, more passive players, fail to make continuation bets often enough. Perhaps they do so only when the flop helped them. This strategy is too weak, and liable to be exploited by opponents – players who bet only when they have a hand are too predictable and easy to read.

The trick is to strike a good balance, and to develop an awareness of when a continuation bet is the right move. Depending on the nature of the game and your opponents, you should probably make a continuation bet somewhere between 50%-80% of the time that you were the pre-flop raiser.

We're going to divide continuation bets into two categories:

- You make a *legitimate* continuation bet if you reckon to be in the lead after the flop. This could be either because the flop helped you, or because you had a strong hand pre-flop and no particular reason to suspect that anyone has overtaken you.
- You make a *speculative* continuation bet if there is considerable doubt over whether you're in the lead or not once the flop has come.

Essentially, legitimate continuation bets are standard, value-based bets. You think you're in the lead, and so you're hoping either to take the pot right there, or to get players with weaker hands to put more money in a pot in which you're favourite.

Speculative continuation bets are closer to bluffs however. You might be in the lead, but you might not. You're mostly hoping that everyone folds, although there's a possibility you are actually in the lead, or will improve to be in the lead, even if you do get callers. The idea behind a speculative continuation bet is that the initiative you generate by being the pre-flop raiser will see you through, assuming other players found the flop similarly unhelpful.

Legitimate continuation bets

If you raised pre-flop, and reckon you're in the lead after the flop, then a continuation bet is usually in order. Circumstances where this might apply are:

> Note: some authors would say that a *legitimate* continuation bet doesn't count as a *continuation bet* at all. They use the term continuation bet only to refer to what we've called a speculative continuation bet.

- You flop two pair.
- You flop top pair with a good kicker.
- You hold a pair in your hand and three undercards to your pair (i.e. three lower value cards) come on the flop.

You might also decide you're in the lead with some weaker hands, e.g. middle or bottom pair, especially if there aren't too many callers and the flop looks fairly safe. Once you've been playing poker for a while, you should find it quite easy to spot the situations where a legitimate continuation bet is in order.

There is a situation where you might not want to make a continuation bet even when the flop helps you – that's where you flop a very strong hand, such as a set or better. In this case you may decide that you can win more money by initially disguising your strength; either by checking and then raising if somebody else bets, or by slowplaying, i.e. checking and calling along.

Note though that if other players are likely to perceive your continuation bet as speculative, and hence not necessarily indicative of real strength, then you'll probably find it more profitable to just *bet out* (i.e. bet rather than check) when you flop a very strong hand, and hope you get raised. These ideas are discussed further in Chapter Ten where we talk about check-raising and slowplaying.

Speculative continuation bets

You will need to develop a good sense of judgment in order to determine the right time to bet when, as pre-flop raiser, the flop doesn't help you. Suppose for example:

- You have two high cards, but didn't pair up on the flop.
- You hold a pair but scary-looking overcards come on the flop.

What are you going to do now? A speculative continuation bet is obviously a possibility, but will it work? Here are the factors that should influence your decision.

Texture of flop. You're in the position where the flop hasn't helped you but it may have helped your opponents – and you're considering betting in the hope that everyone else folds. In this situation, it would be crazy to make a continuation bet if the flop looked likely to have hit someone – they'll surely just call or raise you, and you'll probably end up losing your money. You should be very wary of making speculative continuation bets at dangerous-looking flops.

Number of callers. In a similar fashion, you don't want to make a speculative bet when there are still a lot of players in the hand. Even with a safe-looking flop, it's more likely that one of your opponents will have something playable and take you on.

Position. As always, position is key. If you're in late position and other players have checked to you, then it's more likely they have weak hands and will fold if you bet. Of course somebody *might* be slowplaying a big hand or hoping to raise you if you bet, but that's always a risk in any hand. If you have position on your opponents, a continuation bet is more likely to succeed, and you have a more advantageous situation for the remainder of the hand even if it doesn't.

Your image. Since a speculative continuation bet is mostly a bluff, it requires your opponents to be scared enough of your hand for them to fold. Of course, since you raised pre-flop and then bet on the flop, you've shown quite a bit of strength. And if, for example, you've recently won some big pots or shown down some strong hands, there's a good chance your opponents will take this show of strength at face value and get out of your way. If on the other hand your opponents perceive you as a weak player or prone to bluffing a lot, they'll be much more inclined to call you, and your coup will fail. Table image is discussed in more detail in **Chapter Eleven: Playing styles**.

Other players' style and image. With a speculative continuation bet, you ideally want your opponents to fold; and if they don't fold you want them to call rather than raise so that you can see another card without paying more money. Therefore you should be more inclined to make continuation bets against:

- tight players, who won't call you with weak hands and might even fold hands stronger than yours (although watch out for flops that are likely to have helped tight players – they don't call with rubbish)
- passive players who are unlikely to raise you even if they have a reasonable hand
- weak (i.e. poor) players who are less likely to outplay you in the remainder of the hand.

What you should try to avoid doing is making speculative bets into players that are loose, aggressive or strong (i.e. good). They might call or raise you just because they know the flop probably won't have helped you too much.

Size of continuation bet.

We've talked so far about *whether* to make a continuation bet, but not *how much* to bet if you decide to do so. There are several factors to bear in mind here:

- Legitimate bets must be big enough to get a worthwhile amount of money in the pot and offer your opponents poor odds for drawing out on you.
- If your hand is unlikely to improve further, you should tend to bet more, so you can win the pot immediately.
- Speculative bets must be big enough to make your opponents fold – since you're bluffing, you want to win the pot right there.
- Both types of bets should be small enough that it's not too costly if you get called or raised by a better hand.
- Most importantly, legitimate and speculative bets should in general be indistinguishable from each other so that opponents can't tell too much about your hand strength from your bet size.

Once again, there are no hard and fast rules, and the amount to bet depends heavily on the nature of the game – and hand – in which you're playing. You will need to observe the betting and your opponents to form an opinion of what size of bet is likely to achieve your objectives.

Notwithstanding the above, it usually turns out that a bet of somewhere between 50% and 100% of the pot size will do the trick. In tighter, more cagey games, you can operate nearer the lower end of this range. In wilder games, you may need to bet the size of the pot, or very near it, to have a chance of scaring anybody off.

It's rarely a good idea to bet much more than the pot, although you may occasionally do so, for example:

■ if you have a very good but vulnerable hand that you want to protect, by making sure that opponents pay a high price if they want to outdraw you; or
■ as a bluff, to ensure that poor or average hands will fold.

Summary: continuation bets

As a general rule, if you were the last pre-flop raiser, you should aim to make a bet on the flop 50%-80% of the time. You should be more inclined not to bet if:

■ the flop hasn't helped you and the situation looks too risky for a speculative continuation bet
■ you have a very strong hand and you think you can win more money by slowplaying it.

Your continuation bets should usually be between 50% – 100% of the pot size, depending on the nature of the game and your opponents.

Taking on the pre-flop raiser

Let's now suppose that you weren't the pre-flop raiser, but you've instead called a raise and seen the flop. How are you going to wrest the initiative back from the pre-flop raiser now? How will you deal with him making a continuation bet on the flop, as he is likely to do?

The first question to consider once you've seen the flop is: are you interested in playing the hand any further, or are you just going to fold to any bet? If you're *not* interested, you should pause to contemplate whether your call of the pre-flop raise was in fact justified. Many weaker players are too loose pre-flop, calling raises with under-strength hands, and too tight post-flop, giving up the fight unless the flop improves their hand dramatically.

If you find yourself constantly folding on the flop after having called an earlier bet, you may need to adjust your strategy – either tighten up pre-flop, or loosen up post-flop, or a combination of the two. If you miss the flop, don't be immediately downhearted – always remember that it's likely that your opponents did too.

We'll assume for the rest of this discussion that you are at least potentially interested in contesting the pot in this case. And we'll focus mainly on how you engage the pre-flop raiser in battle rather than any other players who might be in the hand. Don't forget about those other players however – they might have been quietly calling along, but suddenly spring into action.

The next thing to ask yourself is how well you know your opponent (the pre-flop raiser). Do they make continuation bets habitually, or rarely? Have they shown down any hands where they've made continuation bets? Were they legitimate or speculative? Do they seem like the sort of player who tailors their continuation bet strategy to the circumstances, or do they just bet out on a whim? Unless you have some kind of opinion on this, you're playing very much in the dark.

One of the most important factors governing your approach will be whether or not you have position on the pre-flop raiser, for the obvious reason that this determines whether you act before him or after. We'll consider each case in turn.

When the pre-flop raiser has position on you

The pre-flop raiser has position on you, and so you're first to act. You have three main options:

1. You can check with the intention of calling the pre-flop raiser when they bet (as they probably will), or folding if you get too much action from other players. This sort of play is often described as *check-and-call*.

2. You can check with the intention of raising if the pre-flop raiser bets. This is known as *check-raising*.

3. You can take the initiative and make a bet yourself.

Check-and-call is a fairly weak play in this situation. You're making no attempt to take control of the pot, but instead just going along with the other players. You're also out of position relative to the likely bettor which puts you at a disadvantage for the rest of the hand. There are typically only a couple of situations where this play makes sense:

- You have a drawing hand. You think you're probably not winning at present, but would like to see another card as cheaply as possible because there's a good chance you'll improve. If you make this play however, make sure you really do have the odds to call if there's a bet behind you.
- You want to slowplay a very, very strong hand. Checking and calling allows you to disguise its true strength.

In a multi-way pot, check-and-call often works best if you are seated just to the right of the pre-flop raiser. That way you can see how everybody else at the table responds to their continuation bet before you have to make your decision. In other words, if the pre-flop raiser makes a continuation bet, and nobody raises, you know you'll be last to act.

When you're sitting just to the right of a likely bettor like this, we say that you have good *relative position*. In a multi-way pot, that's exactly where you want to be.

Check-raising is the strongest possible play here. You're deliberately allowing the pre-flop raiser to get his bet in first, and then putting in a raise of your own. This means that you're having to commit a lot of chips to the pot with your first bet, and before you get to find out where you stand.

A potential drawback of this play is that, if there is no bet behind you, your opponents get to see the turn for free and may draw out on you. But this makes the check-raise appear stronger still because you're saying you're happy to risk giving a free card in order to get more money in the pot.

So should you reserve the check-raise exclusively for your very strong hands? Not quite. If you're up against a pre-flop raiser who habitually makes continuation bets, many of them speculative, then:

- their bet on the flop isn't as indicative of as much strength as it would be in another player
- because you believe they're very likely to bet, the risk of giving a free card is small.

So you can check-raise with merely good (rather than great) hands if you're up against a serial continuation bettor. But beware of a couple of potential traps:

■ Since you're able to check-raise with a slightly weaker hand, any other player worth their salt – including the pre-flop raiser – may realise that too, and may not give you as much respect as your check-raise would normally imply.
■ Never forget about the other players in the hand – particularly those between you and the pre-flop raiser who, like you, initially checked it round to the raiser on the flop. They may have been planning a check-raise of their own.

Finally, you might decide occasionally to make a check-raise as a bluff. Because a check-raise is such a strong play, it will often persuade other players to lay their hands down. Just make sure though that:

■ you make this play against tight players, who won't call you with weaker hands – a bluff doesn't want to be called.
■ you tend to make this play against aggressive players – because they're more likely to have made speculative continuation bets rather than legitimate ones. (Note that a player can be both tight *and* aggressive, as we'll discuss later on.)
■ you raise enough to scare other players off.

A good time to check-raise as a bluff is when you are due to act immediately before the pre-flop raiser (i.e. you have good *relative position*). You can check to him, he makes a continuation bet, and then you can see what everyone else does before you get to act again. If other players call the continuation bet, a bluff is less likely to succeed because there are several players it would have to knock out. But if all fold except for you then you're playing one-on-one against the pre-flop raiser. If you suspect that their hand might not be that strong, your bluff might well succeed.

Betting out (i.e. betting) lies in the middle ground between check-and-call and check-raising you're effectively saying "I know you claimed to be stronger pre-flop, but the flop hit me – this is my pot!". Betting out is a cheaper and safer way of trying to win the pot than a check-raise. You're not risking giving a free card, and you're not putting so much money in with your first bet. If you get called or raised, you can still get away from the hand reasonably cheaply if you need to.

This however is one of the problems of betting out. Other players may reason: if your hand were that strong, wouldn't you have check-raised? They may view your bet as speculative and try to take the pot away from you by raising. To prevent this happening too much, you must sometimes bet out with very strong hands, hands that would normally justify a check-raise. When other players see you make this sort of play, they'll realise that you're not predictable and that they can't read too much into your betting patterns.

Betting out with a very strong hand has further advantages. If you get raised, you can re-raise – and then your opponents have committed much more money to the pot by the time they find out quite how strong you are. In this way, betting out is likely to extract more money from your opponents when they're strong, even though a check-raise might win you a speculative continuation bet from a weaker opponent.

When you have position on the pre-flop raiser

When you have position on the pre-flop raiser, you have the advantage of being able to see what he does before you act.

If the pre-flop raiser checks then your decision is usually not too tricky. Much of the time you should simply take a view on whether you're likely to be in the lead or not, and bet if so. Otherwise you check. You should however beware of the following:

■ The players who acted *before* the pre-flop raiser may well have been expecting him to make a continuation bet (because he usually will). Therefore one of them may actually be quite strong and planning to check-raise, as we saw in the previous section.
■ If a habitual continuation bettor checks rather than betting then you should at least pause to see if you smell a rat. If the indications are unfavourable for the pre-flop raiser (e.g. lots of callers, poor position, dangerous flop, etc.) then his check might be a legitimate and sensible move. On the other hand, if it's the kind of situation where a continuation bet looks to be in order for him, then you should consider whether he actually hit a very good hand on the flop and has decided to slowplay it. He might be trying to *trap* you.

If the pre-flop raiser bets then you may have a tougher decision to make. It all comes down to how you read him as a player and how you estimate the strength of his hand. If you decide to contest the hand, then you have two choices: to call or to raise.

If you're fairly confident that you're in the lead, then you should normally go ahead and raise. You might be tempted merely to call and hope that the pre-flop raiser bets again on the turn (the next round). But you probably won't get much more money this way unless he has a legitimate hand, in which case he's likely to call your raise anyway. And if he doesn't have much of a hand, you'd rather raise and take the pot now, risk free, rather than give him a cheap opportunity to draw out on you.

If you think you're *probably* in the lead but really aren't sure, then this too is a situation where you should normally favour a raise. By raising, you're putting pressure on your opponent who also happens to be out of position against you. If he calls you – or even re-raises – you know he's got a legitimate hand and you're in for a fight. You may not be that happy about the fact he's hanging in there, but at least he has now revealed his true strength.

As always don't forget about the other players in the hand. Look out for trappers in early position who might be check-raising, and spare a thought for any players still to act after you. If you're worried about too much action from other players then you may be better off folding sooner rather than later.

If you decide to call then please at least make sure you do so with a purpose – not just because you can't decide what else to do. Situations that might merit a call include:

■ You have a drawing hand, would like to see the turn, and believe that you have the odds to make a call profitable.
■ You think you're probably ahead of the pre-flop raiser but you're scared of some of the other players still in the hand. You'll simply call this time, and then bet or raise on the turn if none of them show any particular strength.
■ You have an extremely strong hand and would like to disguise it by calling rather than raising, i.e. slowplay it. You hope that you might draw in other callers by doing so because they'll have odds that appear good (but in fact aren't good enough given the strength of your hand).

Drawing hands

Before we leave our discussion of flop play, we'd like to say a few words on drawing hands. Just to remind you, we defined a drawing hand as a hand that:

- isn't yet complete, in that it's nothing much at the moment
- has the potential to make a very good hand if the subsequent board cards are favourable.

The opposite of a drawing hand is a *made hand*, a hand that doesn't need to improve to be a good hand.

Part-made drawing hands

Drawing hands come in many shapes and sizes. Thus far we've concentrated mostly on straights and flushes, but this is largely because these provide good, clear-cut examples. When you hold a straight or flush draw, you usually don't have much else besides – maybe a pair if you're lucky. And once you make a straight or flush you usually have the best hand, as long as you've been following our advice about being wary of non-nut draws of course.

Therefore when you're drawing to a straight or a flush, you often reckon to lose the hand if you don't make it, and to win the hand if you do. This fits nice and neatly with our general rule: bet if you're in the lead, and call if you're not as long as you have the odds to do so. You should be able to tell, quite accurately, where you stand.

But there are other situations where you're hoping your hand will improve that *aren't* quite so clear-cut. For example, middle pair with ace kicker can be considered a drawing hand, in that you have five outs to improve to two pair or three of a kind. But with middle pair and ace kicker, in contrast to straight and flush draws, it's much more likely that:

- you'll win the hand without improving – because you already have *something* rather than nothing
- you'll improve your hand and still lose – because two pair and three of a kind aren't as strong as straights and flushes.

So is middle pair and ace kicker a drawing hand or not? There's no definitive answer to that, and it would be pointless trying to produce one. It's partly a made hand and partly a drawing hand, and the way you play it will have something in common with both. We call these sort of hands *part-made* drawing hands.

With a part-made hand you can call more readily than you otherwise would. To quantify this: you can add your estimate of the probability that you're already winning to the probability of improving by hitting an out, to get your *total* probability of winning. As long as the implied odds are greater than the odds against this happening, you can call.

Drawing profitably

Some players lose a lot of money on their drawing hands, mostly because they call big bets with them without the proper odds to do so, although there are other pitfalls besides this one. We're going to make a few comments that should help keep you out of this kind of trouble. Here's what you should be looking for with your drawing hands.

Nut draws. When you have a drawing hand, you want to be fairly sure that you'll win the hand if you hit your draw. We're not saying that you should *never* draw to hands that don't make the nuts, but that you should do so more reluctantly and with care. If you have a small suited connector such as 6♣ 7♣, it may be ill advised to chase a flop of:

which gives you the bottom end of the straight draw. Another player may hold, e.g., J-Q, which would negate four of your outs. Similarly if the flop comes:

then you should exercise caution with your seven-high flush draw. Another player may hold two clubs, in which case it's likely that their flush will beat yours if you make it.

In general, you should consider very carefully whether each of your outs really is an out for you. If you're drawing at a straight but there are two of a suit on the board, then you should bear in mind that some of the cards that make your straight might make your opponents a flush. If there are three of a suit on the board then it's even more likely that you'll be beaten if another card of that suit comes, and you may be beaten already.

In similar fashion, you need to watch out if the board pairs when you're drawing at a straight or a flush – somebody may have two pair or three of a kind and be drawing at a full house. In these situations you need to downgrade your number of outs accordingly, and only count those cards that you are fairly sure will give you the winning hand.

Here's a general rule for evaluating these situations more precisely. If you're drawing to a hand that has a significant risk of not being a winning hand, you should multiply your number of outs by the chances of your hand being a winner if you hit one of those outs.

For example, suppose that you're on an outside straight draw but estimate that there's 25% chance somebody has (or will have) a flush or full house if you make it, hence beating you. You multiply your eight outs by 75% (the chance of winning if you do make your straight) to give you six outs. You can then work out whether or not a call is profitable in the usual way, but based on six outs rather than eight.

Many opponents. Drawing hands play best against many opponents because:

- the pot odds and implied odds are more favourable
- good drawing hands don't *mind* lots of opponents – if a (good) drawing hand hits, it'll reckon to be a winner. It's doubly important to be drawing to the nuts, or close to it, against many opponents.

Passive opponents, i.e. opponents who tend to check or call more than they bet or raise. Drawing hands can often withstand a single bet, but are usually unplayable against a bet and a raise. It's fine if one person bets and everybody else calls, but if you're trapped between a bettor and a raiser then you're going to have to throw the hand away. So don't play drawing hands if there are aggressive opponents still to act after you who may raise. Drawing hands are a safer bet if the players still to act are passive.

Loose opponents. Loose opponents (i.e. those who call bets too readily) will give you better implied odds because they're more likely to call; both while you're still drawing and if you hit your hand. Playing drawing hands against tight opponents (i.e. those who play only with good hands) is a much less appealing prospect.

Position. Being in late position allows you to lose less money on your losing hands and extract more money on your winning hands. This is a huge asset when you're drawing because you don't really know whether or not you will have a winning or losing hand. Before you make your draw, you want to stay out of trouble and keep the betting reasonably cheap; and after you make it, you want to get paid off. Being able to see what everyone else does before you act will help you achieve these goals.

Relative position. You should also look out for relative position. If you're sitting to the immediate right of the pre-flop raiser then, if he opens the betting in a round, you're going to be the last to act. If anybody raises, or there are insufficient callers to give you the right odds, you can happily fold.

Big stacks. Drawing hands usually need good pot odds, and often rely on implied odds – i.e. odds based on your opponents' future contributions to the pot – to make them profitable. You can't have these odds if either you or your opponents are short stacked. When your draw hits, you ideally want to be in a position whether you can get a lot of money from it.

Strong draws. Sometimes a draw can be so strong that you don't need to play it like a drawing hand – you can play it like a made hand. Suppose for example the flop is

and you suspect your opponent holds a big pair in his hand. You might hold something like:

- 8♦ 9♦, giving you a straight and flush draw with 15 outs, or
- A♦ 7♦, giving you top pair and the nut flush draw – that's 14 outs to a flush, trips or two pair.

With either of these holdings, you're better than 50% to win the hand if you can play all the way to the showdown. In other words, you're favourite at this point even though you're drawing. If you can get all-in with your opponent on the flop, you should try to do so, because you have the edge. By betting and raising, you may also get him to lay his hand down, giving you a risk-free win.

If you don't manage to get all-in or win the pot on the flop then you may need to slow down on the turn if you don't hit your draw. If that happens, your 14 or 15 outs will make you roughly a 2-to-1 underdog with one card to come. You don't want to put more money in the pot voluntarily as underdog, unless you think you can get your opponent to lay his hand down. You would however have the pot odds to call a pot-sized bet (or smaller) from your opponent, even without factoring in any implied odds.

We'll finish this chapter with a brief summary of how to play the flop.

Summary: flop play

When the flop is dealt you should:

- work out whether the flop helped you, and how much
- consider the texture of the flop and whether it is likely to have helped your opponents
- mentally review the pre-flop betting.

Then form a strategy.

- If you raised pre-flop you should decide whether or not a continuation bet is in order.
- If somebody else raised pre-flop you should decide whether and how you're going to take them on – without forgetting about the other players in the hand. ... continued on next page

- Pots that were unraised pre-flop are likely to be small and unpredictable.
- If you decide to play a drawing hand, make sure the circumstances are genuinely favourable enough for it to be justified.

Quiz: flop play

In all the following questions the blinds are £1 / £2 and there are ten players seated at the table. Unless otherwise stated, all players involved have plenty of money left in front of them. Your job is to say how you'd play each of the following flops.

Question 1. You raised to £6 pre-flop from late position with K♠ K♦ and got two callers – the small blind and a player in mid position. There is £20 in the pot. The flop comes 2♥ 10♣ 9♥ and both players check to you. Do you (a) check (b) bet £10 (c) bet £20?

Question 2. As above, but this time the flop comes A♥ 10♣ 9♥. Do you (a) check (b) bet £10 (c) bet £20?

Question 3. You raised to £10 pre-flop from the big blind with 9♦ 9♣ and got two callers in late position. There is £31 in the pot. The flop comes 4♦ 8♠ J♥. Do you (a) check (b) bet £15 (c) bet £30?

Question 4. Following on from question 3, you decide to bet £30 on the flop. The next player to act raises to £100 and the third player folds. It's now £70 to you and there's £161 in the pot. Do you (a) fold (b) call £70 (c) go all-in for your last £200?

Question 5. You are dealt A♦ K♦ in the small blind. You raise to £8 pre-flop and get three callers, taking the pot to £34. The flop comes J♠ 9♥ 7♠. Do you (a) check (b) bet £15 (c) bet £30?

Question 6. You are in a wild game which has featured lots of loose play and big pots. You are dealt 10♦ J♦ in the small blind. There's a raise to £8 from early position and three callers. You call and the big blind folds making the pot £42. The flop comes K♠ Q♥ 9♠, giving you a straight. You are first to act; do you (a) check with the intention of calling any bet behind you (b) check with the intention of raising any bet behind you (c) bet £20 (d) bet £40?

Question 7. You are dealt 4♥ 4♦ on the button. There is a raise to £6 from mid position and another caller. You call, and everyone else folds. The flop comes A♥ K♣ 4♠, giving you a set. The first player to act bets £15 and the second player calls, taking the pot to £51. Do you (a) fold (b) call (c) raise to £30 (d) raise to £75?

Answers to quiz

Answer 1. This is a pretty good flop for you since there are three under-cards to your pair, no high cards, and no possible straights or flushes on the board as yet. You're very likely to be winning at this point. But you can't let your opponents hang around cheaply in case they have a pair or a nice draw and overtake you on the turn. You have to put in a healthy-sized bet to chase them away, or to make them pay if they want a shot at beating you. You go for option (c) and bet £20.

Answer 2. Your heart sank when you saw the ace on the flop, and you probably wished you'd raised a bit more pre-flop to knock another player out. Your pair of kings might be winning, or it might not. How can you tell whether one of your opponents has an ace? Well, you can't. All you can do is guess and, depending on your opponents, you might guess it's about 50-50.

But look at the flop – it's quite dangerous because of the possible straight and flush draws that are on. This means that anyone in the lead (perhaps you) should be more inclined to bet than check, in order to stop other players seeing the turn cheaply. But your opponents can reason the same thing. If they had an ace and reckoned they were winning, surely they would have bet? Ah – but maybe not if they expected a continuation bet from you and were planning a check-raise.

This line of reasoning could go on all day. On balance, you decide that it's more likely than not that nobody has an ace, and that you'll probably be ceding the pot if you simply check. You resolve to put in a bet to try to win the pot right now. Betting £20 would be quite expensive if you were to be check-raised, so a bet of around half the pot seems in order. This makes it cheaper for any drawing hands to stay in, but you're still only giving them a fairly meagre 3-to-1. You go for option (b) and bet £10. If you get re-raised, you're going to fold, and if you get called you're going to be very careful on the turn.

Note however that, if you had reason to believe that an opponent with an ace would come out betting rather than check, you would be more inclined to make a larger bet yourself if it was checked to you.

What a tough decision that was! Playing a big pair with an overcard on the board is always tricky.

Answer 3. The first thing you remark is that the flop was quite good for you. The overcard (jack) is a potential problem, but it would have been worse had it been a queen, king or ace (because players are more likely to call with higher cards). It's a fairly safe flop.

Both of your opponents called the big blind initially and then called your raise, so they are likely to have some kind of a hand but not a great one. If you are losing, it will probably be to one of the following hands: 10-10, J-J, Q-Q, J-10, J-Q, J-K, J-A, 4-4, 8-8, your reasoning being as follows:

■ It's unlikely that an opponent would flat-call twice with K-K or A-A (they would have raised) so you can probably rule those hands out. In fact, depending on your opponents, even 10-10 and Q-Q may strike you as unlikely.
■ Your opponents definitely shouldn't be in the hand with a holding that would have made them two pair. Similarly jack plus a kicker nine or lower.

Moreover, you shouldn't worry too much at this stage about someone having a set, since it's rather unlikely.

Your biggest concern therefore is jack plus other high card. Yes, it's possible that's what one of your opponents is holding, but you can't let fear of that stop you from betting – on balance you're still likely to be winning. You don't really want a caller because you won't know where you stand and you'll be playing the remainder of the hand out of position. Therefore you must bet a good-sized amount. You go for option (c) and bet £30.

Answer 4. Your opponent is saying that he has you beaten. Do you believe him? If he is particularly loose or aggressive, you might not. Similarly, if you are particularly loose or aggressive, or prone to making speculative continuation bets, he might be trying to take the pot away from you with a bluff or with a hand you can beat. But he raised you whilst another player was still active in the hand, which is more likely to suggest real strength. In the absence of any reason to suspect that your opponent is weak, you should go for option (a) and fold.

Note that calling is the worst of the three options here. Your hand is very unlikely to improve, and on the turn your opponent can check and take a free card if he's losing, or bet again and give you another tough decision. If you take the view that he's trying it on with a weak hand, you should go all-in now.

Answer 5. This isn't looking good. You're out of position against three opponents with nothing but a couple of overcards to the flop. The best you can hope for is that an ace or king comes on the turn and makes you a pair, but even then you need to be worried about flushes, straights and perhaps two pair.

So if you bet, you're betting as a bluff and you want to win the pot immediately. Is that likely to happen? Probably not, since anybody who got a piece of that flop is going to hang around against a pre-flop raiser, who is most unlikely to have hit it.

With fewer opponents and better position, you might have talked yourself into having a stab at this one. But, as it is, you prudently decide to go for option (a) and check.

Answer 6. This is a lovely spot to be in – you have the nuts and there's a table full of loose players who are likely to pay you off. You need to be careful, though, in that your straight is potentially vulnerable: a ten or jack on the board could make a higher straight; a spade could make a flush; and if the board pairs, it's not impossible you'll be facing a full house. Ideally you want to reduce the field somewhat before the turn comes, and make sure that any players who do decide to hang around pay for the privilege.

There are a couple of problems with betting out however. Firstly the next player to act is likely to have a decent hand and call your bet. If that happens, the other players may have odds to call along too, and you may not shake enough players off. Secondly it reveals the strength of your hand before there's much money in the pot.

Note further that you have excellent relative position against the pre-flop raiser who's sitting to your left. If you check, it's very likely that he will bet and hopefully get a few callers or even a raise. Even if the pre-flop raiser checks, surely one of the other players will bet – it's a loose game, remember.

Now when the betting comes round to you, there should be quite a bit of money in the middle. You can then stick in a big raise and you'll either win there and then, or get even more money into a pot in which you almost surely are favourite. The best option is therefore (b), to check-raise.

In some circumstances, you might decide to check and then flat-call a bet behind you (in other words, to slowplay your hand), planning perhaps check-raise on the turn. This isn't necessarily a bad play, but it's a risky one. If the turn is scary, you may be faced with a difficult decision.

Answer 7. Your set of fours is almost certainly in the lead here. Yes, one of the other two players might have a set of aces or kings, but it's rather unlikely. Even if that is what's happened, you're just going to have to pay them off – flopped sets can't be folded unless the circumstances are exceptional.

Apart from folding, making a minimum raise to £30 is the worst of the options. You'd be revealing the strength of your hand without making your opponents pay very much to stay with you. The choice is therefore between calling and making a near pot-sized raise to £75.

Unlike the previous question, your hand isn't particularly vulnerable this time. You have only two opponents, and there's no flush draw on the board and no open-ended straight draw. It's likely that your opponents hold a pair, or maybe two pair (probably ace-king if so) at best. As a result, slowplaying the hand by calling is something you might consider, to disguise your true strength.

In this particular case, which option you choose is up to you. If you don't mind taking the risk of being outdrawn, and think that one of your opponents will bet again on the turn, then option (b), calling, is an acceptable answer. If you want to play more conservatively, or you have reason to think that your opponents might readily call a raise anyway, then you can go for option (d) and raise.

This might strike you as slightly unsatisfactory, and you might want to know which of the answers is the 'right' answer. But there isn't always an objectively right answer in poker, or at least not one you can know before the hand is over. Some decisions will be entirely marginal; others may rely on a fuller knowledge of the scenario than is provided in these simplified examples. If you can develop a good feel for the game, you will find that you increasingly make decisions that turn out to be correct.

Chapter Eight:
Playing the turn

ARE YOU **SURE** THIS IS HOW YOU PLAY THE TURN ?

The turn is the name given to the fourth community card to be dealt, and it is dealt alone. Added to your two hole cards and the three flop cards, the turn is therefore the sixth card in your hand.

In general, play on the turn is less complicated than play on the flop. The flop is where you make most of your important decisions and work out how you want to play the hand. On the flop, three of the community cards are revealed at once. On the turn however, with only one more card having been revealed, there isn't as much scope for the shape of the hand to change. You've probably already formed a good idea of how the hand is likely to pan out, and the turn card often won't affect that.

The money gets bigger

However, despite play on the turn being more straightforward, it's every bit as important as flop play, if not more so. That's because the pot usually has grown in size by then. In fact, given that players tend to size their bets in terms of the pot size, each round of betting can see a *considerable* growth in pot size.

Suppose for example that there's £10 in the pot when the flop comes, and you make a pot-sized bet on each of the flop, turn and river. On each occasion you're called by one opponent. The pot will have £30 in it when the turn is dealt, £90 when the river is dealt, and £270 in it by showdown. If instead you get two callers each time rather than one, the respective figures are £40, £160 and £640! So don't underestimate the importance of playing the later rounds correctly. They are where you can win – or lose – most of your money.

The general approach

Your general approach to playing the turn should be very similar to the flop. You should immediately consider:

- whether the turn card helped you, and how much. As always, make sure you read your hand properly. If the board pairs, did it help you? If you were on a straight or flush draw, did you hit it? If you weren't on a straight or flush draw, do you have one now? So called *backdoor* straights and flushes (those made with the help of both the turn and river cards) are good hands because they are well-concealed. It's harder for your opponents to put you on such a hand, i.e. they won't suspect you of having it.
- whether the turn card is likely to have helped your opponents. Might it have matched one of their hole cards? Could they have made a flush or straight? Could they have picked up a backdoor flush draw or straight draw? Make sure you consider all this given the pattern of their betting.
- the outcome of both the pre-flop and flop betting rounds. Think about who currently has the initiative and what sort of hands they might be betting with. Do you plan on stealing the initiative from them or are you going to give the hand up if they bet again?

Most of the ideas we introduced relating to flop play are relevant in much the same way on the turn, and we won't duplicate them here. There are however a few points worth making relating to continuation bets.

Delayed continuation bets

You make a *delayed continuation* bet when you open the betting on the turn and:

- you were the pre-flop raiser
- everybody (including you) checked on the flop.

In fact, it will usually be a good idea to make a delayed continuation bet whenever these two criteria have been satisfied. By the time the betting gets round to you on the turn, everyone will have declined an opportunity to bet post-flop. There is therefore a good chance that your bet will win the pot right there, even if you're not crazy about your own hand. The initiative you grabbed with your pre-flop raise should see you through.

Repeat continuation bets

If you made a speculative continuation bet on the flop that was called, and the turn didn't help you, you may be faced with a tricky decision.

On the one hand you (presumably) don't have much of a hand yourself, and your opponent or opponents called a bet on the flop indicating some strength of their own. This would tend to suggest that you should check.

On the other hand, your opponent's call on the flop might have been made on the basis that they suspected your continuation bet to be speculative, i.e. not necessarily indicative of much strength. They might not have very much strength of their own in that case – if they did, why wouldn't they raise? This line of reasoning suggests that you should at least consider betting again.

Making a second, speculative continuation bet on the turn in this situation is sometimes called *firing the second barrel*, the first barrel having been fired on the flop. Finding the right occasions to make such a bet requires good judgment, since you're potentially risking a lot of chips on not much of a hand. As a general rule, you will be better off checking in this position more often than not. Then, when you do actually come out betting on the turn, your opponents will be likely to credit it with representing real strength.

But sometimes you *must* bet again on the turn with nothing, especially if you're playing against decent opponents. If other players know that you will check the turn when you don't have a hand then it's too easy for them to call your bet on the flop and see what happens on the turn. If you check the turn, they know they can probably take the pot down with a bet of their own. For a similar reason, you should also occasionally check-raise on the turn with a strong hand. When players see this, they'll know they can't necessarily interpret your check on the turn as a sign of weakness, and they'll think twice before playing back at you.

Making life difficult for your opponents on the turn in this way actually increases the chances of your continuation bets on the flop being successful. What's the point in your opponents calling you on the flop if they know they're likely to face a tough decision on the turn?

Chapter Nine:
Playing the river

Why the river is different

The river is the name given to the fifth and last community card to be dealt, and, like the turn card, it is dealt alone. Added to two hole cards, three flop cards and the turn card, the river is the seventh card in your hand.

You might be tempted to think that play on the river is a simple extension of play on the previous rounds; after all, a community card is dealt, and there's a round of betting. It seems superficially very similar to what happens on the turn, for example. However, play on the river is really quite different, as we'll see.

These differences stem from the fact that the river is the last card to be dealt. This means that one of the sources of uncertainty in the hand – uncertainty about cards still to come – has been removed. The only uncertainty you have to worry about now is what cards your opponents hold. This does simplify matters somewhat, although not perhaps in ways that are immediately or intuitively obvious.

Recall the fundamental betting guideline that has come up time and time again in the preceding chapters: *if you think you're in the lead, you should bet, and you should bet enough so that opponents don't have the odds to call you.* Recall also that one of the motivations for betting when you're in the lead is that you don't want to give opponents with weaker hands the opportunity to see the next card for free, in case they overtake you. This clearly can't apply on the river because there are no more cards to come. So on the river there isn't the same pressure to bet in order to avoid giving a free card. Instead, the river is all about getting as much value as possible from the cards you hold.

We'll start from first principles then, and you should forget about betting just because you're in the lead. It's true that if you think you're in the lead on the river, you very often will bet – but certainly not always. We're going to come up with a new set of guidelines for river play.

Heads-up

To illustrate our point, we'll look at a simple scenario. You're playing in a hand with just one other player remaining and all five community cards (including the river) have been dealt. First we'll *assume* that your hand is better than your opponent's, although neither you nor your opponent actually knows that of course. What would you ideally like to happen during the final betting round?

That should be a fairly simple question to answer. Since you're winning, you want as much money in the pot as possible. In an ideal world, you and your opponent would both go all-in. Then you'd show down your cards, and you'd win a big pot.

In practice though, what do you think would happen if you went all-in? The chances are that your opponent, in the face of a big bet like that, would probably fold. You would win the money that was already in the pot before the river, but nothing extra.

Observe too that, had you and your opponent both checked, you would have won exactly the same amount (because your hand is better than your opponent's, so you still win the pot). It sounds obvious, but the only way you can win extra money on the river (when you have a better hand) is when your opponent puts money in the pot during the final betting round.

Are there any *bad* outcomes for you on the river if you're winning? Yes indeed. What you really don't want to do, is to fold. That would be disastrous for you since not only would you fail to win extra money on the river, you'd also lose the money that was already in the pot.

159

Now let's assume instead that your hand is worse than your opponent's, rather than better. What would you like to happen in this case? Well, if you both show down your cards, you'll lose the pot. This means that you'd ideally like your opponent to fold, which may of course be tricky to achieve since they have a better hand than you. If you can't somehow get your opponent to fold, then at the very least you want to minimise the amount of money you put in the pot. Since you're not going to win it, you don't want to bet and you'd rather fold to any bet by your opponent.

Let's just sum this up. If you're *winning* on the river:

■ you want your opponent to put as much money in the pot as possible
■ you want to avoid folding at all costs.

If you're *losing* on the river:

■ you ideally want your opponent to fold
■ if you can't get him to fold, you should at least avoid putting money into the pot yourself.

This sounds quite straightforward, but it's amazing how the consequences of this line of reasoning elude many weaker players. Suppose for example that you make a bet on the river. For that bet to show a profit, one of two things must happen:

1. Your opponent must call your bet with a weaker hand, or
2. Your opponent must fold to your bet with a stronger hand. (If your opponent folds with a hand that's weaker than yours, you haven't made *extra* money because you'd win in a showdown anyway.)

If neither of these things happens, then your bet hasn't made any extra money. But the problem is that the ideal amount to bet in order to achieve (1) is very rarely the same ideal amount to bet in order to achieve (2). In order to make your opponent fold a better hand than yours, you will normally have to make a fairly large bet – if you bet too small, it's too cheap for your opponent to call. And in order to make a weaker hand call, you will often have to make a somewhat smaller bet – otherwise it's too expensive for him.

So here's the first rule of betting on the river: *make a clear decision on what you're trying to achieve – do you want to make a weaker hand call, or a stronger hand fold?*

In order to make such a decision, you'll first have to consider the relative strength of your hand and your opponent's, and who you believe to be in the lead.

For the time being, to keep things simple, we'll continue to consider the case where you're facing only one opponent rather than several. What you decide to do will depend on whether:

- you believe you're losing
- you believe you're winning
- you don't know whether you're winning or losing!

So read on for our advice on what to do in each of these situations.

If you believe you're losing

If you find yourself playing the river, and fairly sure your opponent is beating you, then we hope that one of the following has happened:

- You had a drawing hand, perhaps hoping to hit a straight or flush, but missed your draw.
- Your opponent had a drawing hand, and he seems likely to have hit it in one of the later rounds.
- You never had much of a hand at all, but there was little or no betting so you were able to stay in till the end.

If none of the above is true, then you probably should have thrown your hand in much sooner.

Anyway, you're here now. If you're correct in your belief that you're losing, your only realistic chance of winning the hand is to make your opponent fold, and to do that, you have to bet (or raise if your opponent was first to act, and bet). When you bet or raise with what you believe to be the worst hand, you are of course bluffing. You need to consider then whether a bluff is likely to work in this situation, and hence whether it's likely to be worthwhile.

To bluff or not to bluff?

Bluffing is discussed in more detail in Chapter Ten, but there are a few differences between bluffing on the river and bluffing during earlier rounds.

For now we'll just make a few simple observations that are relevant to our discussion of river play.

■ A bluff on the river is often more likely to work than a bluff made earlier on in the hand. This is because one of your opponent's potential reasons for calling a bet, namely that his hand might improve on later rounds, obviously can't apply on the river.

■ In earlier betting rounds, a bluff is usually more likely to work if your opponent is out of position and has checked to you. That's because checking on earlier rounds is often a sign of weakness – stronger hands are reluctant to check because they don't want to give a free card. On the river however, there are no free cards, and a check is thus not quite as likely to indicate weakness. Therefore you should beware of your opponent trying to trap you – they may be check-raising with a strong hand, or simply planning to check-and-call with a moderate hand. See the following sections for a discussion of these plays.

■ If you think there is some possibility that you're winning, albeit slim, you should be less inclined to bluff. Good players tend to bluff with very poor hands – because a bluff is the only way a certain losing hand can become a winner – but try to show down not-quite-so-poor hands cheaply, *in case* they win.

Making a crying call

If you decide that a bluff isn't in order for any reason, then you're effectively ceding the pot. You will usually check, and fold if your opponent bets. Sometimes however, you will need to make a *crying call* if the pot odds allow it, i.e. a call with what you believe is probably the worst hand.

Suppose for example that your opponent made bets on the flop and the turn, and you suspect that he has at least top pair, and maybe even a stronger hand. You were on the flush draw and had the odds to call his bet on each occasion, but missed your draw. However, you did pick up a pair on the river. Your opponent makes a small bet, of around a third the size of the pot, giving you odds of 4-to-1. With those odds, you can make the call if you reckon you're more than 20% likely to win the pot.

So if you think there's a good chance your opponent is bluffing, or simply betting with a hand worse than yours, then that call is profitable. Even though you expect that you're beaten, your call will show a profit if you can show down the winning hand more than one time in five.

Remember that last point because it's important. *You don't have to believe you're winning to make a call on the river profitable.* You just have to believe that your chances of winning are greater than the pot odds being offered.

> ## Summary: if you believe you're losing
>
> - If you think a bluff will be a profitable move, go ahead and bluff
> - If not, then make a crying call if you have the odds, and check / fold otherwise.

If you believe you're winning

If you find yourself playing the river and fairly sure you're beating your opponent, then you have the rather pleasant dilemma of how to extract as much money from him as possible. If the pot is of a reasonable size, we would urge you to give this dilemma your careful consideration. Bet sizes get bigger as the rounds progress and much of your potential profit can be earned here.

How you play on the river when you're winning will depend very much on whether you act first or second – this is just one further example of the importance of position. We'll look at each case in turn.

If your opponent acts first

In this situation, given that you believe you're winning, you will normally:

- bet if your opponent checks
- raise if your opponent bets.

Before you do so however, you should pause and contemplate what you will do if your opponent raises you back.

Do you fear a raise?

In some situations, you would be quite comfortable with a raise, for example:

- Your hand is so strong that you're happy to call a raise, or perhaps even put in a further raise of your own.
- Your opponent's raise is a very strong indication that your hand is beaten, so you have an easy fold. (This case shouldn't occur very much in hands where you're fairly sure you're winning, however! It's more likely to happen when you're bluffing with a weak hand.)

However, at other times you might have a much harder decision if your opponent raises you, and you might feel it's a marginal decision whether to call or fold.

The problem with marginal situations like that is that it's easy to make the wrong decision (if it weren't, then they wouldn't be marginal). And in general, you want to avoid putting yourself in situations where you might make the wrong decision, especially if there's a lot of money at stake.

All things considered then, if you think that a re-raise will put you in a difficult position, you may be best advised not to give your opponent another opportunity to bet at all. Instead of raising, you may elect to check (if your opponent checked) or call (if they bet).

Note that we're not saying that the possibility of a re-raise should in itself stop you from betting. Whenever you bet, it's always possible that you'll be facing a re-raise a few moments later. The question is really whether that re-raise will give you a difficult decision, and potentially force you into an expensive mistake.

How much to bet?

If you decide that you're comfortable with a possible raise from your opponent then a bet is clearly in order (or a raise if your opponent bet rather than checking). The question is: how much?

To answer that question, you need to consider the following points:

- What do you think your opponent might have? How strong is he?
- What do you think your opponent thinks *you* have? How strong does he reckon you are?
- Is there any chance your opponent will think you're bluffing?

The first of these is quite straightforward. If your opponent has a strong hand then he will in general call a bigger bet than if he is weak. You need to form an opinion on how strong his hand is. To do this, you should mentally review the betting for the entire hand and try to put the opponent on a range of possible holdings. Don't forget to factor in what you know about him specifically as an opponent, and his playing style, etc.

But your opponent won't consider *only* their own hand when deciding whether or not to call – they'll also consider your hand. If they believe you to be weak for some reason then they'll call a bigger bet than they would otherwise. So ask yourself the following question: from your opponent's perspective, what does it look like *you* might be holding? The best possible scenario of course is if your opponent perceives your bet as a bluff. If he thinks you're bluffing then he might call a sizeable bet with a moderate hand, which is exactly what you want.

Then you can just put these factors together to come up with an answer: given what you think your opponent has, and what he might think you have, how big a bet is he likely to call? Here are some examples of how you might reason it out:

Scenario 1. You've been betting most of the hand, and your opponent has just been calling. You think he's on a draw of some kind but it looks like he missed his draw on the river. Therefore he probably hasn't got much of a hand, maybe nothing at all. You're not going to make much money out of him, and he's certainly not going to call a big bet, especially since you've been showing strength by betting. With any luck he might have hit a pair and call a small bet.

Outcome: you decide to bet one-quarter of the pot, giving your opponent odds of 4-to-1 on his call. Even with a weak hand, there's a reasonable chance he won't be able to resist these odds.

Scenario 2. Your opponent raised pre-flop, made a continuation bet on the flop and bet again on the turn – you called on each occasion, having hit a pair on the flop. The river gave you two pair however, and your opponent checked to you. You suspect that your opponent either has top pair with a good kicker or possibly a big pair in his hand, giving him an overpair. Your opponent must certainly have some strength and is likely to call a reasonable bet. However, he's bound to be wondering why you've been calling along all hand, and whether you're trapping with a very strong hand, or maybe on some kind of

165

draw. On balance, you decide that he's likely to call a reasonably sized bet, but fold to a very big bet.

Outcome: you bet three-quarters of the pot, and hope that your opponent is strong enough to call.

Scenario 3. You raised pre-flop with A-K suited and made a continuation bet on the flop when you hit a four-flush. Your opponent called on both occasions, and you both checked the turn, which didn't help you. The river completed your flush, giving you the nuts, but your opponent came out betting. You suspect that he may have made a flush too – a smaller one than yours of course – or maybe a straight. On the other hand, he may be bluffing with nothing on the basis that you checked the turn and may not have very much yourself. In any case, you think it's most likely that his hand is *either* very weak *or* very strong (but not as strong as yours). If he's weak, he won't call any raise; so if he's going to call any raise at all, he'll probably call a big one.

Outcome: you make a pot-sized raise, hoping your opponent made a straight or flush.

If you act first

Now we'll consider the case where you're heads-up on the river, first to act, and fairly sure you're winning. Here you have a choice between two different strategies:

- You can come out betting.
- You can check and hope that your opponent bets, so you can then call or raise.

Obviously, since you believe you're winning, you want to pick the option that gets as much of your opponent's money in the pot as possible.

Will your opponent bluff?

The first thing to consider is whether your opponent is likely to try a bluff if you check. The following are likely indications for your opponent to try a bluff:

- His hand is weak and has no chance of winning a showdown (otherwise why bluff?).

- Your opponent believes that your hand is not so strong that you're bound to call a bet (i.e. his bluff might work).
- He believes that you're a tight enough player to fold to a bet in this situation.
- He is a player who has shown himself capable of bluffing.

If you believe these conditions apply then you are *much* better off checking and allowing your opponent to bluff. Note that he won't call a bet if his hand is weak, so there's no advantage to you betting – he'll just fold. Your best chance to get his money in the pot is to allow him to put it in first. The stronger you think your opponent is however, the less chance he'll bluff and the more inclined therefore you should be to bet.

The above assumes that the best way to induce a bluff from your opponent is to check, and this is normally true. One tactic that players sometimes employ however is to encourage a bluff by making a small bet, e.g. one quarter of the pot size or less, rather than checking. A *small* bet might look to some other players like a weak bet, or a bluff of its own.

Even if this small bet doesn't produce a bluff from your opponent, it can sometimes have other beneficial side effects, by getting more money in the pot if your opponent decides to call or raise for value, i.e. with a legitimate hand. We don't recommend overdoing this play however, although it might prove effective occasionally.

If your opponent won't bluff

If you believe your opponent is unlikely to bluff, then you should usually make a bet yourself, rather than trying to check-raise (i.e. check and then raise if your opponent bets). The reason for that is that a check-raise is a pretty strong move because it signals a clear intention to get as much money into the pot as possible. Therefore your opponent will usually call a check-raise only with a strong hand. Also note that, if his hand were that strong, he'd be quite likely to raise a bet from you anyway, allowing you to re-raise.

So a check-raise will rarely extract *extra* money from an opponent on the river. And by check-raising, you frequently lose out – because an opponent with a half-decent hand will normally call a moderate-sized bet, but won't make a bet himself.

167

Having said all that, you may decide to check-raise on the river occasionally, either because you have a particular reason for believing you can extract more money that way, or in order to vary your play; if you never check-raise, opponents will infer that you aren't that strong whenever you check.

> ### Summary: if you believe you're winning
>
> You should usually bet on the river unless you think that by checking you'll induce a bluff from your opponent. If you do decide to bet, you can take guidance from the previous section on the size of bet to make – position doesn't really make much difference in this respect.

If you don't know whether you're winning or losing!

We're going to divide this scenario into two, based on which case you think is more likely.

If you suspect you're losing

This case is quite straightforward. You normally won't elect to bluff in this situation because, although you reckon you're probably losing, there's nonetheless a chance you might in fact win a showdown. And you won't elect to bet for value (i.e. to extract money from your opponent rather than as a bluff) because you suspect you have the worse hand.

Therefore you should just check if possible, and call any bet by your opponent if you seem to have the odds to do so, i.e. if the pot odds you're being offered are greater than the odds against you winning. If your opponent bets and the odds aren't there, you should fold.

One word of warning – when players make big bets on the river in low-stakes no-limit hold'em games, they usually aren't bluffing. In these games, players who bluff usually bluff too small, and players with genuinely good hands often make bets that are very big, because they get over-excited about the prospect of a big pay-off.

Therefore if an opponent makes a big bet on the river, unless you have some specific reason to suspect that he would do so with an under-strength hand, you should be very wary of calling without good strength of your own. It can be easy to talk yourself into believing such a player is bluffing, when the evidence in fact suggests otherwise. You could do a lot worse than sticking to this one very simple rule: *don't call big bets with marginal hands.*

If you suspect you're winning

We've looked at situations on the river where you're fairly confident that you're in the lead. We're now going to examine situations where there's a reasonable amount of doubt, and a good chance it could go either way.

In rounds of betting before the river, we have normally encouraged you to bet if you believe you're winning, even if you're not completely sure. On the river, however, things change a little. There are no more cards to come, and therefore:

- you don't need to bet to avoid giving a free card
- there is less incentive for a losing hand to call you, because it has no way of improving further, i.e. you are less likely to be called by a hand that you're beating.

The combination of these factors means that *you need to be somewhat more certain of being in the lead for a bet on the river to be profitable.*

Moreover, you must be particularly wary of making bets on the river that cannot show a profit. Let's have an example to illustrate this.

Suppose that you were dealt:

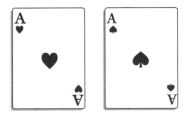

You raised pre-flop and got one caller. The flop came:

You bet and were called. The turn was the jack of hearts, you bet again and were called again. Given your opponent's behaviour during the hand (calling but not raising), and from what you know of his play in general, you have a strong suspicion that he's on a drawing hand, either a club flush draw or a straight draw. Now on the river comes the queen of clubs, putting three clubs on the board. What should you do?

Many inexperienced poker players would reason as follows: "I've got a pair of aces, which is a good hand. Yes, my opponent might have a club flush but he probably hasn't. I'm probably still winning, so I'm going to put in a pot-sized bet so my pair of aces can get nicely paid off."

Can you see the flaw in the logic? The problem is this: your opponent, in all likelihood, now has *either* a very strong hand, if he was on a club flush draw, or a very weak hand, if he was on a different draw and missed it. He probably doesn't have a medium-strength hand. Now, recall that in order for a bet on the river to show a profit, it must either:

- make a weaker hand call, or
- make a stronger hand fold.

But there's no way that a pot-sized bet can achieve either of these objectives in this scenario. If your opponent missed his draw, then he'll almost certainly be too weak to call a bet that size. He'll fold, and you won't win any extra money. But if he hits his draw, he'll call or raise your bet, and you'll *lose* more money in addition to the money you've already put in the pot. In other words, your bet shows no profit in one case, and a big loss in the other.

In this example, it's quite likely that there is *no* amount you could bet on the river and show a profit, since your opponent will almost certainly fold with any hand that's weaker than yours. A small bet might conceivably do the trick, for example if your opponent missed his draw but has picked up some kind of other hand that he thinks might be winning, and is at least worth a small call.

If you're first to act however, a more profitable play would usually be to check and call, in the hope that your opponent missed his draw and decides to bluff.

Here, then, is a very important guideline to follow when betting on the river. *Except when bluffing, don't make bets that are unlikely to be called by hands weaker than yours.* So many poor poker players make this mistake – don't be one of them. Whenever you're contemplating betting for value, always remember that you're looking for a weaker hand to call you. If that doesn't seem likely, then don't bet.

Summary: if you don't know whether you're winning or losing

You need to be slightly stronger than usual to bet on the river, and you should do so only if you are likely to be called by a hand worse than yours. If that doesn't seem probable then you should usually check, and take a view on whether a call is likely to be profitable in the event that your opponent bets.

Multi-way pots on the river

Hands that have three or more people still involved by the river involve a slight change in strategy from those that are heads-up. Here are the main things you should watch out for.

Downgrade the relative strength of your hand. As with any game or hand, the more players left in, the more likely it is that somebody else has you beaten. This coupled with the fact that you need to be slightly stronger to bet on the river than you do earlier on in the hand (as we discussed in the previous section) means that extra caution is required.

Be less inclined to bluff. A bluff may have a reasonable chance of working against one player. But the more players you have to bluff out, the less likely it becomes that all of them will fold.

If you were to assume (hypothetically of course) that there were a 50% chance of each individual player folding, then you have a 50% chance of bluffing one player, a 25% chance of bluffing two players, a 12.5% chance of bluffing three players, a 6.25% chance of bluffing four players, and so on – the probability halves with each additional opponent in an *exponential* decline. Bluffing rarely works well against more than a couple of opponents.

Be less inclined to call if there are callers ahead of you. If there has been a bet and then one or more calls ahead of you, you will need a stronger hand to call than if there were no callers at all. The reason for this is very similar to the reason why you should be less inclined to bluff in multi-way pots. For your call to be successful, you need to beat *all* the other players in the hand. As the number of other callers increases, your chances of beating *all* of them decreases exponentially, as above.

You should contrast this situation with that which occurs in earlier betting rounds. When you have several callers in earlier rounds, the pot is harder to win, but this is offset by the improved odds that the pot is offering you. Why doesn't that same reasoning apply on the river? Because when you calculate your odds of winning on earlier rounds, you're really calculating your odds of hitting your outs – and you assume you're very likely to win if you do so.

On the river however, there are no cards to come, so you have to assess your chances of winning *right now*. This is a wholly different proposition.

Calling can sometimes win you more money than raising. If you find yourself in the following position:

- A player ahead of you has bet.
- You're pretty sure you're winning.
- There are other players behind you still to act.

Then pause for a moment before putting in a raise. In order for your raise to make extra money, you'd need *either* a player acting behind you to call the bet plus the raise, *or* the original bettor to call your raise, or both. But if instead everybody were to fold, you'd make no extra money. Just consider whether you'd be more likely to get extra money in the pot by calling. It's far easier for the players behind you to call a bet, than to call a bet plus a raise – especially considering that the original bettor has the option to re-raise. And if the players behind you all fold to a raise, then your only hope is to get paid off by the bettor.

In each case, you'll need to use your judgment to try to make the right decision. It all boils down to where you think extra money is most likely to come from.

Summary: the river

- Play on the river is quite different from other rounds because there are no more cards to come.
- When you bet, make sure you're very clear in your mind whether you're trying to get a weaker hand to call or a stronger hand to fold. Be very careful not to make a bet that will be called only by a stronger hand.
- The river is often a good time to bluff, or to let your opponents bluff. But big bets on the river in low stakes games usually aren't bluffs.
- Be less inclined to bluff or call when up against multiple opponents.

Quiz: river play

In all the following questions there are ten players seated at the table, each with plenty of money left in front of them unless otherwise stated. Your job is to say how you'd play on the river.

Question 1. You are dealt J♦ Q♦ in late position. There's a pre-flop raise from mid position and you are the only caller. The flop is great for you: Q♥ J♣ 5♠, giving you top two pair. Your opponent bets and you flat-call, hoping he'll bet again on the turn. The turn is the 7♣ and your opponent checks, so you bet the pot and your opponent calls. The river is the 2♥ and your opponent checks. Do you (a) check (b) bet half the pot (c) bet the pot?

Question 2. As above, but this time the river is the A♣. Do you (a) check (b) bet half the pot (c) bet the pot?

Question 3. You are dealt A♣ 8♣ in mid position and call the big blind. The small blind raises and the big blind calls, as do you. The flop comes K♣ 8♠ 7♣ giving you a pair of eights and a flush draw, and the small blind makes a pot-sized bet. The big blind folds and you call. The turn is the J♥ and your opponent and you both check. The river is the 3♦ and your opponent checks. Do you (a) check (b) bet half the pot (c) bet the pot?

Question 4. As above but instead of checking on the river, your opponent makes a pot sized bet. Do you (a) fold (b) call (c) make a minimum raise (d) make a pot-sized raise?

Question 5. You are dealt 5♠ 6♠ on the button. Pre-flop, all fold to you and you put in a (slightly cheeky) raise. The small blind folds and the big blind calls. The flop comes K♥ J♣ 7♥. Your opponent and you both check and the turn is the 7♠. Again you both check and the river is the A♦. Your opponent checks. Do you now (a) check (b) bet half the pot (c) bet the pot?

Question 6. Pre-flop you call from early position with A♠ 5♠. The flop comes 5♥ 10♠ K♠, giving you bottom pair, and overcard and the nut flush draw. You make a good-sized bet, but a player in late position raises and you are the only caller. The turn is the 2♣ and you check. Your opponent bets again, and you call again. The river is the 8♥. Do you (a) check (b) bet half the pot (c) bet the pot?

Question 7. As above, but you check on the river and your opponent makes a bet of around a fifth of the (rather large) pot. Do you (a) fold (b) call (c) make a minimum raise (d) make a pot-sized raise?

Answers to quiz

Answer 1. You need to wonder what your opponent has. Before his call on the turn, his betting was consistent with having a strong pre-flop hand that missed the flop, prompting a speculative continuation bet. But you have to ask why he then called a pot sized bet on the turn. The most likely explanation is that he has *some* kind of a hand, although probably not as good as yours, and perhaps some kind of a draw to a better hand. It's possible that he credits your bet on the turn as a bluff after he checked and showed weakness, therefore allowing him to call with not very much.

At a guess, he most likely had one pair on the turn, with perhaps a draw to a straight or flush as well. The two key points here are that (a) one can't imagine he has a hand that would have been helped by the 2♥ on the river, and (b) there's no other evidence to suggest you're not winning. Let's hope he has a pair of some kind and will call one more bet from you. He's unlikely to call a pot-sized bet with just a pair given the amount of strength you've shown in the hand, but he might well call a smaller bet. You go for option (b), betting half the pot and giving him 3-to-1 for his call.

Answer 2. This is a bad river for you. There are plenty of hands consistent with your opponent's betting that could now be beating you, examples being A-Q, A-J or, less likely, A-5, A-x clubs or K-10. What's more, if your opponent doesn't hold one of these hands, he'll be scared that you do. In short, the chances are much higher that your opponent is check-raising with a strong hand, and much lower that he'll call a bet from you if he isn't. Under these circumstances, betting is not a good move. You go for option (a) and check.

Answer 3. The first question you must consider here is, are you winning? Your opponent must have had a reasonable hand pre-flop, but since he didn't bet on the turn, his bet on the flop looks more like a speculative continuation bet than a legitimate one. It's possible that your pair of eights is in the lead, but it's by no means certain.

If you were to bet, it would be for one of two reasons: to make a better hand fold, or to make a worse hand call. Do you think you could make a better hand fold? It seems likely that your opponent would call a bet on the river with a pair higher than eights, especially as you haven't shown much strength in the hand and the river doesn't look likely to have helped you. So that probably won't work. And it also seems unlikely that your opponent would fold to most bets with anything less than a pair of eights, so you probably won't get a worse hand to call.

Betting doesn't seem to be a profitable move in these circumstances and you go for option (a) and check. In general, if you have a little something to show down it's usually wise to show it down as cheaply as possible.

Answer 4. You should immediately realise that raising is out of the question here, for the same reasons as in the previous question. Therefore it's a choice between calling and folding.

The question is, what are the chances that your opponent has a hand that can beat your pair of eights? If he had a pair of kings or jacks, it seems likely he would have bet on the turn to avoid giving you a free card – since from his perspective you could easily be on a straight or flush draw. And it's very unlikely the river helped him since he probably wouldn't have raised pre-flop with a three in his hand (although he might conceivably be holding a pair of threes).

All things considered, his pot-sized bet on the river looks downright fishy. The pot is offering you 2-to-1 if you call and you reckon there's a better chance than that that he's bluffing (i.e., greater than 33%). You go for option (b) and call. However, if you thought for some reason that your opponent was unlikely to have bluffed, then a fold would also be reasonable.

Answer 5. You have no pair and are losing to your opponent even if he only has an eight or better in his hand. Therefore if you check, you will almost certainly lose the pot. There's no chance of getting a worse hand to call, but perhaps you can make a better hand fold by bluffing. Your opponent has had several chances to bet and taken none of them, despite the weakness you have obviously shown. He will also be a bit nervous about that ace on the river having paired your hand, given that you raised pre-flop.

In this situation, a bet of half the pot should be sufficient for your purposes. Your opponent might be a touch less likely to call if you make a pot-sized bet, but in the end his decision here is more likely to come down to the strength of his hand and whether or not he believes you have an ace. Betting a smaller amount reduces your risk in the case of your opponent having a hand that he intends to call with, and is entirely compatible with a value bet made with a pair of aces. You go for option (b) and bet half the pot.

Answer 6. Well, it should be pretty obvious that your pair of fives isn't winning – your opponent has bet or raised at every opportunity since the flop and is representing a strong hand. Since he surely won't believe that the turn and river have helped you, it's unlikely that a bluff will work.

So you're almost certainly not winning, and almost certain to fail if you bluff. Therefore you go for option (a) and check.

Answer 7. As above, bluffing with a raise is out of the question. Although you're almost certainly beaten, you're getting pot odds of 6-to-1 and it's just possible your opponent is bluffing having missed a straight draw or flush draw. A crying call is in order, and you go for option (b).

Chapter Ten:
Deception

All the way back at the start of Part II we introduced the idea of there being two different types of plays:

■ Value-based plays, where you act in accordance with the strength of your hand

■ Deceptive plays, where you act in a way that disguises the strength of your hand, either by betting or raising with a weak hand (bluffing) or checking or merely calling with a strong hand (slowplaying).

Since then, we've concentrated mainly on the former, and made only occasional references to deceptive plays. Now we're going to take a closer look at deception, and when you should consider using it.

Deception can be carried out in a number of different ways. The mildest form of deception we will describe as *mixing up your play*.

Mixing up your play

In poker, you must avoid being too predictable. If you play the same way in the same situation all the time then it allows your opponents to *get a read* on you, i.e. make good inferences about your holding because of the way you've acted in the hand. For example, if you always make a £10 raise pre-flop when holding a pair of aces but never otherwise then other players are soon going to work this one out.

What you must do instead is vary the amount you raise when holding aces, or raise £10 with other hands as well as aces, or a combination of both. Whatever you do, you mustn't be too easy to read because if your opponents can work out what you're likely to hold, it's much, much harder to get their money.

So you need to mix up your play continually to keep your opponents guessing. The right way to go about this is to determine what you think is the best course of action and then alter this slightly, at random but within certain parameters. For example, if you think a £10 raise is the right thing to do, sometimes you should instead raise £8 or £12, or maybe even £6 or £14. Or if you find yourself with a marginal decision between a call and a raise, then pick one at random. Next time in the same situation, feel free to make the other choice (but don't deliberately alternate – that's too predictable).

One word of caution here. Recall that in general you should simply try to make solid, value-based plays; in other words to bet according to the value of your hand. If you stray too much from this principle in the name of mixing up your play, you will destroy value and cost yourself money. For example, whilst it's correct to vary the size of your pre-flop raise when you hold a pair of aces, it would rarely be correct simply to call with them, even though that would disguise your hand very nicely (as we explained in Chapter Seven).

Similarly, we don't recommend putting in a big pre-flop raise when holding 2-7 off-suit. Sure, nobody will expect you to hold that hand, but that's not going to help you when you show it down and lose.

Whilst there will be many situations where deceptive moves such as bluffs and slowplays can make you money, that isn't what we mean by mixing up your play. Mixing up your play is something you should try to do as a matter of course by varying your actions *within the parameters* of what's sensible and reasonable. Genuinely deceptive plays should be used more sparingly and only when the time is right. (And only after you've read the rest of this chapter.)

Bear in mind too that there's no point in mixing up your play if your opponents aren't watching you carefully. If you believe this to be the case you might as well just work out what you think is the best play, and make it. Departing from the optimal course may cost you money, and that's a risk not worth taking if your carefully conceived manoeuvres will go unnoticed anyway. Situations where this is more likely to apply are:

■ You are playing weak opponents. Poor players are generally less inclined to study the behaviour of the opposition. They tend to focus too much merely on their own cards and bet in a simplistic or formulaic way.

■ You are playing online. The play is faster online, the poker communities are larger (and hence your anonymity greater), and people are often sat at more than one table simultaneously. Players in online games are far less likely to notice and study your betting patterns than those in live games.

Generally throughout this book we've assumed that there is a need to mix up your play. It's an easy enough habit to dispense with if the situation doesn't call for it.

Shortly we'll take a look at the more full-blown methods of deception, starting with those plays that involve underplaying your strong hands (namely check-raising and slowplaying). Before we do so however, we need to look at one of the key risks associated with such moves.

Free cards and cheap cards

One of the consequences of underplaying your strong hands, by which we mean not betting them as strongly as they merit, is that you may allow your opponents to see further cards more cheaply than they otherwise would.

When a player is able to see the next board card without putting any money in the pot, they are said to have received a *free card*. Similarly a *cheap card* results when the total betting during a round is small (in comparison with the pot size). We're going to explain why free cards and cheap cards usually hurt the player with the strongest hand.

Let's suppose for a moment that you're in a pot with one opponent, and the turn has just been dealt. You have the best hand at present but you're not 100% certain to win the hand. In fact there is a 25% (3-to-1) chance that the river will give your opponent the best hand. What happens if both you and your opponent check?

The answer to that question depends on what the last card is of course. Three quarters of the time, you'll remain ahead of your opponent and win the pot (unless you fold on the river). But one quarter of the time, you'll be outdrawn and lose the pot (unless your opponent folds on the river). We can say that your *equity* in the pot, that is, the amount of it you expect on average to win, is 75%. Your opponent's equity is the remaining 25% of the pot.

Now let's look at what happens instead if you bet. If we assume your opponent won't raise with the worse hand, he will have two choices:

- He can fold, in which case your equity increases from 75% to 100% – because you win the pot outright.
- He can match your bet, i.e. call, in which case you now have 75% equity of a bigger pot.

In the latter case, we can see that your equity in the *additional* money added to the pot on the turn is 75% too. Your opponent has added money to the pot, expecting that on average half of what he contributes will in fact go to you. The reason he has made this unfair wager of course is in the hope that, by doing so, he might win the whole pot.

Hopefully you can see that, *whatever* your opponent does if you bet, he is worse off than if both of you check. If you bet and he folds, your equity increases from 75% to 100%; if you bet and he calls, your equity remains at 75% but the pot is larger, meaning that you can expect to profit from the extra money your opponent has contributed.

You should also be able to see that the more you bet on the turn, the more money you can expect to earn from your opponent if he calls. (The fact that you bet more makes no difference if he folds, of course.) If you bet a small amount compared with the pot size, your opponent may have the odds to make a call correct. If you bet a sufficiently large amount, he'll either have to fold, or make an incorrect call which costs him further money.

To sum all this up and get to the main point: *when you're in the lead, failing to bet or not betting enough costs you money.* We really can't stress this enough. So many poor players give cheap or free cards to their opponents when it's not justified.

Whenever you check or merely call with what you believe to be the best hand, make sure that you know exactly how you expect to earn back the money you sacrifice by doing so. Hands that are losing *desire* free and cheap cards; winning hands usually fear them.

Here are some scenarios where you might think you're winning, but should fear giving a free card:

■ You flop top pair with a good kicker, or hold an overpair to the flop – the next card could easily make two pair for somebody with a worse pair than yours.
■ You flop bottom two pair – the next card might make two pair or trips for anybody currently holding top pair.
■ You flop a set, but there are two or three suited cards on the board – the next card might make someone a flush.

Winning hands don't always fear free cards though. One exception is when your hand is such a monster that it's unlikely that anyone will overtake you on the next card. For example:

■ You flop a flush (although it's possible, if unlikely, that someone could make a full house if the board pairs).
■ You flop a full house or four of a kind.
■ You flop a straight flush!

In these situations, you'd love your opponent to improve to a very good hand that is still likely to be second best. But, unfortunately, hands like this don't come along very often.

Summary: deception and free cards

If you're considering making a deceptive move that involves underplaying a strong hand, you *must* give careful consideration to whether you're comfortable giving a free or cheap card. Most of the time you're in the lead, you shouldn't allow other hands the chance to draw out on you too cheaply.

Check-raising

Now let's look at the first of our truly deceptive plays, the check-raise. You do this when:

■ You initially check.
■ A player acting after you bets.
■ You raise when the betting comes back round to you again.

In this case your deception (checking with a good hand) doesn't remain hidden for very long because, as soon as you raise, it's obvious what your true intentions were. Nonetheless, you hope to extract some extra profit in the meantime.

What a check-raise represents

As we saw in Chapter Five, raising once another player has bet represents more strength than making the first bet of the round. This is because a raise says: *despite the fact you've shown strength by betting, I think I'm even stronger.* And the fact that you've *deliberately* allowed an opponent to bet before making your raise usually indicates even more strength still because you have to commit quite a lot of money to the pot in doing so.

Admittedly you will often make this play when your opponent is expected to bet with an under-strength hand, in which case your check-raise doesn't indicate quite so much strength of its own. But nonetheless, it's still a very strong move.

Therefore you should normally check-raise only when you're reasonably confident of having the best hand at the table.

The effect of check-raising

When people bet out (i.e. bet rather than checking), it's often a speculative move. They *might* have a legitimate hand, but alternatively they might for example be bluffing or semi-bluffing (we'll discuss these shortly), or making a continuation bet with a marginal hand. A bet doesn't always indicate great strength. Therefore, a bet won't always knock out many opponents.

A check-raise on the other hand is far more likely to indicate real strength. A check-raise encourages your opponents' money into the pot, and then claims the pot as its own (or tries to). When you check-raise, you'll usually find that all but the strongest hands will fold. A check-raise will often take the pot down there and then.

Benefits of check-raising

The benefits of check-raising are quite simple. You check, hoping that, by feigning weakness, you will encourage one of your opponents to bet with a hand that you can beat, thus getting extra money into a pot where you are favourite. Broadly speaking, a check-raise shows a profit if your opponent has a weaker hand than yours and *either* of the following apply:

■ Your opponent will bet if you check, but would fold if you were to bet; or
■ Your opponent will call your check-raise, but wouldn't himself have raised had you bet.

Hopefully you can see from this that check-raising produces good results against aggressive players who bet frequently, even with relatively weak hands.

Check-raising also acts as a disincentive for other players to be aggressive. If you're having trouble with a player who habitually makes continuation bets on the flop, try check-raising him a couple of times. He'll think harder about making continuation bets in the future, because he won't be able to read your check as a sign of weakness.

Check-raising and position

In heads-up pots you can by definition check-raise only when you're first to act.

When you check-raise in a multi-way pot, it's not so much your position that counts as your *relative* position. You very much want the player that you expect to bet to be on your left, preferably immediately to your left. This is because:

■ you can see what everybody else does before you make your move. If somebody raises, showing strength, you might decide merely to call, or even fold.
■ you might get a few callers before you reveal your own strength, all of them contributing money to a pot you expect to win.
■ the fewer players there are between you and the bettor, the less the chances are that somebody else is planning a check-raise of their own.

So a good time to check-raise might be on the flop, when the pre-flop raiser is immediately to your left. Their continuation bet might induce a few calls from relatively weak hands, allowing you to raise with confidence. If the pre-flop raiser is on the button however, and you're the first to act, you should be more inclined just to bet out.

Problems of check-raising

There are several potential downsides to check-raising, as opposed simply to betting out.

You risk giving a free card. If nobody bets behind you, you have given a free card. We highlighted the dangers of giving free cards earlier in this chapter so hopefully they're still fresh in your mind. Therefore you will usually check-raise only if you're very sure that somebody behind you will bet, for example if you're first to act on the flop when there were lots of callers behind you, or if there was a pre-flop raise from a serial continuation bettor.

Having said that, you might on occasion try for a check-raise even when you're not particularly confident of a bet behind you, as long as you're not unduly worried about giving a free card.

You commit extra money. When you check-raise, you have to commit a significant amount of money to the pot with your first bet. If it turns out you're not favourite after all, it may prove quite expensive.

Suppose that on the flop you decide to check-raise the pre-flop raiser, who you've noticed frequently makes continuation bets. The flop comes, you check, he bets as predicted, and you raise. But then he re-raises! Gulp. Now you're not quite as confident as you were a minute ago – it looks like he hit a good hand – and you're out of position. Not a great situation. If instead of check-raising, you'd simply bet out, then a raise from your opponent would have set alarm bells ringing *before* you'd put so much money at stake. In this sense, check-raising is a high risk move.

You may extract less money. It's frequently the case that check-raising will extract less money from a strong hand than betting out would. If you check-raise an opponent, he's going to realise you have a very good hand and will often fold. Even if he calls, he's going to be wary of you for the rest of the hand.

But if you bet out instead of check-raising, people won't know you have such a strong hand, because betting out is much more likely to be a speculative move on your part. An opponent with a strong hand might call your bet, in which case your hand strength is better disguised on later rounds. Or he might raise you, in which case you can re-raise. This time it is your opponent who will have committed a large amount of chips to the pot before finding out how strong you are.

You will find that betting out is an especially good option if you are the kind of player who frequently makes bets at pots with speculative hands – or who is perceived by your opponents to be such a player. In this case, your strength is still largely disguised.

So check-raising may work well against weaker hands, but betting out is often better against stronger ones – and it's the stronger hands who will really pay you off. Therefore check-raising may earn you some extra money in pots that turn out to be small, but betting out is more likely to win you a really big pot. Since most of your profit will come from the big pots, this is frequently the case you should be trying to maximise.

Before you decide to check-raise then, make sure you consider all the downsides. Is there a chance of giving an unwanted free card? Are the consequences of being called / re-raised too unpleasant? You may decide you can reduce your risk, or perhaps even extract more money, simply by betting out.

Summary: check-raising

You should consider check-raising when there are players behind you that you expect to bet with hands worse than yours, but who might fold if you were to bet first. Check-raising works best against aggressive opponents sitting close to your left.

You may decide it's preferable to bet rather than check-raising if:

- you're not sure that anybody will bet, and you don't want to give a free card

- you're nervous about committing too much money to the pot

- you believe that, were you to bet, there's a good chance that a hand worse than yours will call or raise you anyway.

Slowplaying

If check-raising involves a deception that reveals itself within a single round of betting, *slowplaying* unfolds over a longer timeframe. You are said to slowplay a strong hand whenever you check or call, i.e. do the minimum required to stay in a pot, for the entirety of a round of betting.

Benefits of slowplaying

The benefits of slowplaying are obvious. By not betting or raising, you are disguising as far as possible the true strength of your hand, so it is very difficult for opponents to suspect how strong you really are. You hope that they will bet into you, and ideally keep doing so, in an effort to win your money. In fact, of course, it is you who expects to win their money.

Whenever you slowplay a hand, you are usually rooting for your opponent to improve. The ideal result is for you to hold the nuts – the best possible hand given what's on the board – and for your opponent to hold something near the nuts, slightly worse than your hand. If that happens, all the money will usually go in the pot, and then of course from the pot to you.

As with check-raising, slowplaying works best against aggressive players. If you're not going to bet or raise, you want your opponents to do as much betting and raising as possible.

Slowplaying and position

Position isn't too important when you're contemplating slowplaying. Since you're only going to call or check, and you don't really care too much what other players do, it doesn't matter that much where you're sitting.

Having said that, if you're in late or last position and everyone checks to you, betting may be more advisable than slowplaying. A bet from a player in late position doesn't necessarily represent that much strength and is more likely to attract a call. If you're a particularly aggressive player, then checking in last position might even look downright suspicious. It will certainly look suspicious later on in the hand when you start furiously betting and raising.

Problems of slowplaying

There are two main potential problems with slowplaying, as opposed to faster plays such as betting or check-raising.

You give free cards to your opponents, and hence a free chance for them to pick up a hand that can beat you. Even if somebody bets and you call, you're still giving cards more cheaply than you need to – because you didn't raise. Just remember that *every time you check or call with the best hand you are costing yourself money*.

Therefore, don't slowplay with hands than can easily be outdrawn by the next card – only slowplay with monsters. This becomes even more true as the pot gets bigger – you must make your opponents pay dearly for the chance to win a big pot.

You may extract less money. By slowplaying, you risk getting less of other players' money into the pot than you would do if you just bet. Yes, your opponents might hit a great, second-best hand and pay you off. But what if they have a drawing hand, and miss their draw? They won't call a bet on the river once all the cards are out, but they might have called bets on the flop or turn while their draw was still alive. By not betting you wasted the opportunity to get your opponents' money whilst they still felt they were in with a chance.

So, always bear in mind that your good hands may be paid off more handsomely by betting than by slowplaying. This is especially true if you're perceived by your opponents as someone who often makes speculative or under-strength bets.

Summary: slowplaying

You should consider slowplaying when:

- you're strong enough not to worry about giving free cards
- you want your opponents to improve to a second-best hand
- you believe you can win more money later on by disguising your strength now
... continued on next page

■ you are up against aggressive opponents who are likely to do your betting for you.

However, it's usually preferable to bet or raise rather than slowplaying if you think there's a good chance you'll be called or raised anyway. Most inexperienced players are too inclined to slowplay – if in doubt, just bet.

Bluffing

Now, here's everybody's favourite poker topic – bluffing. Many people new to the game (and some not so new who should know better) seem to think that poker is *mostly* about bluffing. Bluffing is deceitful, it's glamorous and it's daring – surely that's what poker is all about!

The reality is rather more mundane however. Many poker hands go by without a single bluff from any player, and although bluffing should be part of your game, it has no special status and shouldn't be overused. When a well-considered or courageous bluff comes off however, it's one of the best feelings in the world. Or in the world of poker, at least.

What is a bluff?

A bluff is this: any bet or raise that you make when you're sure that you don't have the best hand. Since you believe you're losing, your intention in bluffing is to make everyone else in the hand fold. By definition, a bluff doesn't want to be called.

Bluffs can be made at any time during a hand of hold'em, from pre-flop to the river. They are most common on the river however, for reasons we'll soon discover.

The benefits of bluffing

There are two benefits of bluffing.

- When successful, you force stronger hands to fold, allowing you to win pots you otherwise would lose. If you never bluffed, you would win fewer pots.
- When other players see you bluffing, and know you are capable of bluffing, they are more likely to pay you off on your legitimate hands – because they may think you're bluffing again. When you put in a pot sized bet on the river, you are more likely to get a caller if you've shown a bluff or two during the session. Hence bluffing occasionally can help you earn more money even when you aren't bluffing.

Both of these factors are significant, although which one confers greater benefit will depend on the way you play, and the nature of your opponents.

Problems of bluffing

There's only one real problem involved in bluffing, and that's getting caught. When this happens, you lose the money that went into the pot as part of your bluff.

The trick of course is to make sure that the losses you incur when you are caught bluffing are outweighed by the benefits described above.

Whether or not to bluff

There are two main conditions that suggest a bluff might be profitable.

- You believe you have no chance of winning the pot unless you bluff. This is quite important. It's normally not correct to bluff if you believe that there's a reasonable chance you'll win without bluffing. If you think there's a chance you might win, you should aim to see more cards, and show down your hand, as cheaply as possible.
- You believe that there is a *sufficient* chance that all your opponents will fold if you bluff.

The first of these is hopefully quite clear – a bluff should be seen as a last resort in an otherwise dead hand. The second condition requires closer examination however; in particular we need to explain what we mean by a *sufficient* chance.

Let's have an example to illustrate. Suppose that you were dealt:

You're on the river, about to start the final round of betting, and there's £100 in the pot. The board is:

You missed your straight draw and your hand is now worthless. However, the spade on the river may have made your opponent worry that you've made a flush. You have two choices – you can check (or fold if your opponent bets), and hence cede the pot to your opponent. Or you can bluff.

You believe that, if you make a pot-sized bet, there is a 75% chance your opponent will fold. Should you bluff?

We can work that one out quite easily. If you bluff then 75% of the time you'll win the £100 in the pot (when your opponent folds). But 25% of the time you'll lose the £100 you spent bluffing (you don't 'lose' the money in the pot – money in the pot isn't yours, remember). So your expected gain is:

£100 x 75% – £100 x 25% = £50.

In other words, when you bluff under these conditions, you expect to show an average profit of £50.

Now let's revisit our assumptions and see how that changes things. Do you really believe that your opponent will fold 75% of the time when you make that bet? Maybe that figure is too high, and you decide instead that 25% is nearer the mark. Now you expect to lose £100 on 75% of attempts, and win £100 on 25% of them, for an expected loss of £50. Bluffing clearly isn't profitable in this case.

We can also work out when bluffing with a pot-sized bet is a break-even move. Since you win £100 if it works, and lose £100 if it doesn't work, then you will break even with a pot-sized bluff if you believe it will work 50% of the time. To put this another way, you should bluff with a pot sized bet if you think your opponent is more than 50% likely to fold. Otherwise you should check / fold.

This is quite interesting when you think about it. If you make a pot sized bluff, then you don't have to be particularly confident about it working. In fact, all you need to believe is that it's more likely to work than not.

So far we've considered only pot-sized bluffs. But there's no reason why you couldn't bluff with a different amount, either larger or smaller. Let's suppose that you decide to make a half-pot bluff, i.e. one of 50% of the pot size. How confident must you be of your opponent folding now? It turns out that the break-even point occurs when there is a 33% chance of your opponent folding, in other words if the odds of your bluff working are 2-to-1 against. That seems even stranger – when you make a half-pot bluff, you can legitimately believe that the bluff will fail more times than it will work – yet still show a profit.

There's a general rule here of course. For a bluff to show a profit, the chances of your opponent folding need to be bigger than the ratio of your bet size to the pot size (excluding your bet). So for example:

- A bluff of 20% of the pot must work 17% of the time.
- A bluff of 25% of the pot must work 20% of the time.
- A bluff of 33% of the pot must work 25% of the time.
- A bluff of 50% of the pot must work 33% of the time.
- A bluff of 75% of the pot must work 43% of the time.
- A bluff of 100% of the pot must work 50% of the time.
- A bluff of 200% of the pot must work 66% of the time.

and so on. It might look superficially from this as if your bluffs should be small, since a small bluff can work less often and still show a profit. But don't forget to look at it from your opponent's point of view. A small bet is more easily called, because the pot odds for making the call are more attractive. In practice, if your opponent won't call a bet of 20% of the pot, he may not actually have you beaten – and if he doesn't have you beaten then there's no need to risk a bluff.

To sum up what we've said so far:

- ■ You don't have to be sure a bluff will work in order for it to be profitable.
- ■ The more you bet however, the more sure you need to be.
- ■ But the less you bet, the more likely it is your opponents will call you.

Will a bluff work?

You now have some guidelines for working out whether or not a bluff will be profitable once you've formed an opinion on whether or not your opponents *are* likely to call. But how likely are they are to call? Here are the factors you should consider.

Representing a specific hand. Your bluffs are much more likely to work if they represent a specific hand, or type of hand. If, for example, there are four cards to a straight or flush on the board, then a bluff is likely to work. Your opponent has to believe only that you hold one of the cards that complete the straight or flush to believe that he is beaten. Therefore scary boards (ones that look like they could easily have made someone a big hand) are good for bluffing at. Just remember though that your opponent might have made the hand you're representing.

Maintaining a consistent betting pattern. It's one thing representing a particular hand, but your opponent must also be convinced you're capable of holding the cards that complete that hand. Suppose that on the river, the board is:

  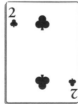  

Before you decide to bluff, hoping your opponent will believe you hold a four and have made the straight, ask yourself what the hand looks like from your opponent's point of view. If your opponent raised pre-flop, and then bet on the flop, what holdings are you likely to have called with on both occasions? Not many that contain a four. If, on the other hand, there was no betting until the turn, and you were in the big blind, then it's much more believable that you hold a four.

To sum up then, before you consider bluffing, re-run the entire hand from your opponent's perspective. If you were him, what kind of hands would you fear, and would you be likely to fold to a bet?

The strength of your opponent's hand. You can't know the answer to this one unfortunately, but you should still consider it. If you believe your opponent is strong then a bluff is unlikely to work. Even if you're representing a strong hand yourself, it may be too much to ask your opponent to lay down a good hand of their own. Therefore you should usually bluff only when you have reason to think that your opponent's hand isn't particularly strong (but nonetheless stronger than yours – otherwise there's no point bluffing).

Later is better. Bluffs tend to be more effective during later betting rounds than earlier ones, and particularly so on the river. This is because on earlier rounds, there are more cards to come, and players may decide to call a bet with what they believe to be the worst hand, just in case they improve. Poor players often call without the proper odds to do so, making a call even more likely. On the river however, with no cards to come, there's no more room for optimism. If your opponents call on the river, they're calling on the basis of their current hand strength alone.

Having said that, a fair amount of bluffing is done on the flop, while all the pre-flop callers are struggling to gain the initiative. A strong bluff on the flop, representing that the flop hit you, is often a good play.

Bluffing pre-flop is fairly rare and should generally be avoided. The one situation where it's most likely to work is if you are in very late position or in the blinds (i.e. one of the last to act) and there are a few callers but no raise. Given that nobody has shown any real interest in the hand, you may be able to pick up a small pot with a healthy-sized raise of your own. Even if you are called you might get lucky and hit a good flop, or perhaps succeed with a continuation bet if you're feeling brave.

Position. Bluffs are more likely to succeed if you're in late position and everyone has checked to you. This is because your opponents:

PLAYING POKER TO WIN

- have shown weakness by checking – if they were strong, they would be more likely to bet in order to avoid giving a free card
- will be more reluctant to play the rest of the hand against you out of position.

Note however that these arguments don't particularly apply on the river. On the river, a bluff is as likely to work if you're out of position.

Number of opponents. The more opponents you are facing, the greater the chances that one of them holds a hand that justifies a call, and so the less likely your buff is to work. Don't underestimate how steeply your chances tail off with each additional opponent – the effect is significant.

Your table image. In order for a bluff to work, your opponents must believe that you have a good hand. If your opponents believe you to be a tight player, who plays only good hands, then your bluffs will be that much more convincing. Note that it doesn't matter whether or not you really are a tight player – what matters is how you are perceived. If you *are* a tight player and don't bluff very much then you are not making the most of your image, and you should bluff more. You'll know when you're at risk of overdoing it when people start calling you with under-strength hands.

If you are perceived as a loose player, you don't need to bluff more – you probably need to bluff less. Players will be more willing to call your bets and your bluff is therefore less likely to work.

Your opponents' image. It sounds so obvious, but is so often overlooked. Don't bluff against loose players – who are likely to call you even with average hands. Save your bluffs for better, tighter players, who are capable of laying down a hand if they think they are beaten.

Bluff size

Once you've made a decision to bluff, you need to decide how much to bet. You should weigh up all the factors above and try to decide to what extent the size of your bet is likely to affect the success of the bluff.

- Your bluff should be big enough such that you aren't giving attractive odds to the kind of hands you want to fold.

196

- Your bluff shouldn't however be so big that it would need a very high chance of success in order to be profitable
- Most important of all, your bluff shouldn't look like a bluff. Don't bet an amount that you wouldn't bet if you had the hand you're representing.

In general, most bluffs will be between 50% and 100% of the pot size. A common mistake made by inexperienced players is to bluff too small, giving themselves no chance of success. A small bluff will occasionally work, however, especially when the pot isn't too big and none of the players has shown much interest in it.

Bluffing more than once at a pot

If you have a bluff at a pot on the flop or the turn, you might sometimes consider having another stab at it on the next round. A move like this is very risky, since an opponent who called your bluff once might very well do so again. If you're going to try something like this, you should at least have *some* reason to think that your opponent might fold on the second attempt, for example if they appeared very reluctant to call the first time. In general however, if you have a bluff at a pot and fail, it's usually time to give it up.

Showing bluffs

If you bluff at a pot successfully, you may sometimes decide – voluntarily – to show your cards to your opponents, to demonstrate to them exactly what you did. Doing so is likely to have the following consequences.

- Players will believe that you're a looser player than they otherwise would, and they will be more likely to play with you in the future. If you are naturally a tight player who struggles to get much action from your opponents, then it may be a good idea to show an occasional bluff in order to get a little more action on your legitimate hands. On the other hand, you may decide to keep your cards to yourself, thereby maintaining your tight image, and simply bluff with greater frequency in the future.

- You will probably earn the respect of most of your opponents for making a courageous move, but it may upset some of them. Not just for the fact that you were bluffing, but that you showed your bluff which to an extent rubs salt into the wound of the player whom you just bluffed out. There's nothing in the rules or etiquette of poker that says you shouldn't do this sort of thing.

In general, it's best to keep your cards to yourself unless you have a good, specific reason for wanting to show them. This is discussed further in the section on advertising in the next chapter.

Bluffy opponents

The strategy for taking on opponents who bluff a lot is straightforward – you simply call them more often.

If you suspect that an opponent is bluffing quite a lot, but aren't sure because they haven't shown down many hands, then you may need to look them up one time by calling. Even if you don't believe you have the odds to make a specific call profitable, calling will achieve two longer-term benefits:

- You will find out information about that player, and build up a better picture of their playing style and betting habits.
- By making a loose call every now and then, you discourage your opponent – and all other players at the table – from bluffing into you in the future. Bluffers don't like to be called, and they don't like bluffing into players with a history of making loose calls.

So if you're up against a bluffer or two, you should plan to make the odd extra call with a marginal hand, just to keep the opposition honest. (There's no point raising a bluffer with a marginal hand however, because they'll call your raise only if they really have got the goods.)

Summary: bluffing

- You don't have to be sure a bluff will work in order for it to be profitable, and you should bluff every now and then to keep from becoming predictable.
- Pick a bluff size that gives you a good chance of making your opponents fold but without risking too much money – usually 50% – 100% of the pot size.
- Only bluff when, from your opponent's view, you could quite easily have a winning hand.
- Bluffs work better later in the hand, from later position and against fewer opponents.

- Only show your bluffs if you want to get more action from other players, or possibly wind them up a bit.
- If you suspect your opponents are bluffing a fair amount, be more inclined to call them with marginal hands.

Semi-bluffing

If you haven't played much poker, you may not have heard much about semi-bluffing, or even know what it is. But semi-bluffs are truly excellent plays that form part of every good poker player's armoury. Semi-bluffs are far more versatile and effective than the pure bluffs we've just discussed.

First of all, for the uninitiated, we'd better tell you what we're talking about.

What is a semi-bluff?

Broadly speaking, a semi-bluff is a bluff you make on the flop or turn *with a good drawing hand*. In other words, you think you have a losing hand at present, but there's a good chance that, even if you're called, you'll end up with the best hand anyway. (See Chapter Seven for a discussion of drawing hands.)

Here's an example. You call on the button pre-flop with:

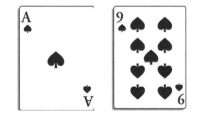

The flop comes:

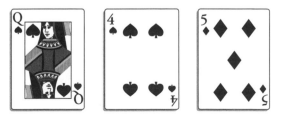

giving you ace-high and a nut flush draw in spades. Everybody checks round to you and you make a semi-bluff bet of three-quarters of the pot size. There are now several distinct ways you can win the pot, the most obvious ones being:

- everyone folds to your bet on the flop, allowing you to win the pot with just ace high; or
- you get one or more callers, fail to improve your hand but win a showdown anyway (admittedly improbable, unless the callers are on a straight draw, or a flush draw like you); or
- you get one or more callers, but improve your hand on the turn or the river.

The last of these possibilities is the characteristic that distinguishes a semi-bluff from a pure bluff, and it's what gives a semi-bluff its real power.

Although in the example above you're almost certainly not winning on the flop, you're actually quite likely to be doing so by the river: you can certainly count any spade as an out; it's likely that aces are outs too (unless e.g. one of your opponents is calling on the flop with something like ace-king – unlikely given there was no raise pre-flop – or one pair plus ace kicker); and it's even possible that nines are outs for you.

This gives you somewhere between nine and fifteen outs. We'll average it out and call it twelve. Your chances of hitting one of twelve outs by the time all the cards are dealt is a very pleasing 44%. In other words you're nearly fifty-fifty to improve to what would almost certainly be a winning hand.

Once you add up all these different ways of winning, you can hopefully see that you're in very good shape indeed.

You might ask however, why betting on the flop is actually better than checking? Since you hold a drawing hand, why not just check and see if the hand hits? The answer is several-fold:

- By merely checking, you're removing one of your ways of winning the pot, namely everyone folding to your bet on the flop.

- If you check the flop, and then your draw subsequently hits, you may not get paid off. If an ace falls, or a third spade comes, your opponents are reasonably likely to be scared off if you bet. By betting on the flop however, it ensures that, if you do hit your hand, you've at least earned some extra money already.

- If you bet on the flop, and your draw subsequently hits, your hand is actually more well-disguised than if you had checked the flop. From your opponents' viewpoint, if you check when there are two spades on the board, and then bet when a third spade comes, it strongly suggests you were on the flush draw and have just completed it. (A similar argument applies to an ace falling of course.) If on the other hand you bet when there are two spades on the board and bet *again* when there are three spades, other players are a little less likely to suspect you of having the flush. Since your hand is better disguised, it's more likely to be paid off.

Note: you can't semi-bluff on the river, because there are no drawing hands on the river – by then, you either have a hand or you don't. You can't really semi-bluff pre-flop either. Although some starting hands are more likely than others to *become* good draws, it doesn't really make sense to talk about *having* a good draw until the flop comes. In hold'em therefore, semi-bluffs are found only on the flop and the turn.

There are just so many ways that the semi-bluff can earn you money – it really is a very powerful play.

When to semi-bluff

A semi-bluff is a two-pronged attack on your opponents:

- They might fold when you bet, allowing you to pick up the pot with a losing hand.
- You might draw out on them in subsequent rounds.

The best times to semi-bluff are when *both* of these factors are working well for you.

Firstly this means that you have to believe there's some chance of winning the pot immediately when you bet. We covered this topic amply under bluffing, and there's not much more to add here. You should be more inclined to semi-bluff if you think that, in the same situation, a pure bluff would have a reasonable chance of succeeding.

Secondly, you should be more inclined to semi-bluff if your draw is of a good quality. In the example above, holding a nut flush draw, you were able to count perhaps twelve outs, which is a very good number. If you held a weaker flush draw or an outside straight draw, you could still count eight or nine outs, giving you chances of 30%-35% of making the best hand. These too are perfectly acceptable holdings for a semi-bluff.

You should think quite a bit harder however before semi-bluffing with fewer outs than that. If you bet with just an inside straight draw (four outs) then you're making virtually a pure bluff. As such you should evaluate your decision almost as you would a pure bluff, and not count on your draw to add much value to your hand.

Another good time to semi-bluff is when you have a part-made drawing hand. (To remind you, that's a drawing hand that has a chance, albeit small, of being the best hand at present). By betting in this situation you prevent any worse hands from taking off a free card.

There's one final key consideration when deciding whether to semi-bluff – that's your position. Semi-bluffs work *much* better from late position than early position. The reasons being that:

■ bluffs of any kind tend to work better from late position (except on the river, which doesn't apply here)
■ semi-bluffs are drawing hands, and drawing hands are best played from late position.

If you semi-bluff from early position, you're more likely to be called or raised, and in more trouble when that does happen. In general you should save your semi-bluffs for late position.

Summary: semi-bluffing

■ Semi-bluffs are generally much more effective than pure bluffs.
■ You should semi-bluff when there is both a good chance of winning the pot immediately *and* a good chance of making the best hand even if you are called.
■ Be more inclined to semi-bluff from late position.

Deception – the pros and cons

The primary purpose of deception is, unsurprisingly, to win you more money. You should be aware however that there are actually two different ways that deception can achieve this, if you use it properly.

Immediate rewards

First and foremost, a deceptive play can show a profit *in the hand where you make it*. When you bluff, for example, you're hoping to win a pot that, based purely on the strength of your hand, you have no right to win.

Similarly, when you slowplay a big hand, you're hoping that by disguising your true strength, you will induce your opponents to put more money in the pot than they otherwise would. These then, are the *immediate* benefits of deception.

Deferred rewards

But deceptive plays may also have *deferred* benefits. If your opponents see you bluffing in one or two hands, they will naturally assume that you are more likely to be bluffing in subsequent hands. Then, when you actually have a legitimately strong hand, they will be more likely to suspect you of being weak and hence more likely to pay you off (i.e. put money into a pot that you are winning).

Similarly, if they see you slowplaying a couple of hands, they will be subsequently less likely to try to push you off pots when they hold marginal strength hands, because they'll worry that you're stronger than you might superficially appear.

Do not underestimate the power of these deferred benefits. By giving your opponents the idea that you're playing in one particular way, you can then extract more money from them in the future when you play in a different way. This is a theme we'll return to in the next chapter.

Deception is good

So with all these benefits, it sounds like deception should be a valuable weapon – and of course it is. If your opponents always knew exactly how strong or weak your hand were, you'd never make any money. You need them to pay off your big hands and fold to your bluffs, and they wouldn't do that if they could see what you were holding.

So from the point of view of luring your opponents into mistakes, deception is paramount. Your opponents won't make mistakes, or at least won't make as many mistakes, if your play is too predictable.

Deception is bad

But we must always remember that this isn't the whole story. You can't continually bet into your opponents with weak hands, because you will often have to show those hands down – and lose. And you can't always check your strong hands because when you have a strong hand you want to get more money in the pot, not less.

So whilst deception is useful for tricking your opponents into making mistakes, it involves, by its nature, making mistakes of your own – albeit deliberate ones. Deception necessitates straying from the true path of value-based play!

Striking a balance

There exists then a perpetual tension in any good poker player's mind. Should I stick to value-based plays and put my money in the middle only when I'm strong? Or should I deceive my opponents, which will induce more mistakes from them but risk destroying my own value?

The answer of course is that you need to strike a balance. When you are learning to play the game of poker, you may find it hard to strike the right balance. You may not like this very much, but here is our advice in this respect: *While you are relatively inexperienced, you should make deceptive plays rarely, if at all.* Some of the reasons behind this are as follows.

■ The weaker players you're likely to come up against when you're learning will frequently be straying from solid, value-based play. You should be able to make plenty of money from them simply by playing a conservative, value-based strategy of your own, without any need to resort to deception.

- Weaker players won't be as good at reading your hand, and may not even pay any attention to it at all. There's no point trying to mislead someone who's not that interested in what you've got in the first place.

- Weaker players often play too loose, i.e. get involved in too many pots with under-strength hands. Bluffing is particularly pointless against such players because they're likely to call your bluff anyway, even when proper strategy might indicate a fold. Similarly, there's less incentive to slowplay against loose players because, if you bet, they will call or raise with relatively weak hands anyway.

- Deceptive plays are harder to pull off than value-based plays and rely on correct judgments of when and how to use them. It's safer to stick to value betting until your judgment is good enough to spot the occasions when deception is most likely to be effective.

Don't professionals frequently use deception?

Hold on a second, we hear some of you thinking, *when I watch professionals on TV, it seems like they're always making moves; slowplaying their big hands, or bluffing like crazy. Why shouldn't I do the same?*

There's a very good answer to that question, or several very good answers in fact. The poker you see on television normally involves coverage of the late stages of big tournaments. These are often characterised by:

- short-handed play, rather than full tables
- games with strong, tight players
- large blind / ante sizes in comparison with stack sizes.

These circumstances favour a very specific brand of play, one in which deception and aggression are significant features of an optimal strategy. Such a strategy would however be a disaster in the cash games in which you're likely to find yourself at the start of your poker career.

On top of this, deceptive plays make better viewing than bread and butter value-based plays – they're understandably a little more interesting to watch. Since poker coverage is normally selective, just showing the more important and exciting hands, deceptive play is inevitably over-represented in the hands that make it on screen.

And finally, we hope we won't cause offence if we remind you that professionals really know what they're doing. They have good enough judgment to make those difficult deceptive plays work, at least more often than not.

All in all, it's safest not to try to emulate the professionals' style of play unless you're playing under similar circumstances, and to a good standard.

Chapter Eleven:
Playing styles

We discussed this topic briefly earlier on in the book, now we'll look at it in a little more detail.

If you're not entirely new to the game of poker, you'll soon notice that everybody has their own style of play. Some players play a lot of hands, whereas others play relatively few. Some players bet and raise a lot, whereas others are more passive. In fact, everybody has their own *unique* style of play, since no two players will always play identically in every situation. To make things even more complicated, many players *change* their style of play over time, and even within the space of a single session.

There are many possible reasons why any particular player should adopt a certain style. It may suit their personality, or may simply reflect how they believe the game should be played. There is however no single 'best' style with which to play the game, and there is considerable variation in styles even amongst the top professionals. There are nonetheless many styles which are clearly sub-optimal, as we'll shortly see.

Know your opponents

As well as concentrating on developing a good playing style of your own, it's important to try to understand your *opponents'* styles, and hence how they are likely to play in any given situation. If you know your opponent well, you have a better idea of what kind of cards he might be holding, and how he's likely to play against you in the remainder of the hand – all to your advantage.

Despite this rather obvious observation, most poker players actually pay relatively little attention to hands in which they're not involved. They chat, look around, daydream, in fact they do anything but study their opponents.

Don't make the same mistake. Keep an eye on your opponents at all times, and watch their betting patterns. Whenever they bet or fold, think about how they played earlier on in the hand, and what it might mean for the type of player they are.

When they show down a hand, you should pay particular attention. Don't just look at the cards, but review their betting throughout the entire hand and adjust your assessment of them as a player if necessary.

Categorisation of playing styles

Ideally you would compile a complete dossier (mental or otherwise) on each of your opponents' playing habits, for example:

- Do they frequently make continuation bets? Do they make speculative continuation bets?
- Do they ever bluff or slowplay? Continually or intermittently?
- Do they check-raise? Do they bluff check-raise?
- Do they call without the proper odds when drawing?

But this rarely turns out to be practical – it's simply too difficult and time-consuming.

Luckily it's possible to categorise players in a much simpler, more broad brush manner. We can still make useful generalisations about the merits of each style, and how best to play against them, but the task is far more manageable this way. (That's not to say that you shouldn't attempt to make a more detailed and refined analysis of your own. The better you know your opponents, the more money you can extract from them.)

In this chapter we will concentrate mainly on two specific categorisations of playing style:

- loose / tight
- passive / aggressive.

We'll take a closer look at each of these in turn.

Loose / tight

We say that a player is loose if they play a lot of hands, and that they are tight if they play relatively few hands. Of course, this implies that there is a whole spectrum of looseness and tightness, from the real gamblers who seem to play almost every hand even if it kills them, to the bores who sit there folding hand after hand until they pick up a monster.

It's possible to be loose in some aspects of your play and tight in others. A trait that is relatively common amongst inexperienced and poor players, for example, is:

- to play too loose pre-flop, essentially calling with anything in the hope of hitting a hand.
- to play too tight post-flop, only hanging around if the flop hits them hard.

In general however, loose players are loose most of the time, and tight players are tight most of the time. If you watch a player for a few hands, you should be able to form a judgment on which they are. If they are calling most hands pre-flop, they're loose. If they show down trash or under-strength hole cards, you know they're loose. If on the other hand they don't seem to enter that many hands at all, and show down only good cards, then you should conclude that they're tight.

Tight is good

Now here's the question: how loose or tight should you play? This is a tough question to answer, but consider this. Only one player can win each pot (split pots excepted). At a ten-seater table, you will on average win only one in every ten pots. You might, if you're a good player, win a little more often than this, although not much more. (Good players tend to make their edge by winning more on the hands that they win and losing less on the hands that they don't win, rather than by winning a higher percentage of hands.) Furthermore, every pot in which you play but don't win costs you money. So, quite simply, don't play too many pots – keep your game tight.

If you follow our guidelines for pre-flop play, you'll probably be playing tighter than maybe 90% of the players you come up against, assuming you're playing at low stakes. But that's simply because these players are playing too loose. If they didn't have such obvious flaws in their game, they'd make more money and probably be playing at higher stakes. If you play tighter than the majority of your opponents at low stakes, most of the time you'll make money.

One reason why many people play too loose is that it can be boring folding hand after hand. If you'd rather play more hands and lose money, that's naturally your decision. A better cure for boredom might be to find ways to keep yourself interested when you're *not* in the hand – for instance by observing your opponents carefully and learning their habits as we recommend above. When you play online, you may choose to play more than one table at a time, so you still get to play a good number of hands even though you're playing tight.

Interestingly, you may find that one time when your opponents are *not* playing too loose is when you're at shorter-handed tables, with perhaps six players or fewer. The reason being that many players don't adjust their strategy properly for short-handed play. As we saw earlier, the fewer opponents you face, the looser you can afford to be. But many weaker players play a very similar strategy in short-handed games to the one they play in fuller games, or at the very least they don't adjust their game sufficiently. If you're playing short-handed, don't forget to loosen up accordingly – every hand becomes more valuable.

But not too tight

Although playing too tight is generally a far less common and serious mistake than playing too loose, it can still cost you money. If you are too tight then:

- You won't win enough pots, and the blinds will eat your stack faster.

- You won't get so much action on the hands you do play – because other players will know that you get involved only with very strong hands.

So don't forget that poker is a gambling game. You have to give action to get action, and you have to take some risks to reap rewards. The very best players are able to tread this line well and play the 'right' number of hands.

Once you've been playing for a while you should be able to do so too – as long as you keep thinking about the number of hands you play and whether you might make more profit by playing either fewer or more.

Passive / aggressive

Whereas tightness is a measure of how *many* hands somebody plays, whether they are passive or aggressive depends on *how* they play the hands in which they are involved.

A player is said to be passive if they tend to check / call much more than they bet or raise, whereas aggressive players will bet or raise proportionally much more of the time. We also say that a player is aggressive if, when they bet, they bet a relatively large amount of money. Betting small on the other hand is a passive trait.

If you're new to the categorisations of playing style introduced in this chapter, you may find the distinction between tight / loose and passive / aggressive rather difficult to appreciate at first. Just try to keep in mind that:

■ how loose you are depends on how often you get involved in a hand at all, and how far you take the hands you do play.
■ how aggressive you are depends on how often you bet or raise compared with the number of times you merely call, and how much you bet.

Aggressive is good

Just as most players play too loose, and cost themselves money as a result, most players are also too passive in their betting. They do plenty of calling, but don't bet or raise often enough. This is largely because, psychologically, it's much easier to *conform* than to stand out – and in poker, conforming means calling. Betting and raising are inherently risky and conspicuous events, and many people aren't that comfortable behaving in this way.

But there is a hard truth here: if you want to make money playing poker, you *must* develop an aggressive playing style. All successful players are very aggressive when the situation demands it, and you must learn to do the same.

The fundamental reason why poker rewards aggression is this: betting is *better* than calling. This is an important idea, and perhaps a surprising one if you're new to it.

It's also a fairly big and bold generalisation, and like all generalisations it has its exceptions. But when you bet (and we're including raising here too) you simply have so many more ways to win money than when you call. Here are a few of them:

1. When you bet, you might win the pot right there (if everyone folds).

2. When you bet, you might not win the pot, but you might force players to fold who otherwise would have stayed in and drawn out on you.

3. When you bet, you might get called by weaker hands who are putting money into a pot in which you have an advantage.

4. When you bet, you might get called by stronger hands but end up the winner anyway (as often happens with a semi-bluff).

5. When you bet, you create harder decisions for your opponents, making it easier for them to make mistakes.

6. When you bet, you usually gain more information from your opponents than you otherwise would, because it forces them to act again, and to act in the face of greater strength from you. As well as earning extra money on the hands you win, betting can – paradoxically – often save you money on the hands you lose because of this information that it solicits.

7. When you bet frequently, you often win more money on your legitimately strong hands, because other players perceive you as someone who bets freely.

This list isn't exhaustive although it encompasses the key advantages. Look down the list and think about what happens when you merely play a check / call strategy. All those lovely ways to extract profit from your opponents are lost.

Admittedly, betting doesn't confer advantages in *all* situations, but most players simply don't appreciate how valuable aggression is. It's possible to be too aggressive and cost yourself money, but there aren't many players at this end of the spectrum. There are usually more weak players sitting at the table endlessly calling and calling, costing themselves money all the while.

Note: calling too much can be a symptom either of playing too *loose* (if you call when you should be folding) or of playing too *passively* (when you call instead of betting or raising). Or it can be a symptom of both.

The gap concept

Now, here's a very interesting and quite subtle point. Because betting is *better* than calling (i.e. it gives you more ways to win), you can often bet with a hand that wouldn't be strong enough to merit a call were somebody else to bet. Let's have a quick example to show you what we mean.

Suppose you're sitting on the button with a very mediocre hand like:

This hand – as you know – is trash and you're probably going to throw it away when the betting comes round to you. But as the round progresses, everyone ahead of you is folding and nobody apart from the blinds is in the pot as yet. Suddenly you're thinking that you might actually play the hand. If they *all* fold to you, you're in a three-way pot with the two blinds, each of whom are playing any two cards. K♣ 8♥ is actually a pretty good hand in these circumstances, and very likely to be winning. You resolve to make a raise of three times the big blind if you get into that position.

But just when it looks like that's about to happen, the player to your right puts in a raise of his own, of three times the big blind. What should you do? You're now looking at a four-way pot and one of your opponents likes his hand enough to have raised. All of a sudden your K♣ 8♥ is feeling pretty sorry for itself. You fold.

So what happened? You had a hand with which you were happy to raise if nobody else had done so, but which didn't even merit a call once another player had bet. In other words, a hand can be strong enough to raise with, but not strong enough to call with. You often need to be *stronger* to call a bet than to make bet or raise of your own, because when you call you lose the advantages that betting or raising confers, and because your opponents have shown greater strength.

This excellent idea – known as the gap concept – was first described by poker author and player David Sklansky. The *gap* is the difference in strength between a hand that merits a bet of its own, and a hand that merits a call if somebody else has bet. The size of the gap varies depending on the circumstances.

A detailed discussion of the gap concept would go beyond the scope of this book, but fortunately you don't need a complete grasp of the theory in order to be a competent player. They key fact to remember is that you can often bet, or even raise, with hands that you wouldn't dream of calling with.

Good players tend to call in much fewer situations than weaker players, preferring instead either to raise or to fold. They will push an edge (by betting or raising) when they perceive that they have one, but often back off (by folding) in the face of any serious resistance. If a good player gets involved in a pot at all, they usually like to be the aggressor.

Extreme aggression

Some of the most conspicuously successful players in the world adopt a very aggressive style of poker, often referred to as *super-aggressive*. Such players are not only more aggressive, but usually a little looser than most of their peers. Super-aggressive players often bet and raise with under-strength hands, and then use more aggression – and their good judgment – to keep themselves out of trouble. They are hard to read because they play a wider variety of cards than most of us would, and their good hands are often paid off handsomely as a result.

The super-aggressive style, in the hands of a player who knows how to use it well, is a potent weapon – plus exciting to behold and rather glamorous. It's no wonder that so many players try to play this way. We would however urge you not to try to adopt such a style early in your poker career. Playing this aggressively *can* be highly effective, but it requires extremely good judgment to make it work. It can be very effective against tight, conservative opponents, and is also well suited to short-handed and tournament play. But it won't work so well in flabby low-stakes games where nobody ever seems to fold.

By all means aspire to become a super-aggressive player if you wish. But first make sure that your skills are up to scratch and that you select the right games in which to employ this style.

Specific player types

We've now identified two distinct categorisations of playing style, tight / loose and passive / aggressive. Each category represents a whole spectrum of behaviour, with players fitting in at some point along each scale. A player may be extremely loose, extremely tight, or anywhere in between. Similarly they may be extremely passive, extremely aggressive, or somewhere in the middle.

There is no particular reason why a player's behaviour in relation to one category should affect or correlate with his behaviour in relation to the other. Tight players can be passive or aggressive, as can loose players. If we look at the two categories in *combination*, we end up with four distinct playing styles:

- Loose-passive
- Tight-passive
- Loose-aggressive
- Tight-aggressive.

Whenever you play poker, you should observe your opponents closely and try to determine what particular kind of style they play. Then you can use that information against them. You should also take note of each player's dress, manner and habits, because it's amazing how frequently poker style correlates well with these characteristics.

Let's take each player type in turn and have a brief look at their profiles.

Loose-passive players are often referred to as *calling stations*. They play too many hands, and they play those hands passively, checking and calling along rather than betting or raising. When they do actually bet or raise, you know they've probably got a great hand and you should steer clear. Calling stations give other players action when they bet, but they don't get action for themselves when they want it. They are great to play against because they're so easy to beat.

Calling stations are more likely than average to be:

- friendly, amiable and laid back
- not particularly loud or brash
- generally indistinctive and dressed unremarkably
- a little dishevelled or untidy.

Tight-passive players are often called *rocks*. They play few hands, and don't bet or raise very aggressively in the hands they do play. This lack of aggression means that rocks find it hard to win much money. But their tightness means that they don't lose very much either. Trying to get money out of a rock is like trying to get blood out of a stone. Sometimes they can make rather dull opposition as a result.

Rocks are more likely than average to be:

■ reserved and self-disciplined
■ neat and tidy
■ careful and deliberate when stacking their chips and making bets
■ less obviously involved in the action than other players.

Loose-aggressive players are known as *maniacs*. They like to gamble, and they like to gamble big. Maniacs bet or raise at every opportunity, and don't worry too much if it doesn't seem to be quite in their interests to do so. Maniacs usually lose their money quickly, but they can sometimes make a lot of money if they hit a good run of cards. For most people, playing against maniacs is fun – and quite scary.

Maniacs are more likely than average to be:

■ loud and brash
■ wearing flashy or ostentatious clothing
■ visibly hyped up or hurried
■ clumsy and careless
■ fond of bragging
■ overtly confrontational.

Tight-aggressive players don't seem to have a specific nick-name for some reason. Not all tight-aggressive players are good – playing winning poker is about more than merely adopting the right style – but almost all good players are tight-aggressive. Playing against tight-aggressive opponents is very difficult. They'll constantly put you to tough decisions for large amounts of money, and you may often find yourself folding with winning hands or calling with losing ones.

Tight-aggressive players are more likely than average to be:

- controlled and disciplined
- neat and tidy
- alert, involved and concentrating on the action
- perhaps not particularly sociable
- winning!

As well as observing your opponents, you should also develop a self-awareness about your own playing style, and strive to improve it.

Most inexperienced players would benefit from playing both tighter and more aggressively, although this isn't always an intuitive combination. If, for example, you cut down on the number of hands you play, it seems almost natural to play more conservatively (i.e. passively) when you do get involved in a hand. But you should resist that temptation. You need to play relatively few hands, but play those hands strongly. *The tight aggressive style is a winning style.*

Adjusting to your opponents' styles

This is a huge subject and goes well beyond the scope of this book. But we can give you a flavour of the way in which you should be thinking about your opponents and their playing styles, and forming a strategy to beat them.

In this section, when we say, for example, a *loose-passive game*, we mean a game in which the players are exhibiting more loose-passive tendencies than average. But it could also apply where you're in a hand up against one or more loose-passive opponents. We've provided an idealised description of each specific game type but in practice you'll find a mixture of player types at each table, and you'll need to weigh up your options accordingly.

Loose-passive games

Loose-passive games are the easiest and safest to tackle. While your opponents are calling along with under-strength hands and doing very little raising of their own, it shouldn't take you long to get your hands on their money. Here are the key points to bear in mind.

The first observation to make is that many pots will be multi-way, because many players are calling and few are raising. As a result:

- it's harder to protect your winning hands – the opposition aren't easily shaken off.
- you will usually have better pot odds (effective and implied) than normal because of the number of opponents and their tendency to pay you off if you make a hand.
- you will on average need to show down a better hand than usual to win, because of the number of players chasing all the way to the river.

This in turn means that your medium strength made hands become more vulnerable. You will need to bet them more strongly (i.e. be more aggressive) in order to stop one of the pack from outdrawing you, or make them pay to try to do so. If you hit a high pair pre-flop, you should make a larger bet than normal to try to thin the field to the one or two callers you desire. Or if you hit two pair on the flop, you should bet it strongly to discourage callers with weak hands hitting a better two pair or trips on the turn or river.

You also need to be a touch more reluctant to play high card hands such as, for example, ace-queen and ace-jack. Even if you flop top pair with these hands, with a large number of players seeing the flop, you are that much more likely to be up against a better hand still or to get outdrawn by the showdown.

Whereas made hands and high cards are more vulnerable under these circumstances, drawing hands become much more tempting. In loose-passive games you can call with drawing hands in situations that would normally be unplayable. The larger number of callers and reduced risk of a raise behind you make for ideal drawing hand territory. Related to this, position generally becomes relatively less significant when your opponents are passive.

You should be less inclined to bluff or semi-bluff in loose-passive games. Since your opponents are loose, they will more readily call your bluffs, making them fail. Slowplays are similarly less advisable. Your opponents will be inclined to call you, even when your hand is strong, reducing the incentive to disguise your strength. And since your opponents are passive too, they won't do your betting for you – this scuppers both slowplays and check-raises.

If you have a strong hand, you should usually bet it. In short, deception is a less effective weapon in loose-passive games – just stick to value-based plays.

Finally, since your opponents are passive, you know they'll usually only bet or raise with relatively strong hands. Therefore calling bets or raises with marginal hands is a bad idea.

Summary: loose-passive games

- Downgrade the value of your high-card hands and made hands.
- Upgrade the value of your drawing hands.
- Worry a little less about position.
- Employ straightforward value-based plays rather than using deception.
- Bet more aggressively when you believe you're in the lead.
- Be less inclined to call with marginal hands.

Loose-aggressive games

Loose-aggressive games are usually some of the most exciting and profitable games in which to be involved. The betting is fast and furious, bluffs are frequent, and the pots can be huge. Because of their volatility however, these games can also be the most expensive if you play poorly or get unlucky.

JOE PERFORMED BEST IN AGGRESSIVE GAMES!

Loose-aggressive games have certain features in common with loose-passive games. Because of the numbers of players in the pot, for example, you should still value drawing hands more highly, and made hands less so. You should still bet your winning hands aggressively to make opponents pay to try draw out on you, and bluffing is again fairly pointless since it's that much less likely to succeed.

But other forms of deception become more effective. Check-raising and slowplaying work well because your loose-aggressive opponents will do your betting for you. This is particularly true when there are other, not quite so loose players in the pot too. The maniacs' betting will attract the tighter players' money, since the latter will expect the maniac to be betting with under-strength hands. That leaves you to step in and pick up a nice big pot once you decide it's time to reveal your strength.

There is a flip side to this of course, namely that *you* shouldn't concentrate so much on the maniacs that you ignore any quieter, less conspicuous players guarding a big hand of their own. Don't let a maniac run you into a monster, as the poker saying goes.

Playing a hand to the river can be quite expensive in a loose-aggressive game. Therefore you want to play with premium hands rather than marginal ones. You should tighten up accordingly, especially as one of the potential downsides of playing tighter – not getting paid off on your good hands – won't apply here.

On the other hand, since your opponents are loose and likely to be playing under-strength cards, you should be more inclined to call with marginal hands in later rounds, particularly on the river.

Summary: loose-aggressive games

- Tighten up your starting hand requirements generally.
- Upgrade the value of your drawing hands.
- Downgrade the value of your high-card hands and made hands.
- Bet more aggressively when you believe you're in the lead.
- Make good use of check-raises and slowplays.
- Call more readily on the turn and river.
- Don't bluff.

Tight-passive games

At the other end of the spectrum to loose-aggressive games are tight-passive games. You may find these eye-wateringly dull – they're hardly rock 'n' roll, just rock 'n' rock! There's a lot of folding, and not much betting and raising. Many pots are won uncontested, as players rush to get out of each other's way. You should be able to make some fairly safe money in these games (because of their passivity) although don't expect to win very much (because of their tightness).

Since most pots are smaller and contested by fewer players, you should downgrade the strength of your drawing hands. When you hit a draw you won't get paid off as well, so the implied odds aren't as favourable. On the other hand, your high cards and made hands become more valuable because it's easier to protect them by betting.

Having said that, it's much harder to bet for value in tight-passive games, the problem being that opponents are generally playing only their stronger hands. When you bet, this makes it much less likely that you'll be called by weaker hands than yours. Therefore you should upgrade your requirements in this respect, i.e. don't bet with medium strength.

With all your opponents playing so tight however, it's much easier for you to steal pots, making bluffs and semi-bluffs more profitable. Tight-passive players don't usually make sneaky plays like check-raises and slowplays so you can be more willing than normal to go out on a limb with your betting, without too much fear of getting in trouble. This is especially true when you're in late position, which is conducive to stealing and bluffing when your opponents have checked. Like your opponents, you too should avoid check-raises and slowplays since nobody else will do your betting for you.

When you come up against a tight-passive opponent who starts betting or raising, you know they've got a big hand. Steer clear unless you've got the goods.

Summary: tight-passive games

- Upgrade the value of your high-card hands and made hands.
- Downgrade the value of your drawing hands.
- Be more prepared to get involved from late position.
- Be less inclined to bet with medium-strength hands, and don't push these hands too far.
- Bluff and semi-bluff more often with weak hands and drawing hands.
- Avoid check-raises and slowplays.

Tight-aggressive games

Tight-aggressive games will be full of players who ... well, who are like you! There won't be too many people in each pot, but the betting will be strong and the play of a good standard (usually, anyway – tight-aggressive players are rarely poor players). The big swings will come when two or more of the players have a legitimate hand simultaneously, and both are trying to push their perceived edge. Many other hands will fizzle out early however as a big bet takes down the pot. You'll find it hard to make money in tight-aggressive games, and it will often feel uncomfortable when you're forced to make tough decisions for a lot of chips.

Since other players are playing tight, you're going to need to play tight too. When those tough decisions come along, you won't want to be sitting there with a marginal hand. As with tight-passive games, you need a stronger hand than normal to bet for value.

There's no need to show any particular bias to either made hands or drawing hands however. Made hands can easily be protected by betting. Drawing hands will usually have inferior effective pot odds – because of the lack of players in each pot – but good implied odds. If you hit a drawing hand against an aggressive opponent holding a good, second-best hand, you can really clean up.

Tight-aggressive players are often sneaky, using check-raises and slowplays to throw their opponents off-guard, and you need to do the same. If an aggressive player is bullying you off the pot with under-strength bets and raises, then you need to defend yourself.

Drop in an occasional check-raise or slowplay, and that should make him back off a little. Bluffing should also be more successful if judiciously used, since your opponents won't hang around with weak hands in the face of strong betting.

Position becomes much more important in tight-aggressive games since each hand is less about hand strength, and more about achieving dominance in the confrontations that arise. Being in late position in the hands you play will help you achieve that dominance more easily.

Summary: tight-aggressive games

■ Be tight and aggressive yourself.
■ Give more weight to good position.
■ Use all forms of deception more frequently.
■ Be less inclined to bet with medium-strength hands, and don't push these hands too far.

Table image

Hopefully by now you've got a good idea of the importance of playing style, and why you need to make judgments on the styles adopted by your opponents. We'll now consider in a little more detail the relevance of a player's *perceived* style to how he and his opponents play.

The term *table image* is used to describe how a player is thought of by the other players in the game at any given point in time. Table image encompasses not only playing style but also any other observable traits that a player may demonstrate, i.e. whether the player is any or all of the following:

■ Loose or tight
■ Passive or aggressive
■ Weak or strong (i.e. a bad player or a good one)
■ Predictable or volatile
■ Calm or upset

and so on.

Weak players usually won't think too hard about other players' table image – they can't see the relevance. They're quite happy to bet their own cards and not worry about these sorts of details. Stronger players on the other hand will pay much closer attention. If you observe a player carefully for a period of time, you may well be able to draw your own conclusions about each of the above, and your profits should improve as a result.

False table images

But here's the interesting thing: a player's table image won't always match the way they are actually playing or feeling. Why not? Because poker is a game of imperfect information. You don't know what cards your opponent is playing, and you don't know what they're actually thinking or feeling inside, try as you might to guess.

Ok, you may say, but why is this relevant? Let's take an example to illustrate. Suppose you sit down at a table with players you don't know particularly well. Within the first fifteen hands, you are dealt some amazing cards: a couple of big pairs, flopped two pair and trips, and so on. Each time you've played these cards very conservatively and rationally, raising pre-flop when it's required, and betting out in the later rounds as you should. But none of the hands you've played has actually reached showdown.

What must your opponents be thinking? They *might* be thinking – wow, this chap must have had some good cards. But, if they're switched on, they're instead probably somewhat suspicious, and thinking – hmm...this guy seems to be a very loose-aggressive player...he's in every hand. From their point of view, this latter conclusion is more likely to fit with the facts with which they've been presented.

The upshot is that you're now in a situation where you're playing sensible, conservative poker, but your opponents think you're a maniac! Some immediate consequences of this for the ensuing play are as follows:

■ You're not very likely to be able to bluff successfully. Next time you bet, because your opponents think you're a maniac, they're not going to give much respect to your hand. Similarly, they won't try to bluff you as readily – you can't bluff a player as loose as you appear to be.

■ Your opponents are more likely to check-raise and slowplay you, since that's good strategy against a maniac. You're going to have to watch out for that.

■ If you hit *another* good hand, your opponents are unlikely to credit it, and they should pay you off nicely. There's no point slowplaying or check-raising with it – just come out and bet it like you have been. It's disguised enough as it is.

So you can see that, simply because you've been dealt a good run of cards that were hidden, you would now be well advised to change the way you play, namely to tighten up and be more aggressive.

Exploiting a false image

But crucially you should also realise that you also have obtained an *on-going* benefit from this run of cards: your good hands are now better disguised. Recall from Chapter Ten that deception is usually a double-edged sword: it misleads your opponent but it destroys your own value. Currently, however, you're in the absolutely wonderful position of being able *to deceive your opponents whilst still making value-based plays.* When you come out betting with a good hand, your opponents just won't actually believe it.

In general, there are many ways that your table image might not match the way you're actually playing, thinking or feeling. For example:

- Your image is loose-aggressive when you're actually playing conservatively (as above).
- Your image is very tight when you're actually playing fairly loose – this could happen when you've had a long run of unplayable hands.
- Your image is weak when you're actually a strong player – e.g. if you make a conspicuously bad play in a hand or two for some reason.
- Your opponents think you're *on tilt* (playing poorly because you're upset or angry) when you're in fact in full control of your game – this could occur if you lose a big hand, and then pick up a couple of good hands immediately afterwards that you bet strongly but don't show down. It might appear that you're simply being reckless.

Whenever you are sitting at a poker table, you should always be asking yourself what your opponents' perception of you is likely to be. If you think there is a discrepancy between this perception and the actuality, then you should exploit that as far as possible. Try to play in a way that seems to conform to your opponents' expectations, while actually confounding them. You tend to make most of your money in poker when you're playing in a way that's directly *opposite* to how your opponents perceive you.

In the example discussed above, where you are incorrectly considered a maniac, you might decide to try the following approach:

- Loosen up a little pre-flop while the pots are small and you can afford to take a bit of a risk.

- Make some speculative calls or raises to further foster your maniacal image.
- While playing these 'extra' hands, you hope to hit a monster. When you do, it's surely pay day.

As always though, try to avoid receiving a dose of your own medicine – your opponents may be trying to exploit their images just as much as you are. By observing them as carefully as possible, you can minimise your risk of being caught out.

Manipulating your table image

We've now seen the benefits that a false image, once established, can confer. In the example above, that false image was delivered courtesy of a run of very good, hidden cards. In general, though, you can't afford to wait around for the fickle finger of fate to hand you such opportunities. Instead you should endeavour to create a false image yourself.

There are several things you can do to go about creating a table image that doesn't quite correspond to your true playing style. The two that we'll consider here are:

- Changing gears
- Advertising.

Changing gears

When you deliberately switch to a different playing style mid-way through a session, you are said to have *changed gears*. If you've been playing tight for a while, for example, then you might try loosening up for a few hands. Or if you've been playing in a somewhat loose or aggressive manner, you might just quieten down for a few hands and see what happens.

By changing gears in this way you make yourself much less predictable, and more likely to catch your opponents off-guard. It gives you a greater chance of deceiving them as to the true strength of your hands, which in turn should earn you extra profit.

Changing gears isn't always easy, not least from a psychological perspective. It can be difficult to play in a way that doesn't suit your natural game, taking you out of your comfort zone, but there is no doubt that you will in the long run benefit from the practice and experience. Doing so will also help you develop a better feel for which styles work in which circumstances, thereby improving your overall game.

As with many of these more advanced techniques, you shouldn't bother changing gears when you're up against weaker players. They won't notice what you're doing, so just play a steady, conservative game and rake in their money. But with tougher opponents, you need to keep moving so they can't get too much of a handle on your game.

Advertising

In a general sense, the term *advertising* can describe anything you do at the poker table to give others an impression of the way you play, representative or otherwise. It is however usually applied in a more specific sense, meaning to show down your cards voluntarily when you're not obliged to. For example:

- if you are playing loose, you may show down a good hand or two, to make your opponents think you're playing tight
- if you are playing tight, you may intermittently show down a bluff or under-strength hand, to make your opponents think you're playing loose.

We suggest that in general you don't show *every* hand simply because it gives away too much information about how you play. (This doesn't necessarily apply if you're not worried about making as much money as possible. If you're playing with friends, for example, showing your cards can make the whole game more interesting and educational.)

It may seem to you that showing down an occasional hand won't fool anyone – they'll just assume that the rest of the time you're playing completely differently. But psychologically it doesn't work like that because people remember what they see much more than what they don't see.

If you show a few strong hands, your opponents will be much more likely to think you're strong in the future and steer clear of you. If you show a few weak hands, they'll tend to give you more action.

You can also try to build associations and images in your opponents' minds. When you advertise to your opponents, it creates a picture for them that links the way you played that hand – including your mannerisms, betting patterns, etc. – with the cards you actually held. When you then play subsequent hands in a similar manner, your opponents are more likely to suspect you of having similar cards, or similar strength.

This effect can be magnified if your mannerisms are distinctive. So if you push your chips quickly and firmly into the middle and then show a bluff when your opponent folds, next time you should try doing the same thing with a legitimate hand. If you've created a strong enough association between the mannerism and your cards in your opponent's mind, they might call even with a weak hand.

In short, clever use of advertising can help you deceive your opponents without actually departing from value-based play.

Chapter Twelve:
Poker psychology

Up until now, we've largely discussed hold'em strategy in a rather dispassionate way. We've talked about how to find the correct play in the various situations you'll encounter, for the most part based on a rational analysis of the factors in play and some relatively simple mathematics. We haven't really said anything of substance that you couldn't, for example, try to teach a computer.

Therefore we have, with the odd exception, ignored the *human* element of the game. Whilst, for example, a computer poker program wouldn't get tired, stressed, cross or misread the board, humans frequently do. A computer would bet in the same, monotonous fashion every time regardless of what it held. And it certainly wouldn't give anything away about the strength of its hand by the way it handled its chips or talked to its opponents. But humans often do.

In this chapter, we acknowledge the frailties of the human mind, and how it sometimes lets us down by revealing more than we want to reveal, or inexplicably behaving in a way that we almost know to be against our own best interests.

But, by doing so, we also acknowledge one of the great *strengths* of the human mind – our sometimes uncanny ability to pick up on the presence and meanings of these behaviours and subconscious signals in other humans. The challenge will be to use this ability to our advantage, whilst at the same time minimising the unwanted intrusion of human flaws into our game.

Tells

Here's our first example of human frailty then, and how you can ruthlessly exploit it. In poker, a *tell* (derived from *telegraph*) is a clue you obtain about your opponent's hand, or its strength, from the way that he behaves.

If you haven't played that much live poker before then you might imagine that this is a very significant element of the game. The poker players you see on television often scrutinise their opponents closely for long periods, or encourage them to talk about their hands, in order to extract from them the information they need to make their decisions. In practice however:

- It is actually harder than you might imagine to obtain useful information from players this way, certainly much harder than getting information from their betting patterns and playing styles.
- Tells are never going to be 100% reliable and shouldn't be used as a substitute for solid and intelligent all-round play.

Notwithstanding these caveats, tells can be extremely useful if you can spot them. Some people are better than others in this respect, and some of the top players are capable of truly remarkable reads of their opponents based purely on tells. Whether or not *you* have any innate ability in this area is something you will need to find out. Like all aspects of poker, however, you'll need to work at it too in order to fulfil your potential.

You also need to be aware that your opponents will be trying to identify *your* tells to extract information from you. Where possible, we've provided advice on how to thwart their evil plans.

Many of the ideas in this chapter have been extensively discussed in publications by Mike Caro, the self-styled 'Mad Genius of Poker', who has done an enormous amount of research into the topic.

Tells are specific to individuals

The first thing to observe is that certain tells may manifest themselves in completely different ways in different players. There's no use looking at a player for the first time when you find yourself head-up against him in a huge pot. You may be able to discern something in his behaviour at that point that helps you, but it's more likely that you won't.

Instead, reading tells is like reading betting patterns, which we discussed in the previous chapter. Just as you need to study a player for a while to form an idea of how he bets in each particular situation, you also need to study him to see which tells, if any, he exhibits in each situation.

For example, one player might push their chips into the middle carefully when they have a legitimate hand, but toss them in carelessly when they bluff. Another player might do the precise opposite. Unless you've been watching a player closely, you won't have any idea what that specific behaviour means in their specific case.

You also need to be aware that tells, even when you've identified them, aren't always 100% reliable. Just because a player tossed his chips in carelessly the last two times he bluffed, that doesn't mean he'll do so next time. The more you study your opponents, the more you should be able to form an opinion on the *reliability* of any tells you discover.

You can get most information from a player when he isn't aware that he's being watched. Therefore, try to do your watching reasonably covertly. One of the best times to watch other players is when they're looking at cards – either their hole cards or the board cards. While everyone is looking at the flop, turn or river being dealt, you should take the opportunity to watch your opponents watching the cards. There's plenty of time for you to look at the board cards yourself once you've noted your opponents' reactions.

In this section, we'll make a few generalisations about tells that usually have the same meaning regardless of who exhibits them. But for the most part we simply highlight the kinds of behaviour that might be revealing, without being able to say exactly what they reveal. You can use the generalisations as rules of thumb when you first come up against players with whom you're unfamiliar. But eventually you should try to identify behaviours specific to each player in each separate circumstance.

Are they acting?

Before you start reading very much into an opponent's behaviour, you first need to ask yourself whether he is acting or not, by which we mean, is he self-consciously trying to affect a particular manner. Most poker players spend the majority of their time at the table behaving normally and naturally, but then become more self-conscious when they get involved in significant pots.

Here's an example. You may be chatting away quite happily, swigging your beer, when suddenly you look down and find you have been dealt a pair of aces. There is a caller or two in front of you – and then a player raises! It's almost impossible not to get a little excited in this situation. You start imagining how much you might win, and the adrenalin starts to flow. No sooner has that happened than you realise you need to get a grip. You resolve not to let your excitement show.

But as soon as this thought has crossed your mind, you're in acting territory. You might try to lock down your behaviour in an attempt not to give anything away, or you might affect even greater casualness or animation. There are any number of things you might do, as we will see. The common theme though is that you will inevitably try to behave in a way that is inconsistent with the way you're feeling – and human beings aren't always very good at that.

So, at any moment in time a poker player may be acting, or not acting. Either way, you can potentially glean information from him, but you need to interpret his behaviour differently in each case. Of course, it won't always be apparent whether or not he's acting. In general, a player is liable to start acting whenever:

- he puts in a big bet
- he is involved in a big pot
- he picks up good cards or has a big hand
- he makes a big bluff.

The first two are self-evident from the context; whether or not the second two may apply is what you're trying to find out.

Weak means strong and strong means weak

Here's one of the most obvious principles underlying many tells you will receive from players *that you believe to be acting*, namely that they act in a manner which suggests weakness when their hand is strong, and which suggests strength when their hand is weak.

Let's suppose you've just made a big bluff at a pot on the river and your opponent is considering whether to call. Obviously you want your opponent to fold, so what are you going to do? Instinctively you're going to pretend that you have a great hand. You might therefore, for example:

- stare down your opponent or look defiant to show you're not afraid (when in fact you are)
- start chatting to them in a way that looks like you are relaxed and welcome a call
- reach for your chips to give the impression that you're going to call any potential re-raise.

But do you think that any of these are going to work against a shrewd player? What would you instead do if you had bet with a great hand? In this case you would be desperate for a call. You would deliberately avoid behaving in a manner suggesting strength because it might scare your opponent off. You perhaps would:

- look down, or away from your opponent
- not say very much
- act in a way designed to convey apprehension.

It is very natural for humans to engage in such *first order* deceptions, i.e. to act in a way that is entirely opposite to how they feel, but this can make them easy to read. All players know instinctively not to jump up and down when they pick up a straight flush. What the unsophisticated player often doesn't realise is how transparent it can be to attempt to appear, say, bored or concerned instead.

With practice you should be able to spot some of these first order deceptions in your opponents. If you're up against an unsophisticated player who you expect to be acting, you can often reason that he is acting in a manner opposite to the way he really feels. Weak means strong, and strong means weak.

If your opponent knows full well that you would never be fooled by a first order deception he might attempt a *second order* deception, or *double bluff*, if you prefer. This is where a player decides to act in a way consistent with the way he feels, rather than opposite to it. In this case, he might actually decide to smile when he hits a straight flush!

As a result, you should be less willing to conclude that 'weak means strong and strong means weak' when your opponent is sophisticated.

We could take this even further and start worrying about triple and quadruple bluffs, but it soon becomes rather pointless. Whenever a poker player is acting, he *wants* you to behave in a certain way, regardless of whatever theatre he performs. It's up to you to try to pick up on that – and then disappoint him.

You should also take care to avoid giving out such information yourself. The most effective way is simply to act the same way all the time, regardless of whether you're weak or strong. You don't have to worry about double or triple bluffs if you just stare downwards, impassively and silently, and wait for your opponent to act. Sure, it can be fun trying to lure in a losing call or induce a bad fold, but it can also backfire. Why not just duck out and avoid giving away any valuable clues?

General demeanour

If you believe a player *not to be acting*, for example when it's early in the hand or when he has no reason to think that anybody is studying him, you should be able to glean some information from his general behaviour. If he is looking bored or distracted, is reclining, or is engaged in conversation with others, he is less likely to have a good hand. If he is concentrating, more involved in the hand, or sat closer to the table, he is more likely to have something playable. (Remember, however, that the opposite may well be true once a player has started acting.)

Make sure you take the time to study your opponents' demeanour, and ask yourself if you could imagine each of them behaving that way with (a) a weak hand and (b) a strong hand. You should ideally conduct this exercise right from the beginning of the hand. If you wait till the point where you really need the information, i.e. when you're mid-confrontation with a particular player, he will by then invariably be acting. If you'd studied him right from the start, you might have had the opportunity to pick up some extra signals before any self-consciousness kicked in.

Speed of action

Sometimes players reveal information about the strength of their hand by the amount of time it takes them to bet.

Simplistically, a player who takes longer than normal to make a decision usually has a difficult decision. Beware of actors here however. Suppose you had raised pre-flop with a pair of aces, and another player now re-raises you, you would usually be well advised to *appear* to be contemplating a difficult decision before moving all-in. By doing so, you are much more likely to tempt in a (highly desirable) call from another big pair.

In contrast, a player who makes a quick decision usually has an easy decision. But note that that player may have been able to start thinking about his decision well in advance of his turn, while other players are acting, or even on the previous round of betting. A player on a draw and out of position might resolve to bet on the river regardless of what comes – as a bluff if he misses, or for value if he hits.

It normally requires a few seconds' preparation to make a bluff, to consider the likelihood of success and summon up the courage. But bluffs can be all the more convincing if planned in advance, and delivered quickly and smoothly. As far as possible, try to think about the future eventualities that might arise in a hand, so you're fully prepared whatever happens

In general you should avoid making decisions instantly, so other players can't see that you have an easy decision. (The exception being situations like the one described above where you want your opponents to know or believe that your course of action was straightforward.)

Therefore if you take a little time for all your decisions, regardless of whether or not you actually need that time, you don't give any information away. Having said that, if you know you're going to fold, then you should usually just fold quickly – you don't need to worry about giving away information when you're about to exit the hand.

Lying eyes

Some people claim that you can tell a lie by looking a person in the eyes. That may or may not be true, but you can often get a lot of information about what a player is thinking by looking at where they're looking. For example:

- A player looking at their chips is more likely to be thinking about betting. Players will often make an almost involuntary glance at their chips when they first discover they have a good hand.
- Players considering a big decision usually need to be aware of the stack sizes of their opponents. If a player is eyeing up other players' stacks, some big action is likely to ensue.
- A player considering stealing a pot would like to be confident that the players acting after him will lay down their hands. Therefore if a player is looking at the opponents following him to check for their interest levels, that player is more likely to be stealing. A player with a legitimately playable hand is in general likely to be less concerned about the other players at the table.

In order to minimise the chances of revealing too much information in this way, many players decide to wear sunglasses at the table so their opponents can't follow their gaze. Plus it makes them look cool. Well, maybe.

Looking at hole cards

You may sometimes be able to get clues to your opponents' hands by noting how and when they look at their hole cards.

- When players are dealt good hole cards, they frequently linger looking at them, or check them more than once before the flop, just to make sure that they haven't made a mistake.
- Most players remember the numeric value of their cards but often don't remember the suits unless the cards are suited. A player who checks his cards when a monochrome flop falls is likely *not* to have two suited cards, but may possibly have one card in the suit that's on the board.

Many players elect not to look at their hole cards until it's their turn to act. By doing so, they can watch their opponents all the more closely as they look at *their* cards. And by not knowing what they themselves hold, they guarantee not to give away any information about their own hand until the last possible moment.

You may decide to adopt this approach if it works for you, but it has its pitfalls. Firstly you get less time to digest your own holding and work out in advance how you want to play the hand as the betting ahead of you unfolds. Secondly you have to make your entire decision while the eyes of the table are on you, and waiting for you. You may not welcome that sort of pressure, at least until you're a reasonably experienced player.

Anxiety

In some players, you may be able to spot visible signs of anxiety on occasions, for example:

- trembling hands or body
- sweat on hands or head
- deeper or more uneven breathing
- a shaky or higher pitched voice
- visible tics or involuntary movements.

It's also likely that if a player knows you are watching them, any anxiety that they may have been experiencing will be magnified considerably. Therefore, feel free to have a good long stare at them, just to see what happens.

You may be tempted to associate such anxiety most closely with bluffs but, in fact, the reverse is more normally true. Players tend to be at their most anxious when they have a very strong hand and are praying that it will be paid off. Bluffs are normally less stressful since players are often resigned to the possibility of losing the bluff the moment their money goes in the pot, and they're certainly not going to carry on any further if the bluff is called.

If you are the sort of player who has a tendency to make their anxiety visible, and if that bothers you, we suggest you clothe your body and head as fully as possible, and invest in a large bottle of beta blockers. Just kidding!

Facial expressions

Some people have more expressive faces than others. In general, however, most people are pretty difficult to read when they're trying to keep a straight face. Some players wear caps to make themselves more inscrutable.

Chips and hand movements

Many people realise that they have to keep their voice and facial expressions under control, but they may be a little less careful when it comes to their hands and chips. Keep a close eye on how your opponents stack their chips, and how they move their chips into the middle when they bet.

Players often reach for their chips involuntarily if they intend to bet or call, even well before they need to do so. It's always a good idea to look to your left before betting or calling, to see if you can spot an opponent limbering up for action in this way.

Many players often use a movement to their chips as a kind of bluff, in order to discourage a bet. If a player wants a free card, but sees an opponent about to make a bet, he may reach for his chips as if to say "go ahead and bet – I'll call", the intention being to stop the bet in the first place. Assuming this player is acting rather than acting instinctively, it's usually an indication of a weak hand or a drawing hand that wants a free card.

Chat

You will see many professionals try to engage their opponent in conversation when contemplating a big call. They may be looking for signs of stress in their voice or conduct, signs which will be more obvious when a player is doing something rather than doing nothing. They may also be trying to solicit a 'weak means strong, strong means weak' kind of reaction.

As we said earlier, you may be best off keeping silent if somebody starts giving you this treatment. You're not actually obliged to respond, and you can't give anything away if you don't get involved.

Emotional responses to poker

We hope you will agree with us that poker is not a game that benefits from the presence of human emotional responses. An injection of passion and emotion certainly may confer advantages in some sports and activities, but poker simply isn't one of them.

Of course, poker does require a good empathy with the emotional states of others (so they can be exploited!) but your results will be at their best when you are thinking clearly and coldly about the game.

Here's the funny thing, though. You know this to be true; your opponents know it; in fact, we all know it. So why is it sometimes so hard to keep our emotions in check while playing poker?

Bad beats and good beats

Let's set the scene. You're coming to the end of a big hand played against a single opponent. You bet your straight nicely and now you and your opponent are all-in on the turn. You both reveal your hole cards and he shows two pair – you've completely outplayed him. There's several hundred pounds in the pot, and it's almost certainly yours. The only thing that will save your opponent is one of his four full house outs coming on the river – you're more than 90% likely to win.

Well, you know what happens next. The river card matches one of your opponent's hole cards making him a full house, and a winner. You watch in dismay as he gleefully rakes in the chips. Absolutely sickening. How could his 10-to-1 shot have come in!

If something like this hasn't happened to you as yet, you can't have been playing poker very long. It happens all the time, in all sorts of games, to players of all standards. In fact, it's such a common occurrence, it's got a name – *a bad beat*. A bad beat happens when you are favourite to win a hand but get unlucky and lose. The stronger favourite you are, the worse the beat. Losing a huge all-in on a four-outer, as in the story above, is a pretty bad beat.

On a more optimistic note, beats come in another flavour too – *good beats*. The only difference between a bad beat and a good beat is which side of the table you are sitting. A good beat happens when you are underdog to win the hand but get lucky and win. For every bad beat in poker, there is an equal and opposite good beat.

People love telling their bad beat stories to other players, but strangely don't go on quite as much about their good beats. Bad beat tales can be incredibly dramatic, although they're usually not quite as interesting for others as for the person who suffered them.

One thing that is certainly true about bad beats is that they are difficult to take for all but the most clinical of players. Quite apart from how much it hurts to have a large amount of money unjustly denied you at the last minute, there is also a risk of such an event affecting your emotions adversely enough to cause a deterioration in the standard of your play.

Tilt

We say that a player is *on tilt* if, because of a temporary emotional imbalance, he is playing in a way he knows to be sub-optimal. You can be on tilt when you are angry, upset, irritated or frustrated. Sometimes in these states of mind it's very easy to make plays that you know – even at the time – to be wrong. You might start playing too loosely or too aggressively, or bluff too much.

Although bad beats are amongst the most common causes of tilt, they are by no means the only ones. Players may go on tilt if they become emotional for any reason, for example after a dispute with another player or after making a bad or humiliating play.

Every poker player goes on tilt at some point in their careers and you almost certainly will too, if you haven't already, and if you play enough. But some players go on tilt more than others, and it can be very costly. The kinds of behaviour that tilt induces – excessive looseness or aggressiveness – usually results in the loss of significant amounts of money. If you want to be a successful player, you will need to avoid going on tilt too often.

If you observe signs of tilt in one of your opponents, it's up to you whether or not you try to exploit that. You might decide that you'd rather not kick a man when he's down , or you might see it as a good opportunity to get your hands on his stack. Some players will even attempt to *induce* tilt in others, if and when they seem prone to it, by winding them up verbally or making the occasional bad play against them – in the hope of giving them a bad beat.

Living with Lady Luck

Your financial success as a poker player depends on precisely two factors:

- your skill level relative to your opponents.
- the luck that you receive when you play.

The first of these, your skill level, is something over which you have direct control (and we're working on that right now, aren't we?). The second factor – luck – is completely out of your hands.

When things go well, and the money comes rolling in, you may feel you're invincible. Yet just as quickly Lady Luck can turn things on their head, delivering you bad beat after bad beat, and eating up your bankroll. Even if you manage to avoid going on tilt in those circumstances, your game may suffer in other ways, as your diminishing funds and eroded confidence upset the balance of your game.

The fact is, Lady Luck is curiously cold and dispassionate towards us; she favours no man, or woman, over any other. In the long run your bad luck and good luck will even out. As we said right at the start of the book, this is an indisputable mathematical certainty.

Yes, lucky and unlucky streaks happen, but these streaks can be identified only with hindsight. If you've had a bad run of cards, you're no more or less likely to be dealt a good hand *next time* than if you've had a good run. How could it be otherwise? It's not as if the cards have any say in the matter. To all intents and purposes, each new deal is completely random and independent of all previous hands.

Despite this, many people do believe in luck, good and bad, and have superstitions or theories about luck, or *feelings*. By all means, entertain these sorts of ideas if you find them appealing or if they fit with your spiritual leaning. But be aware that in poker every time you make a poor decision based only on a *feeling*, it will cost you money.

If you can, try not to give in to the part of your brain that inevitably wants to see patterns in the luck you receive and instead accept that luck has no pattern. One feeling that you're almost bound to succumb to sooner or later is that you're not getting your fair share of luck, particularly when you get drawn out on for the umpteenth time in a week. This can, quite understandably, be rather hard to take.

Part of the problem is that you may have to play for a surprisingly long period of time before the luck balances itself out. If you play at a ten-seater table, you will win only one hand in ten (on average), and win a *significant* pot maybe only one hand in, say, every forty or so. That's less than one big hand per hour (unless you're playing online – more on that later).

Your biggest financial swings will come in these very big hands, and yet they occur relatively rarely. It only takes a little bad luck in a couple of key hands to destroy a session. And it doesn't take much more bad luck across a couple of consecutive sessions to create a losing streak.

The important thing is not to lose heart. Bad luck may be a factor over periods of up to, for example, fifty hours or so of playing time, and you're just going to have to learn to deal with it.

Staying detached

The best poker players are usually pretty good at dealing with bad luck when it comes their way. They don't go crazy, go on tilt, or curse their opponents – all of which are ultimately counter-productive. It tends to be the weaker players who do that.

Here are a few thoughts that should help you come to terms with any bad luck that comes your way. You may want to commit them to memory, and recite them to yourself soothingly in times of need.

Embrace the element of luck. If poker had no luck in it, it would be much more like chess – the good players would always win, or nearly always. This might sound like a superficially appealing state of affairs, but in practice you wouldn't be able to get weaker players to play with you. Would you be willing to play for money against somebody who beat you every time? We hope not.

The fact of the matter is that luck, frustrating as it can be, softens and obscures the cold and harsh realities of the game. It ensures that poor players notice their losses less, and frequently don't realise that they're being outplayed. It's only the fact that poor players *sometimes* get lucky, and hence *sometimes* win, that keeps them coming back for more punishment.

Concentrate on making the right decisions, not on whether you win or lose pots. You can't do anything about the luck so don't worry about it. It will even out in the end. All you can do is try to get your money in the pot when you have the best of it, or at least have the odds to play, and get out of there when you have the worst of it. Don't be happy just because you won a pot, or sad just because you lost one. Be happy if you played a hand as well as you could have, regardless of whether you won or lost.

If you focus on your decision-making rather than your winnings, you will be less emotionally involved, and more attuned to the source of your long-term success – pure good play.

Good players have bad beats, bad players have good beats. If you find yourself thinking that other players constantly draw out on you, yet it never seems to happen the other way around, there's probably a good reason for that. If you get your money in the middle with the best of it, you can either win, as expected, or have a bad beat – you can't have a good beat. If you can't remember the last time you had a good beat, that's probably because you're making good decisions. Good beats are for poor players.

Welcome poor play in others, even if you lose. You may find it incredibly frustrating when a bad player calls your all-in with an under-strength hand, or without the proper odds, and draws out on you. But remember that you had an edge precisely as a result of his bad play, and for that reason you should welcome such calls. In the long run, you wouldn't make any money if opponents always folded against you when they didn't have the odds to call. Accept that being drawn out on occasionally is the price you pay for making money when your good hands hold up.

Poker players behaving badly

Poker tables are often the setting for scenes of conflict. If you manage to survive a whole evening of poker without a single whinge or complaint from any of the players, you're doing pretty well. In many games, full-blown arguments are not too uncommon, although they rarely seem to end in actual fist-fights in these enlightened days.

As a general piece of advice, it usually makes sense to avoid causing or participating in such disputes – for the very simple reason that you don't want games to break up. Tension and confrontation, even if they don't destroy a game there and then, are liable to put people off playing in the future. Good poker games should be nurtured and encouraged to thrive – especially if they're enjoyable and / or profitable (delete according to taste).

Here are a few simple guidelines that you – and in fact all poker players – would be well advised to follow.

- Try to be friendly and courteous to your fellow players at all times. If they feel comfortable with you, they are going to be less unhappy about you taking their money. If you make them cross and stir them to action, it might be much harder to get your hands on their chips.

- Don't criticise weak players for making bad plays, even if they get lucky and beat you. You *want* weak players in the game, and you *want* them to make bad plays, otherwise you lose your edge. By criticising them, you may alert them to the fact that they're playing badly – something they might not actually realise. And if you upset them, they may exercise their right to game selection, and go and play elsewhere. Weak players and bad plays are to be embraced (metaphorically speaking) even if they cause you occasional grief. If you get outdrawn, try just to smile and congratulate your opponent.

- Don't be arrogant or try to prove a point by the way you play, or engage in vendettas against specific opponents. It will interfere with your judgment and may wind other players up. Just quietly get on with the job and let the money do the talking.

- Beware of discussing strategy at the table. You might choose to do so in home games with your friends, for example, but it doesn't always go down that well in public. Good players may prefer it if you didn't give any secrets away to the weaker ones, and the weaker ones may perceive you as trying to intimidate them with your talk of fancy ideas like pot odds that they don't really understand or care about. If in doubt, keep your conversation off the subject of poker, or restrict yourself to innocuous comments such as "my, that was a big pot!".

Poker ethics

Now, we know what some of you may be thinking. Is it right for us to talk so freely and openly about exploiting weaker, more naive members of the population, and doing what we can to get our hands on as much of their money as possible? Isn't that, kind of, you know, immoral or unethical? Well, we're not great philosophers, so we're not going to try to tackle that rather difficult question here (although if you send us £100 we might tell you the answer). Instead we'll restrict ourselves to a few observations.

Firstly, the vast majority of players play for fun. They may lose a bit of money in doing so, but probably not much more than they would during, say, a good night out. If your perception of poker players is that they're all helpless addicts who need to be protected from their own weakness, then your perception is wrong.

Sure, there are some unfortunate souls in this predicament, and we wouldn't advocate trying to clean *them* out. But most players lose no more than they can afford to lose. If they weren't playing poker, they might indulge in even more soul- and bank balance-destroying pastimes such as roulette or blackjack, where there really is no hope of ever winning (unless you cheat).

So although you may have no idea about any particular poker player's motivation, be assured that most of them enjoy the game, win or lose.

Secondly, the kind of exploitation that goes on at a poker table also goes on all around us every day without receiving widespread condemnation. In business, companies try to exploit their rivals' weaknesses in order to make more money for themselves. In racquet sports, a player whose opponent is injured will try to make them run further by moving them around the court, playing drop-shots and so on, in order to make it as hard for them as possible. And we dare not mention what men and women do to persuade their partners to cook dinner, mow the lawn or buy diamond necklaces. Does poker exploitation really seem any worse?

For some reason, when it so directly comes down to money, preying on a poker opponent's inferior playing ability or unbalanced emotional state doesn't seem quite right to some people. But fundamentally, you can play poker for fun, or you can play to win – it's up to you. If you play to win, and if you so choose, then these weaknesses are there to be exploited.

Of course, you may decide that you won't push every edge you have to its ultimate limit, in the interests of not causing your opponents excessive loss or humiliation. You might decide that the money you sacrifice by doing so is amply compensated by the less tangible benefits that maintaining goodwill confers. Incidentally, such small acts of mercy may also help maximise your long-term profits, by keeping the source of your revenue sweet.

How to think

This book can't tell you how to act in every situation – there are just too many different types of player, game and circumstance for that to be remotely feasible. What we have tried to do instead is to teach you *how to think* about each situation and to make considered evaluations and judgements.

Putting this into practice, however, first requires that you *do* actually think when you play! Many players act intuitively and quickly, without properly working through their decisions in their own mind. If you do the same, you are more likely to make poor decisions, and your standard of play will improve less rapidly than it otherwise would. Here's what you should try to do.

Take your time. Don't be rushed into any decisions, especially the more important ones. If you need a few moments to think, it's helpful to say "time please" or similar, so that other players know you're actually thinking rather than simply unaware it's your turn.

Don't take this too far, however. If you find that you are taking much longer than most of your opponents to act, you could begin to alienate them. Slow play can breed even slower play (because other players lose concentration while they're waiting) and eventually spoil a game.

Use *all* the available time. To maximise your thinking time without slowing the game down unduly, try to do as much thinking as possible in advance of your turn. Before the next card is dealt, try to work out what you'll do depending on whether it hits or misses your hand. While your opponents are acting, try to work out what you'll do if they check or bet. Then you can do whatever you're going to do as quickly and smoothly as possible.

Make your thinking explicit, by which we mean reason out your decisions in full in your own mind rather than playing by feel or instinct. Pretend for example that you have someone looking over your shoulder to whom you have to justify your every move. Before you make a bet, work out how you would answer this person if they were to ask you "why are you doing that?"

By constructing explicit arguments to justify your actions you can evaluate those arguments retrospectively, criticise them if necessary, and learn more from your mistakes. You can also minimise the influence of unwanted emotional factors, e.g. tilt, on your thinking. If you can't explain your decisions fully and rationally, they're probably bad decisions.

Chapter Thirteen:
Final thoughts on strategy

This is the final chapter in our (rather long) strategy section. We'll be tying up a few loose ends and discussing some slightly more advanced topics, namely:

■ Multiple possibilities and weighted averages
■ Blind and stack sizes
■ Short-handed play.

Finally we'll round off with a list of the top ten mistakes made by inexperienced or weak players.

Multiple possibilities and weighted averages

We've already discussed in some detail the uncertainties that are a fundamental feature of the game of poker, in particular not knowing precisely what your opponents hold. One thing you should always try to do when making decisions is to remain open-minded about those uncertainties and not jump too readily to specific conclusions.

It may be very tempting to put an opponent on (i.e. conclude that they hold) a specific hand, or make simplistic decisions like "he's bluffing, I'll call", or "he's got a monster, I'll fold". But that doesn't always get you to the right answer. Instead, you should identify and keep in mind *all* the possibilities, and make your decisions based on *all* of them rather than just a single one.

Suppose you're trying to choose between two different actions, e.g. call or fold. Your thought process should be roughly as follows.

1. Make a list of all the scenarios you believe to be possible, i.e. all the feasible explanations you can construct for your opponents' behaviour in the hand.

2. Assign to each of these an estimate of its probability of being true.

3. Work out your expected profit for each of these if you choose one action over the other one.

4. Select the play that shows the highest profit when averaged over all the possibilities, i.e. take a weighted average.

If this is the first time you've come across this idea, it may not be at all obvious what we mean by this. But hopefully a couple of examples will make it all a bit clearer.

Example 1

You are dealt:

and put in a good-sized raise pre-flop. Your opponent, who is usually a tight player, and who initially called from under the gun (i.e. he was the first to act), re-raises you all-in. Do you call?

Your first thought should naturally be, does he have pocket aces? He's certainly representing a very strong hand indeed. But equally you shouldn't jump to conclusions. Even if you suspect your pair of kings might not be winning, that doesn't necessarily mean it's right to fold.

Actually, this is a very important point to bear in mind in this kind of situation, and it can feel totally counter-intuitive. We'll say it again: *Just because you think you're losing, it doesn't necessarily mean it's right to fold.*

Let's try to work through the decision analytically. First of all you need to list the possible hands you could be up against. You might decide that the candidates are:

- Pair of aces – your opponent has made a classic pre-flop play if he's holding aces; it seems to be the most likely explanation
- Pair of kings – highly unlikely because there are only two kings left in the deck, but possible
- Pair of queens – most people would consider your opponent to have played badly if this is what he's holding
- Ace-king – quite possible; your opponent is not much worse than 50% against almost every hand except kings and aces, and even against kings he's still 30%
- Random bluff – making such a move with any hand weaker than these would usually be considered a bluff.

In fact, we will discount the possibility of a pair of kings in this case, because it is so unlikely, and because it will almost certainly result in a split pot anyway, thus not really affecting the calculations.

Next you should assign rough probabilities to each of his holdings. Obviously this depends partly on your opponent and what you know of him, but you decide to plump for:

- Pair of aces – 65%
- Pair of queens – 15%
- Ace-king – 15%
- Random bluff – 5%.

Now you need to work out your chances of winning in each case:

- Pair of aces – you are 18% to win
- Pair of queens – you are 82% to win
- Ace-king – you are 70% to win (a little less if he's suited, but we'll ignore that)
- Random bluff – you are about 80% to win.

Next you take a weighted average of your chances of winning against each holding. You do this by multiplying his probability of having each holding by the probability of you winning against it.

Note: after you've been playing hold'em for a while, you should become familiar with these heads-up percentages. The common situations are covered in **Appendix C: Tables of odds.**

- Pair of aces – 65% x 18% = 12% (roughly)
- Pair of queens – 15% x 82% = 12% (roughly)
- Ace-king – 15% x 70% = 11% (roughly)
- Random bluff – 5% x 80% = 4%.

And then total up the figures. Your total probability of winning is 12% + 12% + 11% + 4% = 39%, or about 1.5-to-1 against. You know what you have to do now – look at the pot odds that you are being offered on your call. If they are better than 1.5-to-1, then a call is profitable.

Now, that was a pretty involved example, and we don't necessarily expect you to make a calculation as accurate and detailed as that while you're sitting at the table contemplating what to do. What we want you to realise however is that the line of reasoning that goes "I think he's got aces – I'll fold" is too simplistic.

The correct line of reasoning goes "He may have aces, in which case I'm a big underdog, but he may have queens or ace-king or be bluffing in which case I'm a big favourite. On balance I think I'm about 40% to win the pot so I'll call because the pot odds are better than that."

If you want to, and are able, you might decide to attempt something approximating to the full line of reasoning but in a simplified form. For example:

- If he's got aces, you're about 20% to win
- If he hasn't, you're probably about 80% to win, give or take
- You reckon he's 70% likely to have aces, and 30% not to
- Therefore your chances of winning are (70% x 20%) + (30% x 80%) = 35%, or just under 2-to-1
- Therefore you need pot odds of nearly 2-to-1 to make the call profitable.

Whether or not you try this sort of thing will depend on your inclination and arithmetical ability. You should be aware though that this is what the best players will do on a fairly regular basis. When they take a long time to make a decision, they're not always sitting there thinking "hmm ... I wonder if he's bluffing or not", although this may admittedly occupy part of their thoughts. They're likely to be making a more detailed analytical assessment of whether or not a call will be profitable.

Example 2

Let's do one more example, a slightly different one this time.

You are on the button and are dealt:

The player under the gun raises to three times the big blind and you are the only caller. (Folding might arguably be a better move than calling but we'll gloss over that for now.) The flop is:

and your opponent comes out betting. What do you do?

From your opponent's betting and what you know of him, you suspect he holds one of the following categories of hand:

1.   A-A, A-K or A-Q, giving him a big pair
2.   Q-Q or K-K, giving him three of a kind.

In either case, you reckon to be losing now, but your flush draw and bottom pair give you a reasonable chance of improving. (We'll ignore the possibility of your opponent having a better flush draw than you since, with two spades on the board, two in your hand, and only one opponent, it's really very unlikely.) How many outs do you have in each case?

1. If he has a pair, you can hit the two remaining sevens in the deck (for trip sevens), the three remaining eights (for two pair) plus the nine remaining

spades (for a flush), giving you a total of fourteen outs. This actually makes you about 50% to win the hand if you play all the way to the river.

2. If he has three of a kind you're in much worse shape. Your own outs for two pair of three of a kind are no good so you're going to need to make your flush win. Even if you do, the board might pair giving your opponent a full-house. Ignoring the full house possibility for now, you just have nine outs this time rather than fourteen. You're less than 30% to win the hand in this case.

However much you think about it, you can never actually know whether your opponent holds a pair or three of a kind, so you can't actually know how many outs you really have. What if your opponent bets an amount such that you have the odds to call if you can count fourteen outs but not if you count only nine? What should you do then?

The answer is that you need to take a weighted average depending on your assessment of the likelihood of each scenario.

- If you are almost certain your opponent has a pair, you count all fourteen outs.
- If you are almost certain your opponent has three of a kind, you count just nine outs.
- If you think it's 50:50 one way or the other, you split the difference and count 11.5 outs.
- If you think your opponent is 80:20 to have the pair, you split the difference 80:20 in favour of the pair and count thirteen outs.

And so on. The fact that you can't actually have 'half an out' shouldn't bother you. Just plug in the numbers and you'll find your answer. Then pick the course of action that reckons to fare best against your weighted assessment.

Size matters – blinds and stacks

Stack size

In no-limit hold'em, the stack sizes of you and your opponents can make a big difference to the way a hand is played. In general, you should aim to have a large stack, one that covers (i.e. is bigger than) most of your opponents' stacks. If you have a big stack then:

- You can get paid off better when you make a great hand. If you have a small stack then you may find yourself all-in when you'd rather have more money left to bet.
- Related to this, with a big stack you have better implied odds when you're drawing, because there's more scope for getting paid off when you make your draw. If you're going to call a pre-flop raise with a small pair, trying to hit a set, or suited connector, hoping to hit a straight, flush or good draw, you need you and your opponents to have large reserves.

In situations like these, you should compare the amount you have to call with the remaining available funds. As a rule of thumb, marginal calls shouldn't be made for more than 10% of your (or your opponents') stacks, and even anything over 5% should give you cause to consider whether the implied odds really are there.

- You can protect your made hands more effectively with a big stack, because you can always make big bets and raises (oversized if necessary) and thus avoid giving opponents the correct odds to call.
- You can more readily intimidate your opponents by bullying and bluffing. Other players will give little respect to a small stack. But if you bet or raise into a player with a big stack, it makes them wonder if they're going to lose all their chips if they get involved. Often the reason a player will fold is not because he fears calling the *current* bet, but because he fears the even bigger bets that may be yet to come.
- You have more money!

There are a couple of downsides to having a big stack.

- You can lose a lot of money quickly, when you lose a big hand.
- You are less likely to be called when you pick up a truly great hand and bet it, because other players will fear a big stack in the way they won't fear a short stack.
- There are some hands, particularly drawing hands, where you would like to see all the cards as cheaply as possible. Being close to all-in with a small stack means that opponents can't bet you off a good draw as easily.

On balance though, the advantages outweigh the disadvantages. In many no-limit games, especially online ones, there is a maximum buy-in when you sit down at the table, i.e. a limit to how many chips you can start with. Typically the maximum buy-in will be somewhere between 50 and 100 times the big blind.

We strongly recommend that you buy in for this maximum, rather than a smaller amount, and that you rebuy chips whenever your stack diminishes to less than, say, 75% of this level.

If you're not comfortable about buying in for such a large amount then you're probably playing at stakes that are too high for you. Drop down to a lower level and buy in for the full amount, and come back up to this level only once your confidence and bankroll have grown sufficiently.

No-limit hold'em is a volatile game, and it rewards those who are prepared to gamble when the time is right. Good players will often lose their entire stack once or twice, or even more, before they start to build a big pile of chips. If you're scared of losing your entire stack, you're effectively handicapping yourself, and you'll be operating at a distinct disadvantage.

Blind size

In most no-limit cash games, the blinds are relatively small compared with the players' stack sizes, typically no more than 1%-2% of the maximum buy-in. In games with larger blind sizes than this, however, you will need to change the way you play. Larger blinds favour looser play because:

- if you play too tight, the blinds devour your stack that much more quickly
- there is more to be gained by winning the blinds, therefore more incentive to bet
- since everyone else will be playing looser, you can afford to play looser too.

Indeed the larger the blinds are, the looser and looser you should play – it just becomes too expensive not to. If you stick to cash games then this is unlikely to be a factor – you don't have to make significant changes until the blinds are over, perhaps, 5% of your stack size.

But it makes a huge difference in tournaments where the blinds increase continuously to make sure that players are knocked out in a reasonable timeframe. Tournaments require a very different strategy from cash games, and much of the reason for this is the different blind structure. We cover tournament strategy in Chapter Seventeen.

Short-handed play

Why play short-handed?

Many old-school poker players seem not to like smaller games, preferring instead to sit at fuller tables with, say, nine or more players. If you play only in live games in card rooms then it's quite rare you'll ever engage with fewer opponents than this.

Increasingly, however, people are becoming more comfortable with the idea of shorter-handed games. Much of this is driven by the internet, where player turnover is high, and games are constantly forming and breaking up. Home games too are frequently short-handed, if only because few people have dining tables that big.

There's no formal definition of short-handed play, but any game with fewer than perhaps seven players might be reasonably described thus. A game described as 'very short-handed' would normally involve fewer than five players.

Short-handed play has some real advantages over fuller tables. The main one is that you get to play much more poker:

- With fewer people at the table, you spend less time waiting for others to act, and can be involved in the action more often yourself.
- This effect is further compounded by the fact that people tend to concentrate better, and act more quickly, because they know they don't have long to wait. Fast play is self-reinforcing.

■ Moreover, many more hands are playable at short-handed tables, for reasons we first introduced when discussing how the number of players in the game influences the way you play (see Chapter Five).

All in all, you might on average expect to play four times as many hands per hour in a six-handed game as you would in a ten-handed one, and you would be actively involved in, say, ten times the number of hands. This means more interest, more practice and, hopefully, more profit for you.

Short-handed play is also less volatile. At a full table, the pots you win are likely to be contested by multiple players and hence be quite large. But you won't usually win pots that often (even ignoring the slower rate of play) because you have to beat that many more players to do so. When you're relying on big wins at long intervals then it's easy to have a losing session if you're dealt a few bad hands.

In short-handed play, the pots are generally smaller, but you will win a higher proportion of them. This tends to even out the luck more quickly, and reduce the chances of stronger players losing money.

And finally, if you become proficient at short-handed play, you should develop a much better awareness of how to cope with what are effectively short-handed situations that arise in fuller games. If many of the early-position players fold pre-flop, you can really consider yourself to be playing short-handed. There's very little difference.

Short-handed strategy

Short-handed play requires you to make adjustments to your playing style that don't come naturally to many people. Here are the main points to bear in mind.

Loosen up. This is the first and most important adjustment you should make. With fewer people at the table, there is less chance that any particular hand will be beaten – simply because there are fewer hands out there. Until you've been playing short-handed for a while though, it's not that easy to get a feel for *how much* you should loosen up as a result. Recall the table we introduced in Chapter Five showing how good a hand you needed to reckon to be favourite to win.

No. of players (including you)	Percentile to be favourite
2	50%
3	29.3%
4	20.6%
5	15.9%
6	12.9%
7	10.9%
8	9.4%
9	8.3%
10	7.4%
11	6.7%

This suggests, for example, that nearly twice as many hands reckon to be winning in a four-player game (20.6%) than in a seven-player game (10.9%). Of course, you don't even have to have what you believe to be the best hand in order to play – you just have to have, at a minimum, the odds to call.

In a heads-up game, one player is the small bind and the other is the big blind. Therefore in the small blind you should at least call pre-flop with almost every single hand, because you'll be getting 3-to-1 on your money. Even in a three-handed game, you might expect to put money in the pot in over 50% of hands.

As well as loosening up your starting requirements pre-flop, you will need to loosen up in the later rounds too. With fewer players seeing the flop, there's less chance that it will have helped someone. You should be that much more willing to bet with hands like middle or bottom pair, or even if the flop misses you altogether.

Always remember then – keep your play tight at full tables, but be prepared to really open up when the number of players diminishes.

Be more aggressive. In short-handed games, with fewer players in each pot, and fewer players making a genuine hand, fewer hands get played all the way to showdown. Therefore hands are often won by the player who competes hardest for them, rather than the one with the best cards. In a ten-player game, you usually have to have the goods when you bet since it's too likely that your opponents will have a good hand of their own. But in short-handed play you can win more pots by sheer willpower. You need to be far more prepared to trust your judgment and simply be courageous. Even with poor hands, you will need to raise and re-raise your opponents on occasions.

Know your opponents. Because you will be playing weaker hands, and therefore playing more speculatively, it's doubly important to know and understand your opponents' playing styles and habits. Otherwise you can get into too much trouble. Fortunately, short-handed play is particularly suitable for getting to know your opponents, because you'll be coming up against each of them far more often. In very short-handed play, you may find betting patterns repeating themselves in these exchanges, with players trying out different variations in order to establish superiority. With so few hands being shown down however, the challenge will be to find out what each pattern means for each player.

Position is key. This follows naturally from the number of hands that are resolved without showing down cards. You are largely trying to 'play the man, not the cards', and position is a huge advantage in such tactical exchanges. Be prepared to go out on a limb more when you're in position, and tighten up when you're out of it.

Value high cards and made hands more than drawing hands. With fewer players in each pot, drawing hands become less valuable – the pot odds and implied odds won't be as good. Pre-flop, you should be less inclined to call raises with suited connectors or suited aces, for example. In general you want to play hands that you can bet on their current rather than future merit, since these are the best hands to play against few opponents. In late position, small pairs can often be played with a raise rather than as drawing hands. And other combinations that you'd normally throw away can be played for a raise too, such as ace-five unsuited, say.

Slowplay big hands more often. With fewer players to draw out on you, you can afford to play your big hands a little slower. A hand like two pair or a set can be a monster in these circumstances, and you want to get as much value from these hands as possible. In short-handed games, your opponents are more likely to try to take the pot away from you if you show weakness, so slowplaying can often be the best way of getting your hands on their money.

Top ten mistakes

Without trying to sound unduly negative, when it comes down to it, poker is all about mistakes. If you induce mistakes from others, and avoid making mistakes of your own, you will win. In the long run, you don't make money because you win or lose pots, you win money by making fewer mistakes than your opponents. If nobody made mistakes, or all players made the same number and type of mistakes, all players would break even. Eventually the luck evens out, and the only thing left to distinguish players is the correctness of their decisions.

We've tried to emphasise this idea in several places throughout this book. It's a difficult concept to understand and absorb because, as players, we're all so obsessed with winning money (or losing it). But you need to see winning as a long-term goal that you will achieve automatically if you make the right decisions, and minimise your mistakes. On a day-to-day basis you should just try to concentrate on making the right decisions and not worry too much about the money.

With that in mind, we'll round up our discussion of strategy with a list of the top ten mistakes made by weak or inexperienced players. If you want to become a good poker player, make sure you eliminate these from your game.

- **Don't play too many starting hands.** Keep your game tight, and follow the guidelines on playable starting hands we've laid out in Chapter Six. If you get bored folding all the time, then concentrate more on learning about your opponents or, if you're online, play multiple tables simultaneously.

- **Don't draw without the proper odds.** Don't call big bets with third-rate draws to straights or flushes. That's for losers!

- **Don't call big bets on the river with marginal hands.** That can be very expensive, unless you have specific reason to think your opponent is bluffing.

- **Don't be too passive.** Don't give free or cheap cards because you're scared to bet. Even if you're not sure you're in the lead, it is often right to bet anyway. If you're worried about being outdrawn, you should be *more* inclined to bet, not less.

- **Don't slowplay without sufficient strength.** Don't mistakenly think your good hands are invulnerable. Don't slowplay big pairs pre-flop. Don't give your opponents free or cheap cards unless you're confident you won't be outdrawn, and that you'll earn more money by doing so.

- **Don't bluff too much.** You want your opponents to fold to your bluffs, so bluff relatively rarely but make it convincing when you do.

- **Don't forget to change gears.** Playing the same way all the time makes it easier for your opponents to read you. Make sure you loosen up in games or hands with fewer opponents.

- **Don't ignore position.** It's almost more important than your cards.

- **Don't ignore your opponents.** Make it your mission to watch and categorise their every move.

- **Don't play at too high stakes, or in games you can't beat.** That's the easiest and quickest way to lose money.

Part III
Online Poker

Chapter Fourteen:
Getting started online

When you play poker online, you'll be up against other people from all over the world and you'll be able to find thousands of willing opponents at any time of the day or night.

To get started simply download the poker software (always free) from your chosen site and then deposit your stake money from your credit card. From there on it's usually only a few clicks of the mouse to choose your game, choose your table and begin to play.

Note: In live games in the UK, stakes are in British pounds. Online it's almost always dollars.

For the latest information, lots of extra resources and links to recommended poker sites, please visit www.playingpokertowin.co.uk

Here are the answers to some frequently asked questions regarding online poker.

What do sites charge to enter real money games?

There is no charge for entry into cash games – the sites make their money by taking a small percentage of each pot, called a rake. Tournaments have buy-in fees ranging from one pound or dollar up to thousands, although typically less than 10% goes to the house.

How much will it cost me?

You can play at any level of stakes you choose. The smallest games might have blinds of a few pence, with average pots of around a few pounds. The largest games frequently have four or even five figure pots!

How does the betting work?

On your screen, you will see four different buttons, up to three of which may be visible at any one time:

- Check (if there hasn't been any bet ahead of you).
- Fold (if there has been a bet ahead of you).
- Call (if there has been a bet ahead of you).
- Bet / Raise.

There is a separate control accompanying the last of these which allows you to specify the size of your bet or raise (although this won't be present in fixed-limit games). This control normally takes the form of a 'slider', although some sites also allow you to type in a number or select from a list. You need to set your bet size before pressing the 'bet' button. If you make a mistake and press the wrong button, tough – you can't change your mind. So be very careful.

Most sites also have checkboxes which allow you, should you know what you're going to do, to select an action in advance. The most useful of these is the advanced fold button, although you will often know you're going to call too (you are prompted again if a raise occurs after you've decided to call). Using the advanced action buttons keeps the game moving nice and quickly, but see our comments on the potential downside of this in the next chapter on online strategy.

How do my winnings get paid?

Poker sites usually pay your winnings either by crediting your credit card or by sending you a cheque. Some sites also support other electronic payment mechanisms that don't rely on you having a credit card.

Is there anywhere I can play for free?

Almost all of the major poker sites have free tables where you can win and lose for as long as you like, for absolutely nothing (hopefully learning a thing or two in the process). Playing on free tables is a good way to learn the basics and familiarise yourself with the game. Having said that, the free tables are where the inexperienced players go, so the hike in playing level increases pretty steeply once you start playing for real.

How do I graduate to money tables without it costing too much?

You can sit down and play at the very cheapest cash games with just a few pounds. However, you must always be prepared to lose what you have in front of you.

If you want to minimise your exposure to an absolute minimum, you might decide to start with tournaments. You'll only be liable for the initial buy-in, which can be as low as $1, but there's still be real money to play for so you'll get good games. Don't forget that tournament strategy is quite different from cash game strategy though.

We discuss tournaments in **Chapter Seventeen**.

Is it safe to play online?

From the point of view of money and credit card security, yes, it's very safe – providing you play with large, reputable and properly licensed companies.

Which is the best site?

We provide a listing of online sites in **Appendix E: Online poker websites** towards the end of the book. Which site is the best is largely a matter of personal preference. The two main factors you should consider are (a) playing community; are there enough people playing your favourite game, at your preferred stakes, and (b) the quality and usability of the software; is it easy and intuitive to play, or is it a pain. There's a lot of variation in this respect.

Is there a lot of cheating going on?

Not really, and especially not at the low stakes because it isn't really worth it. But see Chapter Nineteen for our opinion on cheating online, by players and by the house. Issues concerning (and attitudes to) security and honest play are usually published by each individual site.

How do I recognise other players?

Every player has their own alias on each website, which is the name by which they're always known on that site. Players are not normally able to change their alias, so you can always recognise those you've encountered before, and they can recognise you too.

Can I communicate with other players?

Yes, assuming your chosen site offers a chat facility. Many poker players use a form of chat shorthand to communicate, for example *nh* means nice hand and *ty* means thank you. If you haven't got a clue what people are saying then have a look at our online chat glossary on page 338.

If you do use the chat facility, don't let it distract you, don't use all capitals (shouting), and always be polite and friendly.

What if I need to stop playing for a short while?

Most sites have a 'sit out' feature. They also have rules about what happens when it's your turn but you fail to act. If you're going to be away for a long time then you normally have to give up your seat.

What happens if I lose my connection?

If the entire game server crashes then, typically, all games are cancelled and all chips in play will be refunded. However, disconnections are more likely to be caused by problems your end, when you lose your internet connection for some reason.

Usually the site will give you a short time in which to reconnect and rejoin your game. If you don't turn up for a while, some sites will create a side pot for you while the other players continue betting.

Deliberate disconnections (because you're losing) are another case entirely. Online sites monitor disconnections continuously, and if you're found guilty you can be blacklisted – so don't even think about it!

Can I pull out if I'm losing?

You can get up and leave a cash game whenever you like, although it's not recommended during the middle of a hand since you'll forfeit any money you've already put in the pot. Deliberate disconnections are covered above.

In tournaments, once you've paid the buy-in, you can't get your cash back unless you make it to the prize places.

Anything else I should know?

Yes – always check the house rules on betting, disconnects, etc. before you play. And if you use a cordless mouse, make sure it doesn't run out of battery power at an awkward moment.

The next chapter covers online strategy.

Chapter Fifteen:
Strategy for online play

Online play is more similar to live play than most people realise. It is generally assumed, particularly by those with relatively little experience, that not being able to see one's opponents must make a huge difference. In fact, this discrepancy between the two forms of the game isn't even really the most significant one. In this chapter we'll examine each of the differences, and explain what impact they have on the way you should play.

You should be aware however that almost all of the material presented in Part II, concerning general strategy for no-limit hold'em, is directly applicable to online play. In the discussion that follows, we'll assume that you're already familiar with this material, and will therefore talk mostly about *adjustments* in strategy for online play rather than revisiting the fundamentals.

You can't see your opponents

Well, since this is the main difference that everybody obsesses about, we'll start with this one. Yes, it's true – in online play, *you can't see your opponents*. The question is, does that make much of a difference? Have a brief look over the contents list for Part II of this book and see which sections you think that affects. The fact is that it only makes a significant difference to tells – the clues that you sometimes get about opponents' hands from their behaviour. In online play, there are far fewer tells than in live play.

We'll agree then that cutting out the visible contact with your opponents does impact on your ability to make the right decisions to a certain extent. Inexperienced players might think that it makes a big difference, because they think that poker is about staring down opponents and working out whether they're bluffing or not, like they do *on television*. But stronger players place a greater emphasis on studying the betting patterns of players throughout the game, and making good plays based on pot odds and rational analysis of each situation. These skills are more fundamental, more reliable and, most importantly to our argument, equally applicable to online play.

Note also that we didn't say there are *no* tells in online play – they do still exist. For example:

Speed of action. You can occasionally make inferences about the difficulty of a player's decision based on the amount of time it takes them to respond. Bear in mind however that:

- just because a player took a long time to respond, it doesn't mean they had a tough decision. They might have been watching another table, or the TV, or anything but the hand in question.
- the pace of action that you observe on the screen in front of you doesn't always reflect reality, because of possibly delays in messages going to and from your screen to the poker site over the internet.
- players may use the advance betting controls to select an action before it's their turn. The only such action that's really relevant to no-limit hold'em is *call*. If a player has decided to fold in advance, that's not a tell; and it's rarely possible to plan a bet or raise in advance because of the need to use the slider to select the bet size.

So if you see an opponent make a seemingly instantaneous call, it's likely that they decided to call sometime in advance. Therefore you should avoid using the advance betting controls for calling in situations where you wouldn't want your opponents to know that you were able to make an early decision in that respect.

Chat. Most poker sites have a chat facility that allows you to converse with your opponents. Although there's usually little time to interrogate an opponent while you're making a decision, sometimes you can ask a question and get an answer with some information. Don't bank on it though – most people can't type very fast, and are less likely to respond to computer chat online than they would be to real chat in a live game.

The play is faster

Online play is much faster than live play for several reasons.

- House activities such as dealing the cards, determining the winner and dividing up the pot are performed more or less instantaneously. Very nearly all of the time spent at a table online is spent waiting for players to make an action.

■ Each player is limited to a short amount of time to make each decision, typically thirty seconds or so, and is alerted to the start of their time with a change in their display and, usually, an audible warning. Because the game proceeds faster overall, and because each player knows about the time constraints under which they're operating, players tend to concentrate a little more than in live games. For the most part, anyway.

As a result, you might find your self playing up to fifty hands per hour at a ten-seater table online, or one hundred hands per hour at a six-seater. You'd be doing very well to manage half this number in a live game.

The furious pace shouldn't affect your strategy too greatly. The main problem is having only thirty seconds (or similar) to make a decision. Although you'll no doubt act much faster than that on the vast majority of your turns, it will sometimes pose a problem on the big, difficult decisions.

The only advice we can give here is to try to prepare yourself in advance. If the pot you're involved with is getting large, and your course of action isn't clear, try to anticipate the possible scenarios that might arise. Before the next card is dealt, try to work out what you'll do depending on whether it hits or misses your hand. While your opponents are acting, try to work out what you'll do if they check or bet. This will maximise your chances of selecting the right course of action in the time available.

Simultaneous play

On most poker sites, you are permitted to play at more than one table simultaneously if you so choose, something which would of course be impossible in a live game.

When you first start playing online, you'll probably have trouble following the action at even one table in its entirety – it can take a while to become used to the graphical representations of tables, players and money. After a while however, you'll find yourself increasingly accustomed to the display, and able to play at more than one table without too much trouble. The question of course is, should you do so?

Playing at more than one table has both advantages and disadvantages. The obvious downside is that it's harder to follow what's going on at more than one table as well as you can do so on a single table. You will find that you won't be able to study the habits of your opponents as closely, and that you won't have so much time in which to make your decisions – especially if you get a good hand on more than one table simultaneously. You may also incur the wrath of your opponents if you consistently take too long to act because you're concentrating on other games.

JOE OFTEN WISHED HE COULD DO MORE THAN ONE THING AT ONCE!

But on the plus side, if you make money at one table, and you are able to play multiple tables without drastically reducing your earnings at each individual table, you can in theory make money a lot faster. It's perfectly possible to play over 200 hands per hour online which is a huge number, nearly ten times the number you could play in live games. Most winning players tend to find that they make money more quickly on two tables than on one, but that somewhere around the three or perhaps four table mark their total profits start declining.

Another advantage of playing multiple tables is that you can play tight, yet still play plenty of hands. If you have a tendency to play too loose, or to get bored if you play few hands, then sitting at multiple tables will probably do you good.

You'll have to experiment to find the number of tables that seems to maximise your earnings. It will typically depend on a number of factors, including:

- how many opponents you're facing – ten-player games are much slower than shorter-handed games, and therefore less demanding of your time.
- the game you're playing – hold'em is easier to follow than more complex games, such as omaha for example.

- the software on the site, and how quick and easy it is to use.
- how quickly your brain works!

We'd recommend that, when playing multiple tables, you play the same game at the same stakes on each. The last thing you want to do when you're trying to make a quick decision about a game that you haven't been giving your full attention, is to forget which game you're playing.

As well as thinking about how many tables you should play, it's often useful to look at how many tables *your opponents* are playing. (Most sites have a search facility that will tell you at which tables any particular player is seated.) If a player you haven't come across much is playing at several tables, he's unlikely to be following very closely what you're doing. He may not know whether you've been playing tight or loose, conservatively or aggressively. You are less able to rely on any kind of table image against such an opponent, so make sure you factor that out of the equation.

Larger communities

Online poker communities tend to be larger than their live game counterparts, because a significant proportion of the world's players end up at one of few major sites. These sites will typically have thousands or tens of thousands of players online at any one time.

Even if you play the same game at the same stakes all the time, you will probably find that your opponents are drawn from a very large pool of regular players, with many other occasional visitors who play intermittently. Therefore you will frequently find yourself playing against players you haven't met before, or at least don't know particularly well.

Having said that, you are likely to encounter your fair share of familiar faces, particularly if you're playing games or stakes that fewer people are interested in. Hold'em doesn't usually qualify in this respect (except at very big stakes) since it's the most popular game around – the communities are huge.

So when playing online, with a large and transient community, your anonymity is considerably greater than it will usually be for live games. How will you remember anything about the playing styles of the many players that you come up against infrequently?

Fortunately, the poker sites have already found an answer to this problem – they allow you to make notes on each player individually. Typically you click on a button next to each player and type in whatever you want to say about them – only you will be able to see what you type (don't get player notes mixed up with the chat window!).

Then, when you play against that same player in the future, you will be able to see from the display that you made notes about them in the past, and can click on the button again to see what you wrote. Since players can't usually change their alias, i.e. the name under which they appear on the site, this is a reliable way of keeping tabs on your opponents.

You should make good use of the player notes facility. At the very least, write down whether you think a player is weak or strong, tight or loose. Any other habits you observe that might be useful one day should be recorded too, e.g. *called a re-raise all-in with K-10 suited*, or *doesn't make continuation bets without a good hand*, or similar.

You should treat these notes not only as an aid for the future but also for the game you're currently playing. If you're sat at four ten-seater tables simultaneously, unless your memory is very much better than ours, you're going to struggle to remember who exactly did what.

Online poker seems less real

Here's another difference between live and online poker. You play online poker in the comfort of your own home, in front of a computer. Although you are with other people *virtually*, you're not physically with them and interacting with them.

This makes quite a difference to some people, at least from a psychological perspective. For instance, there isn't the same peer pressure not to look like an idiot.

If you're with other opponents in the flesh, you'll probably concentrate a bit harder and try not to make stupid or embarrassing plays. Online, it's very easy not to care what people think, and hence let go of the inhibitions that often will protect you from reckless play.

What's more, in online poker you don't handle real money or chips, but instead play with numbers that end up on your credit card or bank statement. This further removes you from the actuality of what you're doing – wagering money – and makes it easier to be too loose or aggressive, or otherwise bet irresponsibly. All in all, it's quite easy to make bad plays with the click of a mouse that you'd never make at a live table.

There aren't really any specific ways in which you can exploit these tendencies in your opponents when you observe them; you should just apply the usual strategy that you would against players with manifest flaws in their playing style. But you do need to keep an eye on your own behaviour, and make sure that you give online play the respect and attention it deserves.

Standard of play

In general, online poker games are of a different standard to live games. It would be natural to assume that the standard of play online is generally lower because of the lower barrier to entry. Anyone, regardless of their standard of play, can sit down at a computer and start playing, at any time. Going to a live casino or card room on the other hand is something that would usually be considered only by fairly dedicated and regular players.

This isn't the whole story however and, as it turns out, the standard of play online is usually higher than in live games, at least at the lower end of the stakes. (We're considering a like-for-like comparison here, e.g. a comparison of £1 / £2 *live* games and £1 / £2 *online* games.) Many live game players, when they first start playing online, are not aware of this difference in standard and lose money as a result.

To give you a brief idea of why the difference exists:

■ The cheapest games in card rooms will typically have blinds of around £1 / £2, whereas online games can have blinds of a few pence. In other words, the starting levels are different. If you play at £1 / £2 in a live game, you're playing with the worst players there. If you play at these stakes online, you're actually playing at relatively high stakes compared with many of the beginners and casual players on the site.

■ Recall from our comments above that you can play many more hands per hour online, easily over five times as many, because the dealing is faster and you can sit at multiple tables. And when you play poker, how quickly you win or lose money is more closely related to how much you stake *per hour* than how much you stake per hand. Therefore people playing at, say, £1 / £2 stakes online are often in reality gambling as much money as those playing in £5 / £10 live games.

It's difficult to say exactly how much of a difference in standard there will be in practice, but in our experience £1 / £2 hold'em games in card rooms are typically populated by players who would struggle at the £0.25p / £50p level online. And by the time you reach the £1 / £2 level online, you need to be good solid player with some experience under your belt to have a chance of making money consistently. So don't start playing at these sorts of stakes online until you're ready.

Note: for various reasons that we won't go into here, these arguments don't apply to the same extent at higher stakes.

We'll finish by summing up the main adjustments you need to make for online play.

Summary: online strategy adjustments

- You can't see your opponents, so pay even more attention to the information that you do have – particularly their betting patterns.
- Use the player notes facilities to keep a record of your opponents' habits and playing styles.
- Concentrate even when it's not your turn to act, to make as much time as possible for when it is.
- Experiment with playing on multiple tables, to find the number that's best for you.
- Make sure you don't treat online games less seriously than live games (unless as a conscious and deliberate choice)
- Be prepared to play at lower stakes online than in live games – the standard is usually higher.

Part IV
Poker variants

Chapter Sixteen:
Poker variants explained

As you well know, this book is first and foremost about Texas hold'em. So why, you may ask, are we now about to venture into a discussion of other forms of poker? There are in fact some excellent reasons why it's worth getting to grips with a variety of games:

- The more games you know how to play the more chance you'll have of finding a table at which you're happy – this is especially true for live games in card rooms, where you won't always find your favourite game being played at your preferred stakes.
- You might find that you enjoy playing some games more than others. If you only ever play one game you could be missing out.
- You are also likely to find that you have a greater aptitude for some games than for others. Learning these games will increase your profits.
- Each game requires specific skills, and emphasises different aspects of poker strategy. Becoming proficient in one game will often give you a greater understanding of certain aspects of other games. Learning omaha for example will definitely improve the way you think about many hold'em hands.
- Some of the games we describe below are fairly similar to hold'em. It can be a refreshing change to try something a little different, but not *so* different you've no idea what you're doing.

When it comes to the differences, each poker game has its own rules regarding:

- hand rankings – which hands beat which other hands
- deal structure – hole cards, up-cards and community cards
- betting structure – limits, blinds and antes.

But, in fact, many of these rules are shared by more than one variant. For example, hold'em and seven card stud use the same hand rankings but have different deal structures. Whilst seven card stud, unlike hold'em, is never played as no-limit, both games are often played as either limit or pot-limit games. Some poker variants are more suited to specific betting structures, as you will see.

Games we cover here are as follows:

- Omaha
- Omaha hi-lo (Omaha 8)
- Seven card stud
- Seven card stud hi-lo
- Razz
- Draw poker
- Lowball
- Triple draw
- Pineapple (also known as Irish)
- Indian poker
- Video poker (which isn't real poker, as you'll see).

Finally we describe the betting structure of limit and pot-limit games, and answer some popular FAQs.

Omaha

Omaha is similar to hold'em in that you have the same number of community cards (five) and they are dealt in the same order. The betting structure and hand rankings are also identical. There are however two important differences:

- players receive *four* hole cards on the initial deal (in hold'em you get only two)
- winning hands must be made up of *two* of your hole cards plus *three* community cards. No other combination, however good, is allowed.

Play proceeds as follows:

- The two players on the left of the dealer place forced bets (small blind and big blind) as in hold'em. Each player is then dealt four cards face down on the table – the hole cards.
- A round of betting takes place using the same rules as hold'em, i.e. in a clockwise direction around the table, with players checking, betting, calling, raising or folding in the normal way.
- The second round begins with the dealer placing three community cards (the flop) face up on the table. This is followed by another round of betting.
- The third round sees another community card dealt (the turn). This is followed by another round of betting. Ditto the fourth round (the river).
- Each player still has four hole cards and there are now five community cards on the table.
- When all the bets are in, each player still remaining in the game chooses two hole cards and *three* community cards to make up their hand. As usual, the best / highest hand wins.

Omaha is most commonly played with a limit or pot-limit betting structure, although it's not unheard of for it to be played as no-limit. Omaha may also be played with more than four hole cards per player, sometimes with as many as six or seven if there are few enough players at the table to allow this. In general, the more cards each player has, the more action will be generated.

Omaha hi-lo (Omaha 8)

Very popular in card rooms, omaha hi-lo is a highly challenging, if somewhat complicated, game. It's a *split pot* game which means that you get *two* chances to win some of the pot – one with a high hand as usual, and one with a low hand.

For the high hand, the usual omaha rules apply and the best hand wins.

To make up the lowest hand you must 'qualify' by choosing five unpaired cards of denomination eight or below. When comparing low hands it is the lowest high card that wins, i.e. 3-4-5-6-8 beats 2-3-4-7-8 because the six is lower than the seven.

Therefore the lowest possible hand, known as *the wheel*, is A-2-3-4-5 (aces can be played low). The worst possible qualifying hand is 4-5-6-7-8.

Straights and flushes are completely irrelevant to the low hand, so for example an A-2-4-5-6 'flush' is still six-high, and ties with A-2-4-5-6 of differing suits. Low hands containing pairs, for example A-2-3-3-4, do not qualify.

Players may use the same cards in their high and low hands if they choose, which is why the wheel (A-2-3-4-5) is so strong – it's the best low hand *and* a straight.

Of course, there will always be a highest hand to win the top half of the pot, but not necessarily a lowest hand. It may not be possible to make up a hand of five cards to the value of eight or less when your choice is restricted to two hole cards and three community cards. If there is a high *and* low winner, the pot is split equally. If no-one who shows down their cards is able to make up a low hand, the high hand takes the entire pot.

It's possible for one player to win both halves of the pot, helped by the fact that aces can be played as either high or low. Winning both halves is called a *scoop*.

Play proceeds as follows:

- The two players on the left of the dealer place forced bets (small blind and big blind) as in hold'em. Each player is then dealt four cards face down on the table. These are the hole cards.

- A round of betting takes place using the same rules as hold'em, i.e. in a clockwise direction around the table, with players either checking, calling, raising or folding.
- The second round begins with the dealer placing three community cards face up on the table (the flop). This is followed by another round of betting.
- The third round sees another community card being placed face up on the table followed by another round of betting. Ditto fourth round.
- When all the bets are in, you have the showdown. Each player chooses *two* sets of cards to make up *two* hands – a high hand and a low hand. Both hands must be made up of two hole cards and three community cards. Other combinations, however good, are not allowed.

Seven card stud

After hold'em, seven card stud is one of the most popular poker games around. It's played in card rooms, on the internet and also in the World Series.

Here's a basic idea of how it works:

- Everyone puts in a small ante. (Or, in some games, only the player on the button does so.)
- Players are then dealt three cards – two face down hole cards, and one card face up that everyone can see. Whoever has the lowest card (or highest, depending on house rules) places a bet and the first round begins. In the case of a tie, the player closest to the left of the dealer goes first.
- Betting proceeds in a clockwise direction around the table, with players checking, betting, calling or raising as in hold'em.
- Players are then dealt three more up-cards, each one followed by another round of betting. Everyone now has two hole cards and four up-cards.
- The fifth and final round begins with each player receiving a final hole card face down on the table. Everyone now has a total of seven cards – three hole cards and four up-cards.
- There is a final round of betting and then the showdown in which the player with the best five-card hand wins. Hand rankings are the same as for hold'em.

Note: there are *no* community cards in seven card stud.

Seven card stud hi-lo

Seven card stud can also be played as a high-low game, with a split pot as in omaha hi-lo. The rules are the same as for normal seven card stud, but the pot is split at showdown if there are any qualifying low hands.

This game can also be played without the eight qualifier, so that any hand can take the low half of the pot as long as it's the worst hand at the table. In this case, you might win the low half of the pot with paired hands, or perhaps stronger hands still, if your opponents are all going for the high hand.

What's more, the high-low variant can also be played with a *declaration*. At the end of the betting, but before the showdown, each player reveals whether they wish to compete for the high pot, the low pot, or both.

The winner of the high pot is not (necessarily) the player with the highest hand, but the one with the highest hand *amongst those who indicated they are competing for the high pot*. And similarly for the low pot. If a player declares 'both', they must win (or tie) both pots in order to claim either.

Players usually make their declarations simultaneously, so that no player can gain an advantage by observing other players' declarations. This is achieved by concealing a number of chips in the hand indicating one's declaration: one for 'low', two for 'high' or three for 'both'. Chips are revealed only once all active players have made their decision.

But just to further complicate matters, some people play with sequential declarations, starting to the left of the dealer. This format gives a huge advantage to those players in late position.

Razz

Razz is simply seven card stud played for low only, i.e. with no high hand. Rules determining the winning (low) hand are as in omaha hi-low.

Draw poker

Draw poker was the original form of poker prevalent before hold'em took off in such a big way and it's the variant they play in all the old poker films. It's still popular in some quarters.

Draw poker differs from stud poker and hold'em in that you get to change your cards. There are lots of different versions but here's how you play the basic game:

- All players put in an ante to get some money into the pot.
- Everyone is dealt five cards face down on the table (hole cards).
- The player to the immediate left of the dealer starts off the first round of betting and this continues around the table in a clockwise direction with players checking, calling, raising or folding as usual. Betting is normally fixed-limit or pot-limit.
- Players now get the opportunity to *change their cards* if they so wish. Starting with the player on the dealer's left, everyone is allowed to discard up to five cards. Keeping all your cards and discarding none is called *standing pat*. Discards are placed face down in the middle of the table and immediately replaced by the dealer from the deck, ensuring everyone ends up with five again. If you run out of cards, discards can be shuffled and reused.
- There is now a second round of betting starting with the player who was the first to bet in the opening round.
- Now comes the showdown. Everyone now places their cards face up on the table in front of them, and as usual, the best hand wins.

As with any form of poker, games may not reach the showdown if all but one of the players folds before that point.

There are numerous versions of draw poker – some limit the number of cards you can exchange, or allow more than one draw; some require a payment for each exchanged card, others play lowball (the low hand wins rather than the high hand) or split the pot between the highest and lowest hands.

Lowball

This variant is similar to draw poker, described above, the difference being that the lowest (or worst) hand wins, instead of the highest. You can play:

Deuce-to-seven low – in which aces are high and straights and flushes don't count as low hands. Therefore the best possible hand is 7-5-4-3-2.

Ace-to-five low – in which aces are low and straights and flushes are ignored. Therefore the best possible hand is 5-4-3-2-A.

Ace-to-six low – in which aces are low and straights and flushes don't count as low hands. Therefore the best possible hand is 6-4-3-2-A.

Triple Draw

Triple draw is a variant of draw lowball that's been getting increasingly popular in recent years and is renowned for the action it generates. The play proceeds as follows:

- Two blinds are used as in hold'em.
- Each player is dealt five cards and there's an initial round of betting.
- Players can draw as many cards as they like (zero to five) up to three times each.
- After each round of drawing, there's a round of betting.

Triple draw can be played either as deuce-to-seven low or ace-to-five low. Unfortunately you can't play with more than six players because you run out of cards too often.

Pineapple (Irish)

Generally known as Crazy Pineapple in the US, this is a poker variant that you'll often find being played in home games or possibly in 'dealer's choice' games in card rooms. It's not very popular on the internet though. The game is generally played as fixed-limit in the US and pot-limit in the UK.

The rules are similar to hold'em with two major differences; players initially receive *three* hole cards instead of two and are then required to discard one of them, either before or after the flop, depending on which version is being played.

Play proceeds as follows:

- The two players on the left of the dealer place blinds as in hold'em. Each player is then dealt *three* hole cards face down on the table.
- A round of betting takes place using the same rules as hold'em.
- The second round begins with the dealer placing three community cards (the flop) face up on the table. This is followed by another round of betting.
- At this point all players discard one of their hole cards, bringing their number down to two.
- Play continues with the turn, the river and the showdown, and as in hold'em your five card hand can contain any combination of hole and community cards.

You may encounter many variations on this theme. Rather than starting with three hole cards, players may begin with four or more cards in their hand (although usually all but two are discarded after the flop betting round, as above). High-low variations are also popular.

Indian Poker

Indian poker is an amusing and outlandish poker variant played with any number of players. This is how it works:

- Blinds or antes are posted so there's something to play for and everyone is dealt one card, face down.
- Now you lift up your card and hold it against your forehead so that everyone *except you* can see it. If you peek at your own card, you're disqualified.
- Betting begins with either the dealer or the person sitting to the left of the dealer (you decide), and continues around the table with everyone betting as much as they like on the strength of their unseen card.
- The winner is the last player still remaining in the hand (if everyone else has folded), or the player with the best card at the showdown.
- The next hand should be played with the remaining cards and not a newly shuffled deck.

Trying to second guess what your card is by 'reading' your opponents' faces can be very entertaining, especially after a few drinks. Even harder is keeping a straight face when an opponent bets heavily on a deuce or folds an ace. A good memory is useful for subsequent hands, because you just keep dealing the remaining cards until they're all used up.

There is a variant of this game, known as *blind man's bluff*, which proceeds exactly like hold'em but with players placing their two hole cards on their forehead for all but them to see.

Video Poker

In poker you always play other, real, live people, but video poker is totally different. Here you do *not* play other people. Instead you'll be pitting you wits against a computer or a machine, depending on whether you're playing online on in a bricks and mortar casino. In fact the whole thing is more of a slot machine game than anything else. Always remember that the house has an edge in these games, so you can't possibly win in the long run. The more you play, the more you stand to lose.

However, unlike other slot machine games, winning isn't purely a matter of pure luck – there is a small element of skill and strategy involved. Perhaps that's why it's so popular.

This is how it works:

- First you place your bet by selecting a number of coins from a choice of denominations.
- Next, the computer or machine deals you a hand of five cards.
- You can now reject some, or all, of your cards. Obviously the decision as to which to keep and which to discard depends on the strength of your hand.
- Any cards you discard are immediately replaced by the computer, bringing the number of cards back up again to five. And that's basically it.

Whether you have a winning hand or not depends entirely on the payout scheme which should be clearly indicated, either on screen, or on the actual machine.

There are countless variants of video poker, although *progressive poker* is where you can win the most money. Here, a constantly accumulating jackpot is up for grabs – and these can be worth many thousands. In addition, you have the same chance of winning whether you've been playing for days on end or just a few minutes (you'll need a Royal Flush to win).

Remember that in video poker there is no such thing as a bluff. It's you against the computer and all that matters is the strength of your hand. It's also quite addictive – so practise good money management, remember to take a break now and then ... and know when to quit.

Betting structure variants – pot-limit and limit games

As we mentioned at the beginning of this book, no-limit, limit and pot-limit are not names of poker games; they are terms which define the betting structure used in a particular game, and whether or not the betting is capped. The maximum size of a bet or raise is determined by the type of limit you're using.

Although this book is primarily about *no-limit* hold'em, hold'em can also be played as a limit or pot-limit game. Many games, such as omaha and seven card stud, are played as no-limit rarely, if ever – they are typically played as either limit or pot-limit.

In **pot-limit** poker, all raises must be at least the size of the previous bet or raise, but you may not bet or raise any sum greater than the amount of money already in the pot. In other words, *oversize* bets are not permitted. This of course means that you need to keep track of the pot size, to make sure that nobody tries to make an illegally large bet.

Strategies for pot and no-limit hold'em are really quite similar. The only significant difference is that, since you can't make oversize bets in pot-limit, you have no way to offer your opponents really unattractive pot odds. As we discussed in Chapter Four however, it is rarely particularly desirable to make such big bets anyway.

Limit poker on the other hand (sometimes known as *fixed-limit*) is a drastically different game from no-limit and pot-limit. In limit poker, you have to bet or raise a fixed sum of money. Taking limit hold'em for example, you can only make a bet or raise that is exactly:

- the size of the big blind during the first two betting rounds (pre-flop and flop)
- double the size of the big blind in rounds three and four (turn and river).

The total number of bets or raises that can be made in any one given round (not just the number made by individual players) is also limited, usually to a maximum of four. House rules differ though, so check before you play.

Poker variants FAQ

How do the different betting structures vary across the world?

In the US they play relatively more limit poker than the Brits/Europeans who have always traditionally favoured pot-limit and no-limit. However, big bet (no-limit and pot-limit) poker is eating up limit poker's market share, and is a tougher, more complex and arguably more interesting game – and the one we prefer.

Which game am I most likely to encounter in a bricks and mortar card room?

By far and away, hold'em. In UK card rooms, hold'em is usually played as pot-limit (for which your strategy should be close to that for no-limit); in the US you'll find limit games more common. After hold'em, omaha is likely to be the next most popular. You will also find games of *dealer's choice*, where the players take it in turns to pick a game which is then played for a whole rotation of the dealer's button around the table. These games can be both interesting and lively.

Which games are popular on the internet?

No-limit hold'em is the most popular, by a margin. You will also find plenty of limit and pot-limit hold'em, if that's your thing. But, because it's the internet, and because there are thousands of people online all the time, you will find people playing many other variants, including omaha and omaha hi-lo (limit, pot-limit and no-limit) and seven card stud (limit and sometimes pot-limit).

Which games are played at the World Series?

If you're aiming to win the world championship, no-limit is what you'll be playing. But the World Series includes a host of other big, if slightly less prestigious, events including omaha, omaha hi-lo, seven card stud and deuce-to-seven lowball.

Which is the best game for beginners?

Almost certainly hold'em, because of the simplicity of the rules and the number of people out there playing it to practise against. One could argue in favour of learning limit hold'em before pot-limit or no-limit because it's a less challenging game – but we would disagree on the grounds that it's far less stimulating too.

Can you make up your own variants?

Of course. Once you're familiar with a few of the games, you might start borrowing rules from one game and introducing them into another. If you and your friends are happy playing one of these made-up variants, who are we to stop you? We don't necessarily recommend that you play made-up games *all* the time however – you'll need practice in the more standard variants too for your encounters in card rooms and online.

What are wild cards?

A wild card is a card that can be used as a substitute for any other card in the deck, of any suit. For example: if jokers are wild then Q-Q-Q-9-joker will count as Q-Q-Q-Q-9 (four of a kind) thereby improving your hand substantially.

But you can designate cards other than jokers as wild cards – they can be any denomination, or more than one denomination if you so choose. The use of wild cards can be a fun way to liven up a home game but it's always a good idea to decide in advance how competing hands will be ranked.

For example, if deuces are wild then will

be beaten by a royal flush made without wildcards or tie with it? Will a hand containing two wild cards be ranked lower than a hand with only one? And what will happen in the event of somebody making a five of a kind, which is possible with wild cards but not without?

The usefulness of wild cards can also be restricted if you so wish. It's quite common for jokers to represent *only* aces, or be used *only* as part of high-ranking hands such as a straight or a flush. But so long as everyone is clear on the house rules you can be as creative as you like.

These days, however, wildcards are rarely used in the mainstream games you'll find in card rooms and online.

Chapter Seventeen:
Poker tournaments

Tournaments are a great way to graduate from the free tables without it costing you too much money. This is because you're only liable for the initial buy-in, which can be as low as a few dollars if you're playing online, maybe a little more than that in card rooms. Having said that, some tournaments are huge, with buy-ins costing thousands of pounds or dollars.

How tournaments work

After paying the buy-in and entry fee, all entrants are supplied with exactly the same number of chips and then assigned randomly to tables, typically with ten people on each table (although sometimes fewer than this). You can buy a seat in advance, but a tournament will always begin promptly at a pre-determined time.

The basic rule is that as soon as you've lost your chips, you're out. Survivors carry on playing and the overall winner is the person who ends up with all the chips. In order to ensure that this happens within a reasonable timeframe, the blinds and antes increase regularly during the tournament. You actually need to increase your chip count as time passes, just to make sure that the ever-growing blinds don't eat up your stack.

Tournament organisers (or tournament software) will keep the tables balanced to ensure fairness to all players. For example, with 100 entries, you'll probably get ten tables of ten. As players are eliminated, survivors will be moved around to keep the numbers seated at each table as close as possible. Once ten people have been eliminated, one whole table will be broken up to make up nine tables of ten (rather than ten tables of nine) and so on. The final table will include the last ten or so players.

Although the person who ends up with all the chips is the ultimate winner, other finalists won't go home empty-handed. Typically the top-placed 5%-10%

of all entrants receive prize money, according to the order in which they exit the tournament. Prizes, which may be substantial, are usually paid in cash. Winning a *satellite tournament,* however, will get you free entry into a larger tournament (such as the WSOP).

Some tournaments – known as *rebuy* tournaments – allow you to buy more chips if you lose yours within a certain period of the start, typically during the first hour of play. Tournaments without rebuys are known as *freeze-out* tournaments.

Card rooms and poker websites generally offer a variety of different sized tournaments on a regular basis. The rules can change from tournament to tournament, so check before you start playing.

Strategy adjustments for tournaments

Discussing tournament strategy in detail would make a book in itself, so here we've condensed it into a small number of important tips. The main thing is that you realise that you must play very differently in tournaments than in cash games.

- When blinds are small, with the big blind less than, say, 5% of your stack, you can play 'normal' poker, similar to how you'd play in a cash game.

- If you lose a big hand in a tournament however, you can be knocked out. So, initially at least, play more tightly than usual, and don't take unnecessary risks. In general you should try to avoid big confrontations with players with big stacks unless you hold a premium hand. Stick to taking on those players who can't knock you out or cripple you if you lose.

- Aggression is rewarded even more in tournaments than cash games. A tight, aggressive style is highly effective, so bet and fold much more than you call.

- As the big blind increases to over 5% of your stack, you have to start taking a few more risks, change gears a little, to try to stay ahead of the game. At this stage, you don't need to be reckless, but you should start playing a few more marginal hands, usually by betting or raising rather than calling.

■ Once the big blind is over 10% of your stack then you're starting to get into trouble. You need to pick a hand to make a stand with, and put in a hefty bet or go all-in with it. If you're going to play a hand at all, you need to be prepared to take it all the way.

■ Once the big blind is over 15% of your stack then you're nearly out of time. You should go all-in with any two half-decent cards in the hope that everyone folds, and that you pick up the blinds (which are by now substantial). Even if you get called, you might still win – take a look at the heads-up probabilities in **Appendix C: Tables of odds** to get an idea of these. The main thing is that you make a stand while your stack is still large enough to scare people. Don't let yourself get meekly blinded away.

■ If the tournament uses antes as well as blinds, you'll have to reduce the above thresholds slightly, and loosen up rather sooner (5%, 10% and 15% might become, for example, 4%, 8% and 12%).

■ When the tournament gets near the money (i.e. almost down to the places that pay prizes) then players generally become more reluctant to take big risks in case they leave empty handed. If you are reasonably short-stacked at this point, then you should do the same. Don't get involved with marginal hands – it's not worth it. If you have a relatively healthy stack, however, you can exploit others' meekness. Bullying, bluffing and stealing are more likely to work at this stage since players will be reluctant to risk being knocked out, as they surely will be if they lose a big hand to a big stack.

■ You'll need to be proficient at short-handed play to make it to the final table, and then down to the last few places. If you spend most of your time playing at full tables, you're unlikely to have developed the necessary skills. Read our section on short-handed play in Chapter Thirteen, and get yourself plenty of practice.

■ The last few players in live (but not online) tournaments will sometimes do deals, to split the money more evenly and protect themselves from the huge swings than can happen in short-handed games with large blinds and antes. You're under no obligation to accept a deal if you don't want to, so make sure you're completely happy if you do agree to one.

- Since tournaments pay a few big prizes to a small number of players, you can make a lot of money if you do well in a tournament. But if you have a bad run of cards, you might find you go for many tournaments without even placing.

- Tournaments reduce a large field of players to a single winner within a relatively short space of time – well within the amount of time it would take for all the luck to even out. So to win any tournament, you'll need to get at least a little bit lucky at some stage.

Part V
The money: making it and keeping it

Chapter Eighteen:
Money management

Winner or loser?

We've talked in **Chapter Twelve (Poker Psychology)** about how you should in general pay relatively little attention to your short-term results, because they're too coloured by luck. Quite the opposite is true of your long-term results however, because they are a true measure of your skill as a player. To be clear, by long-term we mean results over periods of, say, fifty hours play or more.

On the back cover of the book, we've made the claim that most poker players lose money more often than not. This claim is justified thus:

■ In poker, any money lost by one player is won by another. In other words, the net winnings / losses incurred by all players at a table all add up to zero. (Poker is therefore called a *zero sum game*, for the obvious reasons.) This means that, all other things being equal, we might expect 50% of players to lose money, and 50% of players to win money.

■ In practice however, winning players win more than losing players lose. There are several reasons for this, most notably that winning players tend to demand a winning edge, and won't play without one. If they can't make a good amount of money at a particular table, they'll probably go elsewhere. Players that consistently lose significant amounts of money on the other hand tend to be more rare.

■ Therefore the poker community is made up of winners, who tend to win big, and losers, who tend to lose moderate amounts. In order for all the wins and losses to sum to zero, you can see that there must be more losers than winners.

■ The numbers are further skewed towards the losers because of the rake or table charge (the money paid to the house for the privilege of playing at their tables). A player who otherwise would break even will be sent into the red by these charges.

It's very difficult to say exactly what proportion of players are long-run losers, but it's probably somewhere around the 80% mark or even higher. What do you think would happen if you took a survey of players and asked *them* how they do? It's not likely that 80% would publicly admit to being losers. In fact, many losing players won't even admit that to themselves. They conveniently allow the memory of their occasional short-term successes to linger on, and forget about their repeated failures. This in turn allows them to pretend that they break even, or perhaps even make money, when the truth is altogether less palatable. In short, they are in denial.

Tracking your results

It's not an exaggeration to say that denial is one of a poker player's greatest potential enemies. If you have no accurate concept of how much you are winning or losing, you have no way of measuring your success or your development as a player. (And this quite apart from the fact that losing money consistently may place undue strain on your general finances. But we're not going to try to tackle the problems of serious gambling addiction in these pages.)

The way to stave off such denial is simple – *just keep track of your wins and losses.* After each session, make a note in a book or spreadsheet of how you fared. We would also recommend that you record roughly how long you played for. This allows you to see not only whether you are winning or losing money, but at what rate. The numbers won't lie to you. After you've been doing this for a while, you'll be forced to confront the truth about your success (or otherwise) as a player.

If you find yourself unpleasantly surprised by the results, then you may need to re-evaluate your approach to the game. Let's suppose that your records tell you that you've been losing money for the past few months. What are you going to do about it? You have two realistic options:

1. Accept these losses and be happy. This could be a sensible course of action if both (a) your finances can sustain the loss, and (b) you enjoy playing poker sufficiently that losing this amount doesn't really matter.

2. Alternatively, resolve to lose less money in the future, or even – dare you hope it – become a winning player. This might seem like a tough thing to make happen, but for most players it's really just a question of changing their attitude.

If the second of these options is your preferred one, then read on to find out what you need to do. If you really care about making money playing poker, then this next section is perhaps the single most important one in this whole book.

Game selection

If you are a losing poker player, it is for one reason, and one reason alone – namely that you regularly play with opponents who are better than you. It can't be because of bad luck, because luck always evens itself out eventually. Don't kid yourself in that respect. How much money you make depends solely on your skill level relative to your opponents.

Note the word *relative*. You can be a very poor player by any objective measure, yet make plenty of money if you are lucky enough to regularly come up against even worse opponents. Or you can be the second best player in the world, and go broke by insisting on playing the best player – as happened to Nick 'The Greek' Dandalos when he took on Jonny Moss in 1949. But that's another story.

If you are *serious* about winning money playing poker, you must strive to improve your relative skill level. Reading this book will of course help develop your game, but that may take time, and there's no guaranteeing how far it will take you. No, the easiest, quickest and most sure-fire way of becoming a more successful player is to seek out worse opponents. This process of picking games based on their likely profitability for you as a player is known as *game selection*.

Game selection isn't just for poor or losing players. Every player can increase his profitability by being more selective about the games he joins. Whereas losing players will lose more slowly or become winning players by doing so, already winning players will win even more.

It's amazing how few people appreciate just how fundamental game selection is. It seems like being a winning poker player *ought* to be solely about how good a player you are, and that's what most people would like to believe. But in fact it's game selection that separates the winners from the losers.

However good you are, unless you happen to be one of the top professionals (and you'll forgive us for assuming you're not), you can always find players better than you if you look for them. If you take on those players, you will lose. If you stick to finding players who are worse than you, you will win. It's as simple as that. Had you thought of poker in this way before?

If it's so easy, you may ask, why don't more people practise good game selection? The answer isn't clear, but it's probably because many people (a) aren't honest with themselves about how much they lose and (b) want to prove themselves in tough games, seeing it as a failure to languish in easy or low stakes games. Instead, they stay in games they can't beat.

We should be glad that such people exist. If they didn't, then nobody could make money playing poker because winning players earn their money at the expense of the losing players. If players never hung around in games in which they lost, then the weaker players would constantly be quitting or moving to softer games, and the stronger players would be constantly chasing these weaker players around, trying to get their money. It would all be very inconvenient, and generally never do.

Recognising softer games

There is an old poker saying attributed to Amarillo Slim that is quoted in almost every poker book or film, and we see no reason to make an exception here: *if you can't find the sucker at the table after thirty minutes of play, you're the sucker.*

This saying wouldn't have stuck around as long as it has if it weren't true. Poor players usually aren't very good at evaluating the skill levels of other players (unless they come up against them time after time and can actually see whether they win regularly or not). But strong players can usually identify poor players quite quickly. If you want to make money, you need to make sure that you're not trying to punch above your weight, and that you can see players at the table who are worse than you, and over whom you believe you have a clear edge. Even if you reckon you're on a par with most of the players in a game, there won't be much profit in it for you. You need a good few soft targets at a table for it to be worthwhile.

Therefore you should constantly be on the look-out for weak players. For example, players who:

- play far too many hands, or show down under-strength starting hands
- call too readily – many poor players habitually call pot-sized bets with flush or straight draws and no chance of getting the pot odds they'd need to make such calls correct
- never bet or raise without a strong hand.

If you can't spot such obvious flaws in your opponents, you may well be the weakest player at the table.

Finding softer games

The easiest way to find games with weaker players is to reduce the stakes you play for, because lower stakes games are generally (but not always) easier to beat. Players who consistently win at lower stakes soon move up to higher stakes, to try to win money more quickly. Therefore it's likely that, within a single card room or website, you can tell which of two tables will be tougher just by the size of the blinds. This kind of *stakes selection* is the simplest form of game selection.

When you begin playing poker, start at the lowest stakes available in the card room / website where you play. Don't even consider moving up from these stakes until you've made money over 30+ hours of play. Many players get too confident too quickly. They move up to bigger games after a few weeks and lose all their money immediately. Make sure you take it slow.

Moreover, if you move from one card room or website to another, and especially if you move from online play to live play, or vice versa, don't assume that equivalent stakes means equivalent skill levels. You might be tempted to think that the $2 / $4 online game will be about as easy as the £1 / £2 game you play in your local card room. In reality though, the online game is likely to be much tougher, for reasons we discuss in Part III. If you're not careful, you might lose a lot of money before it starts to dawn on you that you're out of your league.

More specific than stakes selection is player selection. Once you've seen a player in action a couple of times, you should be able to make some kind of assessment of his ability. Then, if you can spot a game with a few players you recognise and know to be weak, you should be in business.

Alternatively, if you don't see players you recognise, you can simply watch a game for a while and try to form an opinion of the standard.

Look for players making obvious mistakes or losing a lot of money. Online games usually have a maximum buy-in, i.e. a limit on the amount of chips you can sit down with. You will often see one or two big stacks with many more than this number of chips – they've been making money – and a larger number of short stacks who never exceed the maximum buy-in because they've been losing money.

Think of it as the big sharks feeding off the little fish. You may decide not to join the game if the sharks appear too numerous or too skilful, but remember the identity of the fish for next time.

Finding the right level

Maximising your winnings isn't just about maximising the difference in skill between you and your opponents. If you wanted to do that, you could just stay in the easiest, lowest stakes games your whole life. Although playing in such games would virtually guarantee you a win every time, you would struggle to win very much because the amounts of money involved are too small.

In poker, the maximum amount you can realistically win is determined by the size of the blinds. For no-limit hold'em, a good, solid return would be perhaps fifteen times the big blind every hour. For example, if you play in a £0.50 / £1 game and have a clear skill advantage over your opponents, you might expect to make an average of £15 per hour. If you decided instead to play in a £0.25p / £0.50p game, you would have a much bigger edge, and might even make, say, twenty big blinds per hour. But twenty big blinds at these lower stakes is a mere £10, two-thirds of the profit you were making at the higher level. Your increased edge is easily outweighed by the reduced stakes.

Alternatively, you might decide to move up the stakes. You might discover that in an hour in the £1 / £2 game you can make ten big blinds, for a return of £20 per hour. Although your edge is smaller, the larger stakes ensure that you're making more money overall. But in the £2 / £4 your edge is down to three big blinds, £12, per hour, and in the £2.50 / £5 game, you have no edge at all and you break even. You don't even think about joining the bigger games – you'd lose money.

Sample profit curve - reasonably skilled player

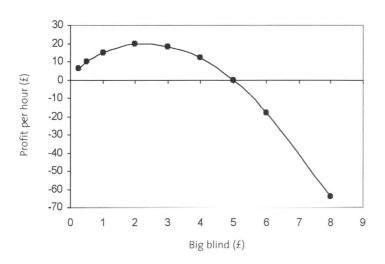

This scenario is typical. If you play at very, very low stakes, you should have a big edge, but won't make very much money. As the stakes increase, even though your edge is diminishing, you will make gradually more money until you reach your *optimum playing level*, the level at which your profit is maximised (£1 / £2 blinds in the above example). Beyond this point, your returns will diminish as the stakes increase. When your average return is zero, it means that your skill level is average for the game – you are at the *break-even level* (£2.50 / £5 blinds in this case). Beyond that point, you'll lose money at an increasing rate as the stakes climb.

Everybody has a curve that looks something like this, regardless of their standard. Weaker players will have a curve that peaks earlier (at lower stakes), tails off more quickly, and has a smaller maximum hourly profit. Stronger players can play profitably at higher stakes, and get much better returns. In practice it's not really possible to determine precisely what your curve looks like because fluctuations in luck obscure the short-term figures, and fluctuations in the skill levels of you and your opponents upset the long-term figures. But if you keep decent records you should, for example, be able to get a rough idea of the kind of stakes that are most profitable for you, and whereabouts your break-even level lies.

We recommend that you try to spend the bulk of your playing time in between your optimum playing level (where you make most money), and your break-even level (where you are an average player in the game). The former will build you a healthy bankroll in the shortest possible time. The latter will maximise your exposure to players better than yourself – which is essential for the development of your game – without actually costing you money. If you decide at any point to experiment with your playing style, and to try different strategies and approaches to the game, be sure to do this at a level where it won't be too expensive if the experiment fails – ideally no higher than your optimum playing level.

You should also be aware of the psychological impact of playing at different levels. If you play at stakes that are too small for you, you might find yourself being too loose or aggressive, because the amounts of money involved are too small for you to care about. Conversely, if you play at stakes that are too high, you are liable to be too passive or tight because you fear losing more than you can afford, i.e. because you care too much about the money.

In theory, the way you play shouldn't depend on the stakes at which you play – it should depend only on the nature of your opponents. However, it's difficult for most people to distance themselves from the money in this way. If you find your game suffering because the stakes aren't right for you, you need to switch to different stakes.

Building a bankroll

If you aim to become a better and higher-earning poker player, then you're going to need to build yourself a bankroll. Broadly speaking, your bankroll is the amount of money you have set aside for poker or, to put in another way, the amount of money you're prepared to lose.

Don't under any circumstances play with money that you can't afford to lose.

If you win money while playing, then your bankroll grows. If you lose money on the other hand, your bankroll diminishes. However, your bankroll isn't quite the same as the historical total of your poker winnings, because it gets adjusted from time to time. Let's give an example to explain what we mean by this.

When you start out playing, you might pay £50 into an account on an online poker site and say to yourself "if the worst comes to the worst, I can afford to lose that £50". Then your bankroll is £50. If you win £100 in your first few weeks, you might now call your bankroll £150 – the £50 you started with plus the £100 you won. You could still afford to lose £150. But a year down the line, if you'd made £2,000 playing poker, you might not be that comfortable with the thought of losing all £2,000. You might decide that your bankroll is £500, and that the other £1,500 you'd won should be put away safely (or spent extravagantly!). You have effectively cashed in some of your bankroll in this case.

Losing players on the other hand will frequently have to top up their bankroll, to cover their losses. Very few people would start out with a fixed bankroll and then give the game up when that's exhausted. More likely they would decide after a while that they could afford to start playing again and top their bankroll up from their earnings.

Anyway, be it big or small, you should decide how big your bankroll is and not simply play without considering the financial implications. The main reason being that the stakes at which you can sensibly play are limited by the size of your bankroll. If you play at stakes that are too big, then your bankroll can be wiped out by a run of bad luck – just like that. There are no strict guidelines here, but if you are playing no-limit hold'em then:

Your bankroll should ideally be at least 500 times the size of the big blind.

So if you're playing £1 / £2 blinds, for example, which may not seem like much, you should be prepared to lose up to £1,000 or so. Or to turn it the other way round, if your bankroll is a mere £100 then you shouldn't play at stakes higher than 10p / 20p with any degree of regularity. (It's ok to dabble at higher stakes for very short periods – just be prepared to get out quick if it starts going wrong.)

If you make money and your bankroll grows, it's fine to move up the stakes – so long as you remember our advice above about game selection and don't take on players who are too good for you. If your bankroll begins to diminish, then move down a level or two until you start winning again.

Note: Different games and betting structures will demand different guidelines. Omaha (when played at pot-limit or no-limit) tends to have bigger pots than hold'em, and so requires even more caution. Limit games on the other hand have much smaller pots and can safely be played at higher stakes.

General money-management tips

Finally, here are a few general pieces of advice that will help you ensure that the size of your bankroll keeps heading in the right direction.

- Always play in card rooms (or on websites) that you believe to be safe. Stick to the big, mainstream operators if in doubt.
- If you play online, look out for the many introductory offers and loyalty bonuses that are out there. Internet card rooms routinely offer hundreds of pounds completely free as an enticement to new players to get on board.
- Beware of playing if you're not feeling 100%. Your play may suffer if you're tired, drunk, angry, unhappy, unwell, stressed or just generally tilting for some reason. Losing is one thing, but if you're beginning to feel despondent, it's time to stop.
- Check your playing record frequently. If you're not entirely comfortable with your results, or how much time you're spending playing, then make sure you do something about it. If in doubt, play less or at lower stakes.

Of course, however well you manage your money, there will always be people out there who want to take it all away from you ... and we don't necessarily mean honestly. This unpleasant thought leads us conveniently into the next chapter which is all about cheating (and how to protect yourself against it).

Chapter Nineteen:
Cheating

A book on poker wouldn't be complete without a chapter on cheating. Many players seem obsessed with it; not because they want to learn how to do it (fortunately most people are essentially honest) but because they're worried they might end up on the receiving end.

This is a potentially valid concern, especially with the rise of internet card rooms. When you play online you can't physically see your opponents, and since there are millions of players out there it can be nigh on impossible to build up a clear picture of how any one person plays, or who they play with (although see **Player Analysis Software** below).

If you're playing online, how do you know that your opponents aren't all sitting in the same room together or communicating by phone or instant messaging? Or that you're not playing a poker 'robot'? Live games are also vulnerable, albeit in slightly different ways. How can you protect yourself?

This chapter covers the different ways people cheat and what you should do to guard against them. We also discuss the methods card rooms and websites use to detect and discourage questionable practices, including the use of performance enhancing software.

First we'll talk about live games. These permit several methods of cheating, ranging from a casual peek of another player's cards to the fully fledged con, as featured in all good poker movies.

Cheating in live play

The casual peek

This is most likely to happen in a home game where players are in it purely for the enjoyment rather than the money. Everyone may be too busy chatting and drinking to notice somebody catch a glimpse of another player's cards.

: *THE CASUAL PEEK!*

It never hurts to guard your hole cards carefully. Getting used to keeping them face down on the table in front of you (as opposed to holding them up and waving them around) will stand you in good stead for the day you venture out into bricks and mortar card rooms.

Try to get into the habit of looking at your hole cards once at the start of the hand and then committing them to memory. Checking your cards frequently not only means they're more likely to be seen by other players but can occasionally reveal information about your hand itself. See Chapter Twelve for more on such tells.

Doctored cards

Cards can be marked or doctored in numerous ways, usually to denote the high or picture cards. For example:

- Punching – tiny holes or indentations are made with a dedicated card punch. These little holes or dents are felt by the dealer as he distributes the cards and allow him to identify each card in turn. Players in the know can also identify punched cards by looking at their backs.

- Changing the design – some cheats favour changing the design on the back of specific cards. This is done so subtly that even the closest inspection won't rumble it.

Obviously these methods require quite a bit of preparation – they're not the sort of thing you can initiate in the middle of a game. Having said that, there are card cheats out there who are quite adept at surreptitious scratching, bending or tearing. So if you don't know and trust your opponents implicitly, use new packs of cards regularly, look out for damaged cards and supply your own cards whenever you can.

Shuffling tricks and unfair dealing

As every magician will testify, manipulating cards isn't that difficult once you know how. It's quite possible to appear to be shuffling the cards thoroughly, when in reality you're keeping some or all of the cards in the same order. Moving cards to the top or the bottom of the pack, manipulating the order of cards in order to deal yourself a monster, and even substituting cards are all underhand tricks that have been employed by cheats ever since poker was invented.

Mostly these tricks involve the dealer and one other player. That way it's not so obvious that the dealer is winning, and it means that the dealer and their accomplice can effectively hand each other cards.

Fortunately it's most unlikely to happen in casual home games since most players are there for the enjoyment and camaraderie. It's big games that are most at risk, especially where players don't know each other.

If you're worried about this kind of activity, don't let the same person shuffle and deal. Ideally have one person shuffle, another cut the deck and a third deal.

Chip cheats

Scams involving chips rather than cards are altogether more common. In their simplest form, a player secretly brings his own chips to a game or card room, adding to his funds without actually contributing any money.

This sort of thing isn't likely to happen in home games unless you've invited a complete stranger or two; although who's to say your best mates aren't capable of cheating? Card rooms protect themselves against chip cheats by rotating different sets of chips (so you don't know which set is going to be used on any given day) and by using unique chips that are hard to copy and can't be bought elsewhere – just like cash in that respect.

Another cheating technique involving chips is *palming*. This is the rather underhand practice (no pun intended) of stealing chips from the pot. A variant is where a player deliberately under-bets, calling say, £35 but actually just throwing in six £5 chips rather than seven. Alternatively he puts in two £25 chips and takes out too much change.

To combat this, simply insist that players place their bets slightly in front of them, for all to see, rather than tossing chips directly into the pot. Then let the *dealer* give change and gather the chips together at the end of the betting round. It's also a good idea to insist all chips stay in full view – pocketing chips is against the rules.

Collusion

This is where two or more players around the same table help each other out, to the detriment of honest, unsuspecting players. Collusion can be passive or active. Passive collusion is simply avoiding your accomplices when they have good hands, i.e. staying out of each others' way. This practice mostly helps prevent both of them losing their money to a third player with a strong hand – but it doesn't stop one of them from losing.

Passive collusion can also include:

- Signalling to one or more accomplices using pre-arranged phrases, coughs or gestures to indicate the value of one's hand or to coordinate betting.
- Allowing the accomplice to see hole cards.

What distinguishes *active* collusion is the practice of raising and re-raising with the intention of driving out other players.

Collusion, if performed adeptly, is difficult to spot at first because the players involved will never have to show down their hands. But after a while, it should become apparent if the same players keep repeating this sort of pattern. It also takes rather a lot of practice, time and effort – which is why if it's going to happen, it's more likely to happen in high stakes games.

But do watch out for strange or unusual phrases or gestures that get repeated frequently, or the same group of players frequently raising and re-raising each other. If you suspect something is amiss, walk away from the game or find another table.

What about collusion in casinos?

Players colluding in games and tournaments in casinos and card rooms don't usually get very far, and they're certainly nowhere near as successful as the movies would have you believe.

The fact is, casinos are extremely vigilant. Apart from employing their own dealers and supplying their own cards, casinos watch (and record) punters continuously. Anyone playing with the same people and winning consistently will quickly attract attention.

To sum up, the main forms of cheating in live games involves either some form of physical manipulation of cards, chip cheating, or collusion between players. Luckily all these methods are difficult to pull off for all but the most professional card cheat, but it never hurts to be on your guard.

Things are a little different when you're playing online.

Cheating online

With online play, the cheat has no opportunity whatsoever to mark cards, palm chips or indulge in any sort of illegal shuffling tricks. Collusion, however, is a different matter altogether.

Online Collusion

Collusion is a real threat in online play. Accomplices don't have to bother with covert gesturing or surreptitious showing of cards; they can simply play in the same room. In fact, you don't even need an accomplice – you can just play two or more hands on the same table yourself if you manage to get two separate accounts with one poker site.

Poker sites try their best to make it difficult for two people to play using the same computer or in the same location, for example by cross-checking credit card billing addresses and network (IP) address ranges. Having said that, it's still fairly easy to get space on the same table as your best mate who just happens to be round at your place or 'working' in the same office.

And there's not much that can be done to combat players communicating with each other by phone, text or instant messaging.

The good news for honest players is that, although it's not too difficult to sit down at an online game with an accomplice, getting away with active collusion is another matter.

Virtually all of the big sites, and many of the smaller ones now use sophisticated anti-collusion software to spot players deliberately co-ordinating their betting. During online play, computers monitor who plays with whom and how they bet, and look for unusual betting patterns. As with live games, you as a player still can't see your opponent's mucked hands – but the poker sites can. Similarly, they can also spot players continually raising and re-raising inappropriately and any other tell-tale signs. Poker sites also make it very difficult for players to change their aliases (on-screen names).

If a player is discovered, or even suspected of, attempting to defraud a poker site, he will be banned, his account funds seized and his name placed on a blacklist. And this applies to any form of cheating, not just collusion.

All of which makes life harder and a lot more risky for all but the most determined cheat, and a lot safer for the rest of us.

Performance-enhancing software

Yes, you guessed it. It's now possible to buy software which runs on your computer while you're playing poker online and assists you in your play. There are several different types of program but they all have the same aim – to give you an advantage over your opponents.

Hand analysis software. Hand analysis software looks at your cards (your hole cards and the community cards) and then lets you know how good your hand is and the odds of winning. This can be very useful, especially when you're starting to play seriously or when you just need a bit of instruction on how good a specific hand is.

You could in theory learn a thing or two from using such software, and it might improve your game a little, but there are also a number of disadvantages. It can only be used for online play and doesn't always come cheap. More importantly, it can't tell you anything whatsoever about your opponents.

Because of this last point, most poker website operators aren't too worried about card analysis software – it's more educational than anything else and good players won't benefit much from using it anyway.

Player analysis software. The next step up from hand analysis, player analysis software keeps a record of the way all your opponents play and what they do in each situation. This information is compiled into a database which you can then consult during play, often via a head-up display. Once you've faced an opponent a few times, the software will tell you whether they are loose or tight, what sort of hands they play, how often they check-raise or bluff, and so on.

The poker websites generally don't mind people using this sort of software too much either. After all, it's only collecting and processing information that would be available anyway. Yes, using such programs doesn't quite seem to be what poker is all about, but we won't deny that the information they provide can be extremely helpful.

Player databases. Now we're getting into rather murkier territory. It's possible to buy databases which have the goods on large numbers of people who play regularly on the main poker sites. We're talking tens or hundreds of thousands of players tracked on a daily basis. These, used in conjunction with player analysis software, can form the basis of a very powerful playing aid.

The poker sites take a dimmer view of trading in player databases. It's one thing to use software to enhance one's own game, but another thing entirely for people to be sharing information about the playing habits of a whole community. Our advice would be to steer clear of this sort of activity.

Poker robots. Another worry for honest players and poker sites alike, is the rise of the poker robot, which is a piece of software that plays online poker on your behalf. The idea is that you set up a poker robot to play multiple games simultaneously, possibly using multiple aliases. All you then have to do is collect the money – or at least that's the theory.

The first potential problem is one of detection – the poker sites have started to introduce methods of spotting these robots. Having said that, there are some elaborate ways of virtually guaranteeing you go undetected.

The main drawback however, and the reason why the current crop of poker robot programs isn't a serious threat, is simply because they're not much good. Most of them play about as well as a poor human player, and they are notably much worse at no-limit and pot-limit poker than limit poker. (Limit poker is an easier game to play by rote, at least at low stakes.) At the time of writing therefore, you're unlikely to make much money by acquiring an army of poker robots.

Having said that, there are plenty of programmers out there trying to teach their computers the human arts of deceitfulness, cunning and duplicity – and perhaps it won't be too long before they succeed. The winner of the 2005 World Poker *Robot* Championship was itself comfortably beaten by top (human) player Phil Laak in a heads-up limit hold'em match. But it may well be only a matter of time.

Why cheat at all?

Where's the fun, enjoyment and *skill* of a good game when you're simply cheating? Why risk your reputation and your opponents' trust? What's the point?

The answer is simple. Some people aren't interested in poker – they're interested in making money any which way they can, and if that means being dishonest, then fine. Cheating at poker is a means to an end, albeit a risky one. Money aside, there are also people out there who simply enjoy the challenge of trying to devise clever and foolproof schemes.

Fortunately, as we commented earlier, most people are essentially honest. That fact, plus the increasingly sophisticated detection software now employed by online sites, gives the shady player and his accomplices less and less room in which to manoeuvre.

Cheating by the house

Many players worry about the possibility of online card rooms rigging the deck in order to make a bigger overall profit. This is usually just paranoia at work. Players who moan about bad beats and unfair deals are normally the weaker players who don't win as much as they'd like, or who don't understand the true nature of randomness and chance.

Having said that, online poker sites aren't charities – they're in it for the money – and there are reports of unreliable and even downright dishonest sites on the net. The biggest problem seems to be late- or non-payment of winnings. A judicious web search will quickly bring up a number of sites listing the worst offenders. The mainstream operators do not typically feature on such lists.

Another favourite accusation seems to be that dealing on poker sites isn't 100% random, and that it's rigged in order to produce more bad beats or big confrontations than would normally be expected. You could argue that by dealing strong hands to all players, more money will go in the pot, and the rake (house charge) will be bigger. The house would benefit from this in some small way if it got away with it.

We hear this sort of complaint so much but we've yet to see any convincing evidence for the practice. The fact is that a big poker site like Ladbrokes or Party Poker will make so much money from the rake that they don't need to increase their takings by rigging the deal. If you've got a licence to print money legally, why would you jeopardise it by doing anything illegal?

All we can say is that, as far as we can see, the big, reputable sites are completely above board, both in terms of timely payouts and honest dealing. If you're unlucky enough to fall foul of a dodgy site or you begin to suspect any sort of cheating is going on, find somewhere else to play; preferably one of the major sites with a bigger reputation to lose.

To conclude, we believe that the risk of being turned over by poker cheats is actually very small. We've played a fair amount (which is something of an understatement) and neither of us has ever felt that any significant amount of dishonest activity has been going on.

Chapter Twenty:
Increasing your earnings

Becoming a good poker player isn't easy. Unlike many other competitive games, and especially in contrast to most sports for example, you will not become significantly better just by playing a lot. No, in order to improve you will need to dedicate some serious time to studying the game, and working on developing your abilities.

For some reason, many poker players never seem to do this. They just play the game more or less the same way they were first taught it, and either assume that they don't have anything else to learn, or don't have any interest in doing so. If that's your choice too then of course that's up to you. But if you've made it this far through the book, it's likely that you have loftier aspirations.

So – here's the important point. If you really want to make a go of improving your poker, and try to fulfil your potential in the game, you *must* spend a comparable amount of time studying, thinking about and discussing the game as you do playing it. We really can't emphasise this enough. There is so much to learn, if you really set your mind to it. Here are the best ways to go about it.

Read more

The more you read, the more you'll learn. You will discover that the game is far more subtle and complex than you ever imagined. You will come across all sorts of ideas that you will need to digest and then put into practice. You will develop an understanding of just how much better the top professional players are than your average card room wannabe, and hopefully get some insight into why.

There are hundreds of poker books available in book stores and online, and some of the large poker sites have their own e-magazines and newsletters as well. There are also a multitude of websites and discussion forums offering information and opinions on every aspect of the game.

It's true you shouldn't treat everything you read as gospel, but there's a lot more good advice than bad out there and in time you'll learn to tell the difference.

We list a few of our favourite poker books in **Appendix D: Further reading**.

Discuss strategy during games

If you play in a home game where the money isn't too serious, it's an excellent idea to discuss interesting hands amongst yourselves. As long as the conversation is handled sensitively, it can be very illuminating to listen to others comment on the merits, or otherwise, of your play, and vice versa.

In poker, it's easy to get into ruts whereby you doggedly adhere to a flawed approach or tactic. Talking to others can show you the light and help shake you out of these bad habits.

Obviously such discussions are more fruitful if everybody reveals their cards at the end of the hand, so you will first need to check if people are willing to do so. Some players insist on keeping their cards totally secret (except when showing them down) because they believe they lose too much of an edge by revealing them.

Although this is to a certain extent a valid point, *occasionally* playing more openly with the right company can be of enormous educational value. We suggest in fact that the long-term benefits such discussions confer may well outweigh the short-term benefits gained by concealing your playing style.

Play jointly online

You can try this as an alternative to the above. You'll need to get together with one or two friends and all be in the same room. One of you sits at the computer and plays online, either in a cash game or tournament. The rest of you discuss each hand and decision, and agree each of your moves jointly. You may also choose to split any winnings or losses amongst you, which will allow you to play at higher stakes more affordably. (By the way – this doesn't count as cheating or collusion and is totally above board. If more than one of you were actually sat down and playing at each table, that would be a different matter.)

As it turns out, this is a tremendously educational way of playing the game. You all get to discuss each hand openly, and from the perspective of a single player. Where you disagree, try to work out (retrospectively if necessary) what the correct play was. With any luck, you'll all be able to pick up the better ideas and habits from your fellow players.

Practice makes perfect

Once you've spent a while reading books and discussing strategy with others, you'll no doubt have a vast number of ideas in your mind about how you can potentially improve your game. It's almost certain that the first time you experiment with a new idea or strategy, it won't always go according to plan. You'll have to review your play during and after each session, to make sure that you identify and learn from your mistakes. The very best players have a huge knowledge of the game – but they also have the experience to know how to apply their knowledge correctly in each situation.

Part VI
Resources

Appendix A:
Odds and probabilities

In this appendix we'll give you a quick overview of the terminology and techniques associated with calculations involving probability.

To illustrate this we'll assume that you have removed the four aces from the deck

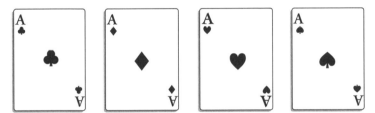

You turn these four cards face down and shuffle them. If you now turn the topmost card face up, what is the probability that it's the ace of spaces?

There are four cards here and only one of them is the ace of spades. Therefore we say that the probability of picking it is *1-in-4*. We can express this another way, as a percentage. Since there are four cards and one is the ace of spades, the probability of picking it is one divided by four, or 25%. A 25% chance is the same as a 1-in-4 chance; there's no difference between them.

There is one other common way of expressing this. Since there are three cards that aren't the ace of spades and one that is, the odds against picking the ace of spades are *3-to-1*. In other words, it is three times more likely not to happen than to happen. This is the notation that bookies use when they display gambling odds, and it's the notation we use in this book for expressing pot odds. It looks a bit similar to the 1-in-4 notation described above, so make sure you don't get them mixed up. However, note that we don't use the 1-in-4 notation in this book. We express odds either as percentage probabilities or as something-to-1 against.

Here's a table showing some selected probabilities expressed in each of these three ways.

Percentage probability	Odds	1-in-?
16.6%	5-to-1 against	1-in-6
20%	4-to-1 against	1-in-5
25%	3-to-1 against	1-in-4
33.3%	2-to-1 against	1-in-3
40%	1.5-to-1 against	1-in-2.5
50%	1-to-1 (evens)	1-in-2
66.6%	2-to-1 on	1-in-1.5
75%	3-to-1 on	1-in-1.33
100%	-	1-in-1

For those interested in the mathematics, we can express these relationships as formulae. If P% is the same as X-to-1 against (i.e. they represent the same probability) then:

P = 1 divided by (X + 1)

And:

X = (1 − P) divided by P

Note: Events that are odds-*on* rather than odds-*against* are more likely than not to happen, i.e. have a probability of more than 50%. An event that is 2-to-1 *on* to happen, for example, is twice as likely to happen as not to happen.

Appendix B:
Expectation

In poker, the *expected value*, or *expectation*, of any bet is the amount of money that you will on average earn by making it. Although you don't actually need to calculate expectation whilst playing poker, it can be useful to have an understanding of how it works.

Example 1

To take a simple example first, suppose you play a game with a friend where you toss a coin repeatedly. If it falls heads, he pays you £20. If it falls tails, you pay him £10. What is your expectation for each toss?

With probability 50%, you will win £20. With probability 50% you will lose £10. You then just take a weighted average of your profit over all the possible outcomes. In other words your expectation is:

$$(50\% \times £20) - (50\% \times £10) = £5.$$

Every time you toss the coin, you expect to win £5 on average. Although it's quite likely there would be significant variation from this figure if you played only a few times, the luck would even out in the long-run. If you played 1,000 times, you would expect your average winnings to be near to £5 per play.

Example 2

Now let's look more closely at the hand example we introduced in Chapter Four. To recap, you hold A♥ 9♥ and the board is Q♥ 2♠ 4♥ 7♦. Assume you will win if you make a flush on the river, but not otherwise, and your nine outs make you just under 20% to do so. There is £100 in the pot and your opponent bets £20. What is the expectation if you call?

If you call, there are two possible outcomes:

- 19.6% of the time you will make your flush and win £120.
- The remaining 80.4% of the time you will miss your flush and lose the extra £20 it costs you to call the bet.

So your expectation is:

$$(19.6\% \times £120) - (80.4\% \times £20) = £7.40.$$

Note: We have rounded the numbers slightly.

Appendix C:
Tables of odds

In this appendix we provide information on the probabilities of a variety of different events happening. You should at least be familiar with the more important of these since they may affect the chances of you winning a hand, and hence how you should play that hand.

Head to head match-ups

This section deals with the chances of one hold'em starting hand beating another if they play each other heads-up all the way to showdown. This is particularly useful for tournament play where players often go all-in pre-flop as their stacks diminish in relation to the blinds.

You should be aware that the ranked list of starting hands given in Chapter Six bears no resemblance to the likelihood of one hand beating another in a heads-up (one on one) battle.

For example, a lowly pair of twos is actually a slight favourite against the mighty ace-king in this case. But against more than one opponent, 2-2 goes rapidly downhill – because the likelihood of other players pairing the board becomes too great, and any pair will of course beat a pair of twos.

Moreover, ace-king is only a very slight underdog to *any* pair of cards from twos all the way up to queens. However, 2-2 is a massive underdog to any other pair. So ace-king stands up far better than 2-2 against multiple opponents and a variety of other holdings, whereas 2-2 is extremely fragile. If you hold a pair of twos, you're either a slight favourite or a big underdog – a situation you should try to avoid.

Here are percentages for some sample heads-up confrontations. These figures have been rounded to the nearest one percent (and hence don't always sum to 100).

Your hand	Opponent's hand	Win %	Lose %	Split %
A♣ A♠	K♣ K♠	82	17	1
A♣ A♠	K♦ K♥	81	19	0
A♣ A♠	2♣ 2♠	82	17	1
A♣ A♠	A♦ K♥	92	7	1
K♣ K♠	A♦ K♥	70	30	1
3♣ 3♠	2♣ 2♠	79	16	5
7♥ 7♠	2♣ 2♠	82	17	2
7♥ 7♠	A♣ 2♠	70	30	0
10♣ J♣	A♦ A♥	22	18	0
10♣ J♠	A♦ A♥	18	82	0
10♣ J♣	2♦ 2♥	53	45	1
10♣ J♠	2♦ 2♥	50	48	1
10♣ J♠	A♦ K♥	37	63	0
10♣ J♠	2♦ 3♥	66	33	1
10♣ J♠	A♦ 2♥	46	54	0
9♣ J♠	10♦ Q♥	36	63	1
A♣ K♠	A♦ Q♥	72	24	5
A♣ K♠	A♦ 2♥	71	24	5

We can generalise the most common match-ups as follows:

- ■ Overpair vs. underpair: roughly 4-to-1 favourite
- ☐ Pair vs. lower unpaired cards: roughly 4-to-1 favourite
- ☐ Pair vs. higher unpaired cards: slight favourite
- ☐ Pair vs. one overcard and one undercard: roughly 2-to-1 favourite
- ■ Pair vs. one shared card and one undercard: roughly 10-to-1 favourite
- ■ Pair vs. one shared card and one overcard: roughly 2-to-1 favourite
- ☐ Unpaired overcards vs. unpaired cards: roughly 3-to-2 favourite
- ☐ Overcard and undercard vs. unpaired cards: slight favourite
- ☐ Shared card plus higher kicker: roughly 3-to-1 favourite.

Pre-flop odds

The following table shows the probability of being dealt various hands pre-flop.

You are dealt	Probability	Odds
A pair	5.9%	16-to-1
A particular pair, e.g. aces	0.5%	220-to-1
Suited cards	30.8%	3.25-to-1
Connected cards	14.5%	5.9-to-1
A suited connector	3.6%	26.6-to-1

Flop odds

The following table shows the probability of flopping various hands given your pre-flop holding.

You hold	You flop	Probability
Unpaired cards	No pair	67.6%
Unpaired cards	One pair	29.0%
Unpaired cards	Two pair	2.0%
Unpaired cards	Trips	1.3%
Unpaired cards	Full house or quads	0.1%
A pair	No set	88.2%
A pair	A set	10.8%
A pair	Full house or quads	0.1%
Connectors (4-5 to 10-J)	Outside straight draw	9.8%
Connectors (as above)	Inside straight draw	18.9%
Connectors (as above)	Straight	1.3%
Suited cards	Flush draw	10.9%
Suited cards	Flush	0.8%
Suited connectors (4-5 to 10-J)	Straight flush	0.02%

The following table shows the probability of unwanted overcards coming on the flop when you hold a pair in your hand.

You hold	Probability of overcard(s)
K-K	23%
Q-Q	41%
J-J	57%
10-10	69%
9-9	79%

From flop to river – hitting outs

The following table shows the chances of hitting one of your outs in a hand of hold'em, depending on the number of outs you have.

No. of outs	On the flop, with two cards to come		On the turn, with one card to come	
	Percentage	Odds-to-1	Percentage	Odds-to-1
1	4.26%	22.5	2.17%	45.0
2	8.42%	10.9	4.35%	22.0
3	12.49%	7.0	6.52%	14.3
4	16.47%	5.1	8.70%	10.5
5	20.35%	3.9	10.87%	8.2
6	24.14%	3.1	13.04%	6.7
7	27.84%	2.6	15.22%	5.6
8	31.45%	2.2	17.39%	4.8
9	34.97%	1.9	19.57%	4.1
10	38.39%	1.6	21.74%	3.6
11	41.72%	1.4	23.91%	3.2
12	44.96%	1.2	26.09%	2.8
13	48.10%	1.1	28.26%	2.5
14	51.16%	1.0	30.43%	2.3
15	54.12%	0.8	32.61%	2.1
16	56.98%	0.8	34.78%	1.9
17	59.76%	0.7	36.96%	1.7
18	62.44%	0.6	39.13%	1.6
19	65.03%	0.5	41.30%	1.4
20	67.53%	0.5	43.48%	1.3

Appendix D:
Further reading

Here's a list of some of our favourite books on poker and poker strategy.

■ *Caro's Book of Poker Tells* – Mike Caro

■ *Super System 2: A Course in Power Poker* – Doyle Brunson

■ *Harrington on Hold'em* – Dan Harrington and Bill Robertie

■ *How Good Is Your Pot-Limit Hold'em?* – Stewart Reuben

■ *How Good Is Your Pot-Limit Omaha?* – Stewart Reuben

■ *Killer Poker Online* – John Vorhaus

■ *Poker 24/7* – Stewart Reuben

■ *Pot-Limit & No-Limit Poker* – Stewart Reuben and Bob Ciaffone

■ *The Psychology of Poker* – Alan N Schoonmaker

■ *The Theory of Poker* – David Sklansky

Appendix E:
Online poker websites

Each of the big online poker sites offers some or all of the following:

- Free-to-play and low stakes tables

- Hundreds of games, tournaments and satellites

- Big tournaments with huge pay-outs

- Thousands of players online, day or night

- Loyalty bonuses

- Secure, encrypted network connections

- Statistical data on your own play

- An online chat facility

- Comprehensive playing guides, tutorials, strategy advice and poker glossaries.

For the latest information, lots of extra resources and links to recommended poker sites, please visit www.playingpokertowin.co.uk

Here's a selection of some of the biggest names on the internet:

- www.ladbrokespoker.com

- www.partypoker.com

- www.interpoker.com

- www.coralpoker.com

- www.gamingclubpoker.com

- www.pokerstars.com

- www.pokerroom.com

- www.pacificpoker.com / www.888.com

- www.paradisepoker.com

- www.fulltiltpoker.com

Other interesting poker sites

Here's a list of some other interesting sites offering a variety of resources for beginners and more experienced players alike.

- www.online-poker-beginners-guide.com. An easy to understand and informative site.

- www.whichpoker.co.uk. Has reviews and stats on the largest UK poker rooms. Includes tournament listings, rules and beginner guides.

- www.homepokertourney.com. Offers advice on how to run your own no-limit hold'em tournaments.

- www.pokercoach.us. Has the rules of the game according to Bob Ciaffone, a leading authority on card room rules.

- www.harrahs.com/wsop/rules.html. The official WSOP rules.

- www.pokerpulse.com. Provides up to date traffic rankings for online poker rooms.

Glossary

Ace high – a hand containing five cards of distinct values, the highest of which is an ace.

Aces up – a hand with a pair of aces and one other pair (can be any value or suit).

Action – betting, money going in the pot.

Active player – a player who is involved in a hand, i.e. hasn't yet folded.

Advertise – to give others an impression of the way you play, often by showing hole cards voluntarily when not required to do so.

All-in – to have all your chips in the current pot.

American Airlines – two aces in the hole.

Ante – a sum contributed to the pot by each player at the start of a hand.

Backdoor hand – a hand made on the river that relied on both the turn and river cards to complete.

Bad beat – where one hand loses to a worse hand in unlucky fashion.

Belly-buster – see inside straight draw.

Bet – chips that a player adds to the pot.

Bet out – simply to bet, as opposed to checking with the intention of subsequently calling or raising.

Bet the pot – to bet an amount of chips equal to amount currently in the pot.

Betting structure – defines the limits, blinds and antes of a game.

Big blind – the larger of the two compulsory bets made before the deal, made by the player sitting two places left of dealer. See also small blind.

Blue chip – a high-denomination chip.

Bluff – to bet or raise with a weak hand with the intention of making other players fold (because they fear a strong hand).

Board cards – the same as community cards.

Boat – another name for a full-house.

Bricks and mortar casino – a real casino where live games are played, i.e. the opposite of an online casino.

Bullets – a pair of aces.

Bump – see raise.

Burn card – the first card dealt in each round is burned, i.e. discarded, to reduce the possibility of cheating.

Button – a flat round disk that moves around the table in a clockwise direction to indicate the position of the dealer in each hand.

Buy-in – the entry fee for a game or tournament.

Buy in – to obtain chips and sit down at a game.

Call – to match the largest bet previously made in the betting round by adding chips to the pot.

Calling station – a loose-passive player (see **Chapter Eleven: Playing Styles**).

Change gears – to switch playing style mid-way through a session.

Cheat software – a computer program which give the user an unfair advantage.

Check – to neither bet nor fold, but to remain in the hand but without contributing chips to the pot. Checking is permitted only when everyone who acted previously has checked too.

Check-raise – to check and then subsequently raise within a single round of betting

Chip leader – in a tournament, the player with the most chips.

Chips – small, round, coloured counters used for betting in live games.

Coffee-housing – to discuss a hand in progress for strategic purposes, e.g. to mislead or manipulate opponents.

Collusion – where two or more players at the same table (either in a live game or online) covertly help each other out to the detriment of unsuspecting, honest players.

Community Cards -– cards dealt face up in the middle of the table which can be used by any player.

Connected holding or connector – cards with consecutive values. See also suited connector.

Continuation bet – an opening bet made on the flop by the last (or only) player to raise pre-flop.

Crying call – a call made, usually on the river, by a player who doesn't expect to win.

Deal structure – the rules that govern the dealing of cards in a game, i.e. hole cards, upcards, community cards, etc.

Dealer – the person dealing the cards. The deal moves clockwise around the table after each hand.

Dealer button – see button.

Deck – a pack of cards.

Declaration – in high-low (split pot) games, a phase after the betting has finished but before showdown where players indicate whether they wish to compete for the high hand, the low hand, or both.

Designated dealer – a person who deals every hand.

Dominated hand – a hand that is (a) weaker than another hand and (b) has cards in common with it, making it particularly unlikely to win.

Drawing dead – playing a hand that can't possibly win the pot even if it does improve.

Drawing hand – a hand that isn't yet complete but has the potential to be good if subsequent cards are favourable.

Draw poker – a class of poker games in which cards can be exchanged.

Equity – your equity in a pot is the amount of it you expect on average to win.

Expectation – expected profit.

Face-to-face play – live play around a real table.

Family pot – a hand in which all the players at the table are still involved.

Fish – a terrible player.

Flat-call – to call, rather than raise.

Flop trips – when a hole card matches two board cards, making three of a kind.

Flop – in hold'em, the first three community cards which are dealt face up on the table after the first round of betting.

Flush – any five cards of the same suit.

Flush draw – a hand that could improve to a flush.

Fold – to place one's cards face down on the table and withdraw from the current hand.

Four flush – four cards all of the same suit.

Four of a kind – four cards of the same value plus one other card, e.g. 7-7-7-7-9 or, at its best, A-A-A-A-K.

Free card – when a player is able to see the next board card without putting any money in the pot.

Freeze-out tournament – a tournament in which you're out as soon as you lose your chips. See also re-buy tournament.

Full House – a hand made up of three of a kind plus one pair, e.g. Q-Q-Q-A-A.

Gap concept – Why you sometimes need a stronger hand to call a bet than to open the betting yourself.

Good beat – the opposite of a bad beat; where one hand beats a better hand in lucky fashion.

Gutshot – see inside straight draw.

Hand rankings – the order of winning hands.

Heads-up – playing just one opponent.

Holding – your hand.

Hole cards – cards dealt face down to each player.

Implied odds – the odds you are offered by the pot after factoring in likely future bets, calculated as total pot size plus likely future donations to the pot by other players, divided by bet size (how much you have to call).

Inside straight draw – a straight draw missing a card in the middle. Typically four cards in the deck will complete the straight – the four with the missing number.

Kicker – an odd or extra card, which may be used to break a tie between otherwise identical hands.

King high – a hand containing five cards of distinct values, the highest of which is a king.

Limit – players may bet or raise a fixed sum only.

Limp / Limp in – to call the big blind pre-flop rather than raising.

Live play – the same as face-to-face play.

Loose – somebody who plays a lot of hands.

Lowball -– a class of poker games in which the lowest hand wins.

Made hand – a hand that doesn't need to improve to be a good hand, i.e. the opposite of a drawing hand.

Maniac – a loose-aggressive player (see **Chapter Eleven: Playing styles**).

Mark – a sucker, a terrible player.

Marked cards – cards deliberately marked or altered in some way (scratched, dyed, punched, etc.) so they can be identified from the back.

Middle pin – see inside straight draw.

Monochrome flop – a flop in which all cards are of the same suit.

Monster – An extremely good hand.

Moody rule – a rule that forbids coffee-housing. The Moody rule is enforced less and less these days.

Muck – the spot in the middle of the table where all discarded and folded cards are placed, face down.

Multi-way hand – cards that play better against many opponents rather than just a few; or a hand in which multiple players participate.

No-Limit – describes games in which players may bet or raise anything up to the amount of money or chips they have in front of them, irrespective of the pot size.

Nut flush – the best possible flush, i.e. ace high.

Nuts, the – an unbeatable hand, or the best possible hand at any given point.

On tilt – see tilt.

One Pair – two cards of the same value plus three other random cards.

Online card room – an internet site where you play poker against other people.

Online casino – an internet site where you play blackjack, roulette, video poker or other games against a computer.

Open the betting – to be the first person to bet in any given round.

Out – any card which will improve your hand.

Overcard – any card higher in value than any other card or cards.

Palming – to steal chips from the pot.

Part-made drawing hand – a drawing hand that might possibly win even without improving.

Pass – to withdraw from the current hand, i.e. to fold.

Play money – tiny stakes or pretend money.

Pocket cards – cards dealt face down to each player (also called hole cards).

Pocket rockets –- a pair of aces in the hole.

Poker robot – software that plays online automatically.

Position – your place in the order of play, as determined by your location relative to the dealer button. If you are one of the last to act you are said to be in late position, which confers a playing advantage.

Postillion – a playing-card sized piece of plastic that sits under the deck, concealing the bottom card.

Pot – money or chips that accumulate as the hand progresses. The winner of each hand takes everything in the pot. See also side pot.

Pot-limit – a game in which the size of your bet is limited to the amount of money or chips currently in the pot.

Pot odds – the odds offered by the pot to a player for a bet, calculated as total pot size (including bets already in) divided by bet size (how much he has to call).

Pre-flop – describes the phase of a hold'em hand before the flop is dealt, i.e. the first round of betting.

Qualifier – a rule in high-low, or low-only, poker games, ensuring that only reasonably low hands can win the pot.

Robot – see poker robot.

Odds – Another word for probability, the chance of something happening.

Overbet the pot – to make an oversize bet.

Oversize bet – a bet that is larger than the pot size.

Queen high – a hand containing five cards of distinct values, the highest of which is a queen.

Rabbit hunt – to deal the remaining board cards even when the hand is complete (i.e. when all but one of the players have folded before the river) so players can see what hand they would have made.

Rainbow flop – three flop cards with different suits. See also monochrome flop.

Raise – to exceed the largest bet previously made in the hand so far, i.e. to match the previous bet and then add extra chips.

Rake – the amount the house takes from each pot.

Re-buy tournament – a tournament in which players can buy more chips if they lose theirs.

Re-raise – the second and subsequent raises in a round of betting.

Relative position – your position in relation to the bettor / raiser. In general, the closer you sit to his right, the better.

Reload – to buy more chips after losing your stack.

River, the – the fifth and final community card dealt face up on the table after the third round of betting.

Rock – a tight-passive player (see **Chapter Eleven: Playing styles**).

Royal Flush – the highest ranking hand – 10-J-Q-K-A of the same suit.

Sandbagging – see slowplaying.

Satellite – a tournament in which the prize is free entry to a larger tournament. Many WSOP hopefuls win their seats this way.

See a bet – old fashioned expression meaning to call.

Set – three of a kind, usually meaning two in your hand and one on the table.

Short-handed – a game with few players, typically between three and six. See also heads-up.

Shuffle – to mix the cards before they're dealt.

Showdown – where remaining players in a hand show their cards, the best hand winning.

Side Pot – once a player is all-in, remaining players place their bets in a new, or side pot. The all-in player can win only the chips in the main pot, i.e. the one to which he contributed.

Singe – a shuffled pack.

Slowplay – to check or merely call with a strong hand (rather than bet or raise) to hoodwink opponents.

Small blind – the smaller of the two compulsory bets, made by the player sitting on the dealer's immediate left before the deal.

Split pot – the outcome of a hand in which two or more players tie and hence share the money.

Split pot game – a game in which there are two pots to be won, usually a high hand and a low hand.

Stack – a player's chips or funds that are on the table and in play.

Stack the deck – to deliberately manipulate cards in the deck.

Starting hand – cards received at the beginning of the hand, i.e. hole cards.

Steal – to bluff.

Straight – five consecutively numbered cards of mixed suits.

Straight draw – a hand containing four cards to a straight, which will become a straight if the remaining board cards are favourable.

Straight Flush – any five consecutively numbered cards of the same suit.

Stud – the class of poker games in which players receive their own cards dealt either face up for face down. There are no community cards and no exchanges of cards. The most common form is seven card stud, covered in Part IV.

Suited cards – two or more cards of the same suit.

Suited connector – two consecutively numbered cards of the same suit.

Table stakes – the rule that says that a player cannot be exposed for more money or chips than he has on the table in front of him.

Tell – a clue about an opponent's hand from the way he behaves.

Texas hold'em – most popular poker game in the world and the main subject of this book.

Three of a kind – three cards of the same value plus two other random unpaired cards.

Tie – two or more identical winning hands, resulting in a split pot.

Tight – describes somebody who usually plays only when his hand is very good.

Tilt – to play badly because of a temporary emotional imbalance.

Trap – to slowplay or check-raise with a strong hand in the hope of earning extra money.

Trips – three of a kind, usually meaning two on the table and one in your hand.

Turn – in hold'em the fourth community card dealt face up on the table after the second round of betting.

Two pair – two pairs of cards of the same value plus one other random card.

Under the gun – the position to the left of the big blind, i.e. the first to act pre-flop.

Unraised pot – pre-flop, a pot in which nobody has raised, i.e. everyone has either folded or called the big blind.

Upcard – in stud games, a card which is dealt face up for everyone to see.

Video poker – a poker slot-machine game played against a computer.

Wager – to bet or raise.

Wild card – a card (usually a joker) which can represent any card a player wishes. Wild cards are not used in most mainstream games.

WSOP – the World Series of Poker, a huge annual tournament held in Las Vegas.

Online chat glossary

Here's a list of some of the more cryptic phrases you may encounter when playing poker online.

BRB – be right back.

CYA – see ya, goodbye.

FFS – for flip's sake (often in response to a bad beat).

GG – good game.

GN – good night.

GL – good luck.

LOL – laughing out loud, an expression of mirth.

NH – nice hand.

NP – nice play.

TY – thank you.

WP – well played.

YW – you're welcome.

ZZZZZ – you're playing too slowly. Hurry up!

Index

Trash hands, 112-13
Triple draw, 288
Turn, the, 37-8, 154-7
Two pair, 15
Uncertainty, 54-59
Underplaying hands, 69
Unfair dealing, 315

Value-based play, 33-5
Variants of poker explained, 281-93
Video poker, 291

Weighted averages, 248-53
Wild cards, 294
World Series of Poker, 6, 293
WSOP *see* **World Series of Poker**